MICRO-LEVEL RURAL PLANNING

Principles, Methods and Case Studies

Edited by

R.P. Misra

R.N. Achyutha

CONCEPT PUBLISHING COMPANY PVT. LTD.
NEW DELHI-110059

ISBN-13: 978-81-7022-296-5

First Published 2016

Published and Printed by

Concept Since 1974

Concept Publishing Company Pvt. Ltd.
A/15-16, Commercial Block, Mohan Garden
New Delhi-110059 (India)
T: 25351460, 25351794, *F*: 091-11-25357109
E: publishing@conceptpub.com, W: www.conceptpub.com
Editorial Office: H-13, Bali Nagar, New Delhi-110 015, India.

Cataloging in Publication Data--Courtesy: D.K. Agencies (P) Ltd. <docinfo@dkagencies.com>

Micro-level rural planning : principles, methods and case studies / edited by R.P. Misra, R.N. Achyutha.
pages cm
Contributed articles.
Reprint. Originally published: 1990.
Includes bibliographical references and index.
ISBN 9788170222965

1. Rural development. 2. Rural development--Developing countries. 3. Rural development--India. I. Misra, R. P., 1930- editor. II. Achyutha, R. N. (Ramaswamy Kanne Narasimha Setty), 1949- editor.

HN49.C6M53 2016 DDC 307.1412 23

Contents

Introduction

INDIA has been engaged in micro-level planning at the district or lower level for quite some time. In recent years, greater emphasis has come to be laid on grass-root approach to planning and a number of area development programmes were launched to meet this end. Most of these, however, had only a marginal success. There appears to be three basic reasons for the poor performance of these programmes :

1. They were poorly formulated;
2. They were too loosely integrated with other programmes; and
3. They were haphazardly implemented.

Over a decade ago a serious effort was made at the Institute of Development Studies, University of Mysore, to evolve a workable methodology of district planning. A team of ten faculty members worked day and night and conducted library and field researches with great devotion for about five years. One of the redeeming features of this effort was a close co-operation between the University of Mysore, the people of Karnataka State and the government agencies – both Central and State – and the United Nations. Such collaborative efforts have now become rare.

The output of this venture was a series of district and block level development plans, a joint training programme for intermediate level IAS and State cadre administrators in district planning operated jointly by the United Nations, Planning Commission, New Delhi, and the Institute of Development Studies, and a series of evaluation reports on ongoing projects. These studies and programmes were backed by several academic programmes, such as Master Degree in Development Planning (MDP), Master Degree in Regional Planning (MRP), Master Degree in Agricultural Marketing (MAM) and a number of diploma courses. The Institute became an important centre for planning studies in India. It developed close links with various UN agencies and international institutions.

Among the several important publications of the Institute (IDS) having practical relevance for micro-level planning and development was a series on development planning. It was brought by the Institute in several volumes and since then has been widely used by students and practitioners of planning, both in India and abroad. The copies of the volumes have now become rare. A number of interested persons have been pressing us to reprint them. But, in view of the changed situation and also because the volumes needed revision and updating, we did not undertake this work.

Now with renewed emphasis of the Government of India on District Planning and Panchayati Raj Institutions, the demand for reprinting has been revived. We have, therefore, decided to permit the reprinting of relevant portions of various volumes.

This volume aims at explaining the methods and techniques of plan formulation including their integration with other programmes and projects. The report consists of eighteen chapters, one leading to the other. Starting with the concepts pertaining to area development, it covers problems and methods of selecting areas for development, methods of integrating area development plans sectorally and spatially, models of development, general analytical methods useful in planning, land-use planning, watershed planning, evolving efficient rural structure and network planning for rural areas. The last chapter deals with the methods of project formulation and evaluation.

The objective of the volume is to provide a ready reference to administrator planners on how to prepare an integrated rural area development plan. The emphasis is, however, on methods, for the lack of knowledge of these appears to be the weakest link in the plan formulation process at present. Special care has been taken to present even the mathematical methods in the simplest language possible.

A number of chapters of the book have been drawn from various sources and some of them have been contributed by other scholars closely associated with the training programme of the Institute of Development Studies. Credit has been given to authors of reproduced or edited material at appropriate places.

We are confident that the volume will also be of help to all those leaders in government and people who want to promote micro-level planning; and all those teachers and students who are involved in research and training in development from below.

R.P. MISRA
R.N. ACHYUTHA

1

Approaches to Rural Development

Multi-Dimensional Approach

As mentioned in the introductory part of this book, developing countries are paying increasing attention to rural development, and many approaches have been adopted to bring about sustained growth in rural production, employment and incomes. Some of these approaches have emphasized agricultural development while others food production only. Reform of the land tenure system and in agrarian relationships has loomed large in yet other approaches. Development of rural infrastructure–physical, economic and social–is another approach that has engaged the attention of policy-makers and planners.

However, these approaches have not had the desired impact in reducing unemployment, under-employment and poverty in rural areas. Agricultural programmes have mostly benefited the more well-to-do farmers; food production has languished for the lack of a viable marketing infrastructure; implementation of land and agrarian reforms has been blocked by local power structures and rural infrastructure development has been impeded by the lack of investment resources.

It would appear that each of these approaches by itself cannot solve the wide range of problems that arise in rural areas which are undergoing modernization and transformation. Yet, taken together and formulated into a set of inter-related actions, they can provide a viable approach to rural development.

Since agricultural development can be taken as a key to self-sustaining growth in rural areas, a rural development model can be designed around an agricultural development strategy which will not only benefit the well-to-do farmers but also a substantial number of poor farmers and which can provide the basis for other development activities in rural areas.

The elements of such a rural development model are suggested below, drawing on the experience of a number of countries, notably, India, Israel, Pakistan, the Phlippines, the Republic of China, Sri Lanka and Tanzania.

Labour-intensive Agriculture

Since shortage of capital and excess of labour are characteristics of the rural areas, low-cost labour-intensive, rather than capital-intensive, techniques should be introduced to the greatest extent possible. This will involve the development of simple, indigenous technologies which are more productive than the traditional methods, for example, those involving improved animal-drawn ploughs, transplanting in preference to broadcast sowing, improvements to the quality of compost manure, etc. Such labour-intensive agriculture, which minimizes costly capital inputs, is conducive to a more equitable distribution of the benefits of agricultural growth than from capital-intensive agriculture. The promotion of labour-intensive agriculture, which is mainly directed towards the poorer farmers, would not preclude the well-to-do farmers from using capital-intensive methods in their production as well as making use of the labour-intensive methods where feasible and economical.

Minor Infrastructural Works

Since even labour-intensive agriculture is unlikely to provide year-round full employment in rural areas with surplus labour, employment generating minor development works with high labour content can be carried out with under-employed and seasonally unemployed rural labour. These works include construction and repair of minor roads, irrigation and other waterworks, school buildings, clinics, etc. To minimize housing and other transport costs, construction activities should be concentrated as much as possible in areas with the greatest excess of labour and timed to coincide with the slack seasons in farm activities. In addition, local materials should be utilized wherever possible, because their use provides employment locally and reduces, transport costs.

In China, peasants have constructed irrigation, flood control, terracing and other works as well as re-forested local areas. In Bangladesh, rural populations, mobilized at the local administrative levels were employed in a rural public works programme to construct roads, bridges, embankments and other works. In Sri Lanka, local labour is extensively used to construct and repair minor roads, improve water reservoirs and maintain irrigation canals, particularly in times of drought or crop failure. In India, small capital formation projects have provided supplemental incomes to small cultivators and landless agricultural workers.

Light Industry

Small-scale, labour-intensive, light industries with low capital requirements can be established in rural areas to supplement employment opportunities in agriculture and at the same time to provide some form of skilled training to rural workers who are pushed out of the agricultural sector because of modernization of production. The types of industries most suited for rural areas were mentioned in the previous section dealing with the strengthening of rural-urban interaction through location of industries in rural areas. Initially two types of industries seem to be more appropriate, namely, those which process agricultural commodities produced in the area, for example, fruit and vegetable canneries, flour and rice mills, creameries, wood-working factories, brick-making, etc., and those which fabricate inputs to agriculture, for example, fertilizer plants, manufacture of farm implements and packaging materials, etc.

Popular Support and Self-reliance

This means that those communities which stand to benefit from a rural development programme should assume responsibility for raising a reasonable proportion of the resources needed. In the conditions prevailing in most developing countries at the present time, the share of resources available for rural development is most likely to fall far short of what is needed. Local support can come in various forms: funds allocated by local authorities for specific development activities, local taxes, community labour, individual or community contributions in kind, such as land for specific purposes.

What constitutes a reasonable proportion for a community depends on the size of the population, the degree of economic backwardness, its growth potential and other relevant circumstances. Where local areas are completely dependent on outside grants and loans, rural development planning becomes a matter of drawing up "shopping lists" of desires for outside funding without making the hard allocative choices which realistic planning requires. But if the regions, sub-regions and localities are to participate in the planning process, as good planning requires, it is likely that the choice of rural investments and their quality and reliability as well as their management will be improved if the people in the area involved are required to raise significant quantum of their own resources.

At the local level, the concept of self-reliance implies a full participation by small farmers, through their own organizations or through other institutions where they feel they can freely express their views and be heard during the formulation of rural development plans and projects. It is unrealistic to expect farmers to help implement programmes which do not reflect their needs and objectives. In addition, the participation of farmers in savings schemes can represent both a means of self-help and in time a source of capital for investment in agriculture or other forms of rural production.

Organizational Adjustments

The preparation and implementation of a programme of rural development is necessarily a long-term task which requires much government effort and continued farmers' support.

Such an effort usually requires major adjustments in government organization for rural development, because each ministry, department or agency tends to concern itself only with its own functional sector or sub-sector. However, a rural development programme requires coordinated action among many ministries, departments and agencies which cuts horizontally across the vertical organizational set-up, which is typical of most governments.

Experience in countries which have adopted rural development as a national policy indicates that it is normal for government structures and procedures to be adjusted accordingly. Each ministry establishes appropriate groups and administrative procedures to facilitate the coordination of its own activities with those of others on a continuing basis. At national and regional levels inter-ministerial bodies are established to synchronize the related activities of the different ministries and agencies. This is not an easy task. It requires a strong political will to establish the structures and an inter-disciplinary orientation of all the concerned officials in the various ministries and agencies to understand the inter-dependence of each one's contribution to the total rural development effort. It is important, however, to start the organizational structures required as quickly as possible after the inception of a rural development programme and to make them operate as soon as possible, for, it takes a long time to institutionalize the organizations and the hierarchical relations among them.

Development Centres

Technological and organizational potentialities for industrial decentralization exist at the present time. It has already been pointed out, for instance, that there are many kinds of industries that do not require a big city location. To avoid congestion of economic activities and of population in a few large towns, some countries have used what has been described as "service centres"; that is, specially designed large villages or small towns which act as centres of development within small regions. Their purpose is to retain the population in the rural areas by providing them with economic opportunities over and above those available in farming and with socio-cultural facilities. At the same time, the service centres provide the farming community in the surrounding areas with the necessary services and equipment and may also, where appropriate, develop industries for processing of local agricultural produce and for meeting local agricultural needs. In favourable circumstances, there can also be industries serving the needs of national production.

The scheme is based on a system of "micro-regions", each served by service centres of varying sizes. Precise standards or norms for social equipment (kindergarten schools, libraries, hospitals, etc.), for administrative services (municipal services, post offices, etc.) and for economic facilities (shops, wholesale establishments, banks, etc.), are worked out. Norms for the equipment and facilities vary with size of the locality and the region served. Industry is generally of small and medium size. For a service centre to be viable and to fulfil the functions required of it, the complex must be large enough to maintain an effective level of services. It is difficult to determine the optimal size, because it varies from country to country and from time to time. In any event, it can be assumed that the minimum size required for the effective functioning of the centre should guarantee that all villages coming within its sphere of influence will have satisfactory services at a reasonable distance.

With the progressive development of agriculture and the transition from mixed farming to specialized farming, small centres may no longer meet the needs of the localities, and the centres might have to be functionally differentiated into various categories such as : (a) the village-group centre, providing civic and economic services for four to eight villages, (b) the area centre, designed to serve ten to twenty-five villages, providing services and facilities of a higher standard and scale, for example, cultural and social institutions and certain economic enterprises; (c) the inter-area centre containing mostly economic enterprises designed to serve a broad area comprising twenty-five to fifty villages; and (d) the regional centre in which the large-scale enterprises are concentrated and shared by the whole region containing the village-group, area and inter-area centres and the villages served by them.

The success of rural development rests on a precise combination of all the above-named elements. Experience indicates that a combination of these elements–labour-intensive agriculture, minor infrastructural works, labour-intensive light industry, organizational adjustments, development centres and an atmosphere of self-reliance–offers good prospects for developing the rural areas. This can, in turn, provide increased incomes for poor farmers and rural workers as well as the necessary savings for social overhead facilities and services required for self-sustaining rural development.

Although the ultimate solution to rural under-employment in many countries may lie in the permanent migration out of agriculture of surplus labour, a viable programme of rural development can provide preparatory training for rural workers who eventually migrate to urban centres. It can also be instrumental in spreading migration over a period of time and thus ease the problem of absorption of the migrants into urban life and employment.

Since labour-intensive agriculture is the backbone of self-sustaining rural development, it should have the highest priority of all the elements in the model. Since it is difficult to organize agriculture based on labour-intensive techniques, time should be allowed for such organization to become effective. Social overhead facilities and services should be correlated with the growth in agricultural component over time to ensure that earnings from agricultural output in the area can contribute to the support of these facilities.

As this model is drawn mainly from the individual experiences of a few countries where rural development has been attempted, it does not correspond to any model adopted by any one country. Rather, its six elements constitute a composite based on particular methods which appear to have been fruitful in these countries as well as others. As a composite of the apparently successful elements in rural development programmes, it is not presented as a model to be followed in its entirety by any country. Rather, they are elements which a developing country could find useful in devising a rural development model of its own.

Integrated Approach

Serious study of rural development strategies and programmes that have been adopted by various developing countries and of their effects on the intended beneficiaries of such programmes makes it increasingly clear that a sectoral approach is no solution to setting in motion a development process that is far-reaching and dynamic as it affects the rural areas in particular and national development in general. Agricultural development, although basic to rural development, cannot make much headway without concomitant intervention in the sphere of education, training, and raising the levels of aspirations of the farmers. Introduction of light industry cannot proceed too far without giving simultaneous attention to occupation training, infrastructure and the linkages to markets and consumers. Infrastructure and transport development will have to be related to the production patterns and potential in the area. Education will have to be oriented towards occupational patterns and employment possibilities in the area. There is, admittedly, a close inter-dependence between sectoral services and inputs as they converge on the needs and problems of a particular locality.

Serious thought, therefore, is being given to an integrated approach to rural development. The concept is still rather vague, but it is generally based on the assumption that rural development is a system of inter-dependent and interacting elements. They have to be recognized and the interventions to improve them so harmonized that there will be an optimum utilization of natural resources and mobilization of the human resources in a particular area in order to maximize the economic and social returns from the development efforts to the people of the area. As can be seen, this has many implications for development planning and programming. Specific programmes for increasing productivity, improving levels of understanding and motivation, providing social services, improving transport and communications, etc., although needed and desirable in their own right, will not have the maximum sequence. In effect, it is a systems approach and analysis to the inter-dependency of development components and their interaction within a given operational framework.

In order to understand the rural development system more clearly and manage it more rationally, one can think in terms of various sub-systems which make up this system. For example, the production pattern can be identified as one sub-system; other sub-systems can be the rural settlement pattern, the infrastructure network, the employment pattern, rural organization and institutional system, etc. By their very nature these sub-systems are inter-related. Thus, the settlement pattern is a function of the production pattern in the area; the production processes will dictate the employment pattern; this, in turn, will affect rural, social and institutional organization.

Each sub-system will have a number of development components. Under the agricultural production pattern, for example, there will be such components as land and water for cultivation, land tenure practices, agricultural production techniques, credit, processing and marketing, institutional arrangements, etc. Under the human settlement sub-system there will be such questions as location of production and commercial enterprises, services and institutions, transport and communications, social and cultural facilities, etc. Lack of attention to any of the critical components within a sub-system can seriously jeopardize the results expected from that particular sub-system and indirectly affect the development process within other sub-systems. For instance, lack of water or uneconomic land-holdings will limit possibilities of increased production within that sub-system, although the necessary inputs, credit and market facilities are made available. Limited production will reduce the income of the farmer and affect his levels of consumption expected within the social development sub-system.

An approach to integrated rural development is, therefore, to identify the development components within each sub-system, analyse their interdependencies within the sub-system in relation to the actual conditions obtaining in the area, establish their connections with other development components in other sub-systems making up the rural development system and determine on the basis of certain principles and criteria what mix of the development components will have the maximum effect in achieving a particular objective. The principles and criteria will largely depend on the objectives selected for the development effort—employment, diversification of agricultural production, better distribution of population, higher levels of income and consumption--and in the main related to the problems and needs expressed by the people living in the area.

The thirteenth FAO regional conference for Latin America defined integrated rural development as "an integrated set of planned and coordinated actions carried out at different levels by government agencies and the population itself to bring about the progressive and sustained development of a rural area. It is understood that this development shall result in a qualitative improvement of the life of the rural man, in terms of his own real and felt needs".[1]

The design of an integrated rural development programme is determined by existing local conditions and the policies followed by governments. A number of countries are taking action to develop comprehensive rural development schemes and, in most cases, under a variety of different organizational structures and administrative systems. However, there are certain general principles which have to be taken into account.

There are two main aspects in an integrated rural development actions. The first is the proper integration of a host of factors involved in the drawing up of mutually complementary programmes, that is, programme packages. The second is the orientation of these packages toward integration of both the rural inhabitant and his territory into the general socio-economic development process. Both aspects are intimately inter-related.

The region or area is the level on which the integrated approach to planning works best, because the area of diagnosis can coincide with the geographic area in which action is to be taken. However, to avoid the accumulation of large number of planned but unfeasible activities, it is essential to set up an order of priorities. The task is to identify bottle-necks and determine key points on which to concentrate in order to achieve a meaningful impact.

Integration on the institutional plane involves the agencies functioning in the field of agriculture, finance, research, trade, education, health, public works and others. These agencies will have to integrate their operations in accordance with the objectives and goals.

Given the dependence of rural areas on farming, the agricultural sector is a fundamental plane of integration. This integration will have to encompass agricultural production, extension, credit, the supply of inputs and machinery, processing, marketing and distribution; food and nutrition; natural resources conservation; import and/or export and other aspects. All these variables will have to be integrated into a basic agricultural policy that can serve as underpinning for the body of rural development. The following basic requirements should be kept in mind : opportunities for productive, remunerative psychologically and socially satisfactory employment; a more equal distribution of material and non-material incomes, access to service and social security; better management of the environment; increased participation of the people in the decision-making process and in programme execution.

To make the general approach operational, it is necessary to elaborate a check list of all elements relevant to integrated development; to establish a general matrix showing their potential inter-relationships; to assess carefully their importance and weight under specific conditions; and to identify the bottlenecks.

It is not possible to work out a list of relevant elements in the abstract. However, the following list includes the elements that seem to be the most important to be taken into consideration:[2]

Natural resources
- agricultural (including forestry and fisheries)
- non-agricultural

Human resources
- quantitative
- qualitative

Pattern of social organization
- values
- social stratification and mobility
- power structure
- land tenure system

Economic structure
- agricultural production structures
- agricultural industries
- other industries
- market relations

Technology
- agricultural
- non-agricultural

Infrastructure
- physical infrastructure, including transport and communication
- social infrastructure

Institutions and organizations
- administrative structure
- people's organizations

Services
- marketing
- credit
- extension
- social security

Education and training
- formal
- non-formal

General principles or guidelines should be adjusted in a particular region or area within the country to take into account the stage of general economic development, the geographic and climatic conditions, the population density and natural resources, the structure and value system, etc. The main principles of integrated rural development must be followed by country case studies which will choose the suitable approaches and suggest practical measures to help them. The area development approach is the most suitable approach for integrated rural development, which makes it possible to deal with the differentiated regions and their problems individually and to apply the most effective measures for rural development.

REFERENCES

1. See FAO, "Thirteenth Regional Conference for Latin America", Panama City, Panama, 12-23 August, 1974 (Document No. LARC/74, 5 July, 1974, p. 1.
2. Adapted from: *FAO Monthly Bulletin of Agricultural Economics and Statistics*, Vol. 23, No. 4, April 1974, p. 10.

2

Planning for Integrated Development

IT is conceivable that planning for rural development can be undertaken at the level of the individual community in a rural area. This was a method that was adopted in community development programmes at the beginning. However, its limitations were soon recognized, particularly where such programmes to meet purely local needs and problems had to be related to national policies and objectives or harmonized with programme planning to meet obvious needs of the larger area in which the communities were located.

The current trend in planning for rural development, therefore, is to look for an area larger than the small community, at the level of which national policies and plans can be meaningfully translated into programmes and projects which will meet the development requirements common to the communities in that area. Issues and constraints at the local level can be better analysed and evaluated at the level of the area, and more effective solutions can be sought. For instance, the location of educational facilities for the children in the various communities can be more rationally planned at the area level than at the individual community level; or the transport needs of the communities can be aggregated more meaningfully at the area level for planning a more effective infrastructure network. The area also becomes a more convenient scale for identifying inter-related issues in planning and for dealing with them through cross-sectoral analysis, for example, issues related to production pattern, processing, storage, transport and marketing.

Many examples can be cited of this area approach to rural development; the Gezira Settlement Scheme in the Sudan, the Comilla project in Bangladesh, the Puebla project in Mexico, the intensive agricultural district programme in India and the Lilongwe land development programme in Malawi, to mention a few which have been studied and documented. Each of these had its distinctive emphasis in planning and programme implementation. Thus, the Gezira scheme emphasized irrigation, crop production (cotton), new settlements and, at a later stage, the provision of social services and infrastructure. The Comilla project gave special attention to improve local organization, increasing rural incomes, involvement of local leaders and community members, training, co-operative activities and rural public works with the participation of the people. The Puebla project had as its main objectives improvement of crop yields, increased incomes and improved nutrition. The Indian programme was mostly concerned with increased production and the organization and delivery of the necessary inputs. The Lilongwe programme had broader objectives and was concerned with a variety of activities and functions, notably improved crop yields, physical planning of centres for markets and services, provision of infrastructure (roads, bridges, water supply, health clinics and service buildings), consolidation of land-holdings, community organization and village committees for local participation and credit schemes. The Lilongwe programme seems to be the closest to an integrated approach to area development.

The task of planning for a wide variety of rural development objectives in an integrated manner can become very complicated.

First, there are the three major systems which have to be taken into account. There is the *spatial system* which comprises the location of production enterprises, settlements, physical infrastructure and land-use. Some of the enterprises will have a fixed location, for example, agricultural, mineral and forestry activities, while others, particularly industries and services, are locationally flexible. Settlements are also to some extent predetermined in a historical, cultural and physical sense. Yet, there are other considerations of expansion, land-use, re-location and planned lay-out in their development. Physical infrastructure in terms of road and transport networks and public buildings has to be related to the settlement and productive patterns. There is the *economic system* which includes production patterns, investments, movement of products, prices, sales, etc. Then there is the *social system* in terms of social services provided, employment, security and social organization and institutional development.

Secondly, there is the need to relate and co-ordinate the local planning exercise with regional and national plans for the various sectors. In planning for agricultural sector, for example, farm production models would have to be co-ordinated with the agricultural plan for the area and related to national targets. Experience indicates that inconsistencies often arise between aims projections of local planning and national plans. This happens because micro-planning deals with individual units of production and aims at optimizing employment and income to the producer. It is linked to human behaviour and social environment and involves factors which do not always lend themselves to qualification.

Because micro-planning is concerned with real life situations, it is seldom in complete accord with the goals and targets determined at the level of micro-planning. Soil conditions, availability of water and the educational level of the farmer will prevent production on a particular farm from approximating the national growth rate set for that particular crop, say, rice. Or the quality of labour and the technology available at a given time to a manufacturing enterprise can affect its output which may be lower than the national target for that commodity, say, textiles. The aim, therefore, of co-ordinating vertically the local planning exercise with regional and national plans is essentially to integrate as far as possible these two functions in such a manner that what is desirable at the national level is made worthwhile and feasible at the level of actual production.

Thirdly, there is the need to formulate inter-sectoral plans and projects and establish inter-system relationships among them at the level of local planning. For example, within the economic system any plan to increase crop production will have to include, among others, the technical aspects, financial aspects (incentives, credit, investments, price stabilization, etc.), processing aspects, storage, marketing and sales aspects. These will form the inter-sectoral consideration. At the same time, such an inter-sectoral plan within the economic system will have to establish linkages with the spatial system in such matters as location of processing and storage facilities, transport requirements for the movement of goods, etc., and linkages with the social system in such matters as labour requirements, occupational training, education and health facilities, availability of goods and services commensurate with higher incomes generated by increased production, etc. This can be termed horizontal integration as distinct from the vertical integration mentioned in the second requirement above.

Fourthly, a dynamic relationship will have to be maintained between planning and implementation through an in-built system of monitoring and evaluation. This will ensure the necessary feedback to assess the relevance of the initial plans to the changing circumstances caused by plan implementation and to enable the necessary changes and adaptations to be made before bottlenecks arise which can affect adversely both plan implementation and the objectives and targets envisaged by the plan.

The *Planning Process* consists initially of a preliminary comprehensive survey of the basic data of the selected area covering :

(a) the natural conditions, including mineral and water resources, soil characteristics, land-use patterns, climate and topography;
(b) population, its structure, distribution, migratory patterns, employment living standards, level of income and consumption;
(c) the economy of the region with sectoral characteristics, performance data, market and potential for further growth, role in the national economy and ties with other areas of the country;
(d) social development of the region, including manpower supply and training, education, literacy, health, family and child-care services, help for the elderly and youth programme;
(e) spatial structure, including the settlement pattern, hierarchy of urban centres and their functions, development of metropolitan areas, location of infrastructural facilities;
(f) institutional aspects, particularly pattern of land ownership and tenure, administrative and political structures, social organization.

Ideally much of this information should be in as much detail and accuracy as will permit valid conclusions to be drawn for planning purposes. However, the present state of information gathering, classification and recording in many developing countries leave much to be desired for such analysis. Yet there are many sources from which relevant data can be gathered. Sectoral authorities and various regional and national bodies often collect information for their own purposes which could be used judiciously for area development planning.

Special skills will be required on the part of those carrying out the task of information gathering for rural development purposes to select those data which are relevant. In some instances special surveys might have to be undertaken, and, to the extent possible, the local population should be involved in such exercises, not as passive providers of the information desired but as active participants in the tasks of gathering and recording it. Co-operation of the local people can be assured, if the purpose of the surveys is clearly explained to them, and the local leadership is actively involved.

A common criticism of this phase of information gathering and analysis is that it is time-consuming and fails to suggest immediate solutions to the pressing and urgent problems confronting the rural population, on the one hand, and that it causes delays in implementing the national development plans, on the other. To meet such criticisms it would be possible to undertake a quick empirical survey of the area which will yield certain issues and problems that can then be studied on a priority basis and in sufficient detail to help in policy formulation and planning. This will in no way be a substitute nor make redundant the need for a detailed and comprehensive analysis as a long-term exercise, which alone can provide a rational basis for integrated development.

Such analysis, either partial or comprehensive, should lead to the identification of various development components which require attention, their inter-dependence and interaction and make it possible to group them into sub-systems within the rural development system. This should logically lead to the formulation of an overall development plan for the area, taking into consideration both national development plan objectives and the suggestions and goals of the local populations. This could then be elaborated into detailed plans for the different projects making up the overall plan — in agriculture, manufacture, infrastructure, education, health, institutional reforms, etc.

Having such an integrated plan does not necessarily mean that *implementation* should be undertaken immediately and simultaneously on all the elements in the plan. Urgency of the problem, the resources available and the gestation period of the project would generally dictate what aspects of the plan should be taken up initially. From the point of view of the local community, urgency will largely depend on the priority accorded to the problem by the people, for example, a regular supply of water for cultivation, educational facilities for the children, or ready access to health services. In such instances high motivation and involvement of the people can be expected in planning and implementing the project. Local resources can be mobilized, and to that extent the share of the national resources can be reduced. From the point of view of the national authorities, priority will be accorded to those problems which are of national importance, for example, increased food production or development of natural resources so far unexploited, such as new agricultural land or a mineral deposit. In such instances the major burden will fall on the government to plan and carry out the project, the incentives offered will have to be sufficiently attractive for the people to identify themselves with it and be involved in it.

The gestation period of the project will also influence decisions on whether it should be started within the time span of the plan. The construction of a dam to impound water for irrigation involves many activities —engineering studies, procurement and transport of the needed equipment and materials to the site and actual construction–which would spread over two, three or more years, and it might have to be started at the beginning of the plan period. On the other hand, the selection, orientation, migration and settlement of the peasants on the land to be irrigated by the dam water may require only one year or be initiated later.

If the plan component which receives priority attention is within a well-defined sub-system, then other related components will also require simultaneous attention. The construction of a sugar factory will require parallel action to ensure that sufficient quantities of raw sugarcane are available to maximize sugar production when the factory is commissioned. This will require a series of activities, such as selection and preparation of the land for sugarcane cultivation, the extent of the land that should be set apart for that purpose, introduction of new hybrids of sugarcane, new methods of cultivation, actual planting, harvesting, transporting and stocking the sugarcane in time for production to start. All these activities might take as long as the construction of the factory, and action on the two projects will have to proceed simultaneously. In other instances action on inter-related components might have to be taken sequentially. In a new settlement, the infrastructure in terms of roads, water service, power and other community amenities would have to be planned and provided before housing, public buildings and landscaping can begin.

The strategy for rural development can, therefore, be visualized as a series of events, for example, completion of the dam, settlement of the people, establishment of the factory, which are preceded by activities that make the event possible and followed by activities that make other events possible. Integration in implementation will occur when backward and forward linkages are established between these activities and events, and their occurrence is related to a time schedule which clearly establishes the sequence of operations. Models of systems analysis and planning have been developed for various activities, single as well as multi-purpose. It is not impossible that such a model could be constructed for integrated rural development programmes also.

Such planning and implementation will call for a unified approach by many professionals and technicians acting under an authority which has the power and can take the responsibility to take decisions on the timing of project activities and the integrative measures that need to be taken at appropriate points in the course of implementation. Some development projects are undertaken by one particular ministry or other established agency of the government. In such instances, a problem arises from the fact that the different elements of such a project lie in fields that are normally the responsibility of different governmental agencies. This often leads to conflicts of jurisdiction. Furthermore, the administrative integration of the different elements of a project should, as far as possible, be accomplished at the level of the project itself, and this may lead to conflicts where one or more elements of the project have a live relationship to regional and national administrative units concerned with that type of activity, for example education or road construction. The most suitable arrangement might be to make the land area covered by the project conterminous with that of an established administrative unit of the government, so that project integration becomes administratively feasible and realizable.

Due to the lack of effectiveness of authority and responsibility of Central Government ministries in carrying out integrated rural development, various other organizational devices have been tried. A special commission for rural development established at the national level, regional planning and development authorities, rural development corporations for specific areas, etc., have been adopted from time to time in many of the developing countries, depending on the administrative structure and the political climate obtaining in those countries.

The effectiveness of such organizations will, of course, depend on the powers conferred on them, the resources made available to them and the expertise and trained personnel they can mobilize. What is important to note is that the best plans and strategies for integrated rural development can flounder on the bedrock of inefficient administration, organizational shortcomings and lack of adequate resources to carry out the planned programme.

Two other elements which are crucial to the success of any integrated approach to rural development deserve serious consideration.

One element is the need for institutional reforms in many developing countries. It is difficult to achieve the desired results of any development plan without prior institutional adjustments. Take, for example, the organization of agricultural production which is of prime importance in the developing countries. It is reasonably easy to calculate the quantity and composition of agricultural commodities that would be required to satisfy demand. Estimates of consumption needs and levels of income would give the planner a sufficiently accurate picture of what is needed to be done. The difficulty lies in the inability of the producers to respond to this demand. The lack of response derives from a number of reasons, the most important of which is defective institutional arrangements that prevent the producers from introducing the necessary changes in the utilization of resources.

The introduction of high-yielding varieties of grain on a large scale could help developing countries resolve many of the acute socio-economic problems of their rural areas. However, the "green revolution" has helped yet only those cultivators who had the necessary resources at their command. It has been the land-owning and entrepreneurial class which, because it had access to resources through political, social and economic status, invariably benefited from the use of the new inputs. Moreover, owing to the high profitability of this type of cultivation, this group has in many cases bought out marginal farmers and forced small tenants out of their farms.

Thus, the experience of many countries indicates a clear and urgent need for comprehensive structural change. Most of the population in these countries is now pressing for changes in the power structure, regulation of the economic system, re-organization of the administrative machinery and the adoption of a new set of political, social and economic values. Participation has become a worldwide popular demand, which implies, particularly, access to productive resources and decision-making.

The main elements of relationships of the farmer which are affected by institutional changes are in respect of changes in administration, land tenure and ownership and settlement, agricultural credit, co-operation, and in policies relating to education, medical services, extension, etc. New forms of community organization, of the supporting system and of various social institutions could provide the basis for the attainment of development objectives — an increase in production and the standards of living of the population and overall socio-economic development of the rural areas.

The other element is the need to involve the people in planning and carrying out programmes and projects which directly affect them. Any rural development project is for rural people and should be undertaken by rural people. This is the idea However, in practice, a development project almost never arises primarily in that fashion. Almost invariably, they are designed and launched by some outside group for the rural people. The projects that endure and thrive, however, are usually those which have the benefit of considerable participation by the rural people in various aspects of decision-making, plan implementing, and, over a period of time, modifying and even administering the projects.

The need for popular participation should be recognized from the inception of the planning exercise. The potential beneficiaries should be made fully and continuously aware of what is planned. For some parts of a project, popular approval is necessary from the very beginning; for other parts, approval cannot be expected until after some concrete results have been achieved. Popular participation in planning, administration and implementation is likely to come slowly, but it is unlikely to come at all if it is not consciously promoted from the beginning.

How the people perceive the development measures as they touch their way of life, their work, their relationships with one another and their future will largely determine the degree of their involvement and commitment to the programme objectives. Their perception will be positively influenced to the extent that they are made partners, either individually or as members of groups and through their leaders, in the tasks of identifying the problem, elaborating the issues, assigning priorities, planning and in the execution of the plans. Depending on the nature of the programmes and projects and their aspects, the people can be involved selectively to ensure effective participation and a genuine sense of involvement. The degree of involvement of the people will, of course, depend on their stage of development in terms of education, understanding, outlook and aspirations. Yet this should not preclude giving them opportunities commensurate with their stage of development to contribute their share of decision-making on matters which would have a profound effect on their future growth and change as partners and beneficiaries of the development process.

3

Case for District Planning

DISTRICT Planning pre-supposes the understanding of the processes of district development. This knowledge is either derived from surveys and studies or from intuition. As is the case in India today, district level studies are very scarce. Social scientists in India have tended to take up national problems for investigation, leaving the local and regional problems and issues unanalysed. The techniques and methods used in a few available micro-level studies are often the same as found in macro-level studies. For example, the input-output analysis, a powerful tool of sectoral integration at the national level, cannot be fruitfully applied at the regional and local levels in the present context of information system. Sectoral approach to development, important as it is at the national level, cannot be equally important at the regional and local levels. Lower the level, less relevant is the sectoral approach.

There is a sort of in-built inhibition among social scientists and development institutions to study local problems. Even the National Institute of Community Development, Hyderabad, has no study on Community Development problems of the area it is located in. Every one tends to portray a national or international image by studying problems which are nationally and internationally important, and which require less academic and technical rigour to handle.

One can then understand why the processes of development of a region or district are yet to be understood. We do not know what really brings a major economic change in a region. We are unaware of the processes of social change. Our contribution to the understanding of social development in India has been through the theories formulated in environments not necessarily similar to those in India. This is not to say that theories or concept formulated elsewhere need be rejected. They are parts of the tools that must continue to be used to sharpen our own tools. But if we also develop concepts or theories which explain the indigenous environment better, we will not only add further to the store of knowledge but will also help social scientists in other parts of the world to improve their own conclusions. There is thus a need, nay a great and urgent need, for Indian Social Scientists to engage themselves in micro-studies and thus to improve our understanding of the processes of development, economic, social, technological, etc., at the local levels.

There is almost complete lack of understanding of area or regional development. While the nation as a whole prospers, we find areas and regions develop slowly, stagnating or deteriorating both economically and socially. We do not have the "Instrumentalities–public, private, federal, state and local–adequate to cope with regional and local situations, or endless variety and complexity". (Perloff, 1963).

District Development Process

District development is the combined product of a variety of decisions made at different levels in politico-administrative hierarchy (external forces) and the relative preparedness of the local populace to grab the opportunities for development (internal forces). The two forces must work harmoniously; one cannot be a substitute to the other. Deficiency or weakness in one can only partly be compensated by the other.

We will now further examine these two forces and the harmonious blending of them in order to achieve rapid economic development and social change.

External Forces

The national development programmes have their impact on the district level, as the local economy is closely knit with the national economy through a network of communication, administrative and socio-economic channels. When a new steel mill gets located somewhere because of the national level decision, the relation of the constituent territorial unit of a country such as the district with the whole national economy and the economy of the surrounding regions undergoes a change. Similarly, when a new national policy on agricultural prices gets implemented, it has its repercussions on the economy of the district. To take another example, added emphasis or de-emphasis on the growth and expansion of a particular sector or industry, in the national economic plan, benefits regions endowed with matching resources better than those with resources not so relevant to the chosen sector or industry. Green revolution in the wheat growing irrigated tracts of the country can be taken as another illustration.

Technological changes also have influences on regional economies. Since the capacity of various regions to adapt to new technology is variable, certain regions benefit more than the others from new technological developments. In the same way the national transport network consisting of trunk railway lines, air routes, highways and waterways have varying impacts on the economy of regions because of the wide differentials in accessibility. Improvements in transport technology do not favour all the regions equally, partly because of accessibility and partly because all regional products or industries do not need the same quantity and quality of transport services.

One of the very important factors which influences regional development is the degree of urbanisation. The region which is endowed with growing urban centres is likely to have better infrastructure, social, capital and development than those which are mainly rural. The degree of urbanisation and the location of urban centres, however, considerably depend upon a variety of national policies on urbanisation, taxation, etc.

Internal Forces

The external forces mentioned above only induce changes; they are often catalytic but only when the internal forces are ready to accept the change brought about by external forces. In a tribal region, a steel mill of modern sophistication would be of no avail even though it might be of greatest economic significance for the nation. This has been very well demonstrated by the Bhilai and Rourkela Steel Plants in India. The location of these plants was determined partly by the backwardness of the regions. The contribution of both the plants to national economy is great indeed, but they could do precious little for the region they are located in.

One cannot forget the basic reality underlying all natural phenomena, i.e., uneven distribution. Whether it is water or petroleum or thorium, it is not found everywhere. Only a few ubiquitous sources of energy, like light, are abundantly found on the earth; but even in the case of light, the polar regions are not endowed with the same amount as the tropical regions, for instance. Added and related to this are the variations in the population distribution. Thus the raw materials for productive purposes are not found equally everywhere, nor are the markets for the finished products equally distributed.

The above variations lead to variations in the cost of production. The industries seeking location are of three types. Some are space bound–they are input oriented or market oriented. Others are foot-loose and can be located anywhere. The primary activities such as agriculture, mining, fishing, forestry are space bound and space utilising. The manufacturing (secondary) activities can be located either at the site of raw material or market or in-between the two. Whereas the tertiary activities, such as transportation, banking, marketing recreation, etc., have to be at or near the market. Different regions offer different locational advantages for different types of activities. This naturally leads to regional variations in locational patterns.

Apart from the above locational factors, the factor of past decisions, is of considerable importance in locational decisions. Past decisions have led to concentration or dispersion of activities. These together provide the market inputs and transfer factors. Once a location decision is made, inter-industry linkages evolve and more industries get located at the same place, other things remaining the same. This would happen so long as the sunk costs are high. A time, however, comes, when the location costs overweigh the location advantages. New locations are sought then.

The advantage that a region has at a particular time often fades with change in technology, change in demand for goods produced and discovery of alternative inputs. The region would grow only if it has a relatively larger share of the activity which is increasing nationally. As Perloff has mentioned, it may also grow if it has a relatively declining share of a declining industry. There can be very many combinations in-between the two extremes. They must be understood, then and then alone a sound basis for regional development can be created.

Typology of Regions/Districts

Different regions exhibit different growth potentials. There are several classifications of regions but from the point of view of growth, the one formulated by Perloff appears to be most rational and detailed. This typology is based on the principle of accessibility. It indicates the limitations within which each region (in our case, the district) functions. The region, which has poor access to inputs as well as market has almost no potential for development.

The above typology helps us to achieve two things. First, it classifies regions on the basis of growth potentials and hence helps us to choose strategies for regional development. Secondly, it helps us to understand the role or place of a particular region in the national economy. A region's growth often depends upon its ability to produce export goods or services at a competitive advantage with respect to other regions. As exports increase, the income flows into the region. This in turns expands internal market by improving the purchasing power of the people. This is known as multiplier effect. The multiplier does not, however, work equally in each region. Much depends upon what the people do with the extra income generated from exports. In any case, this leads to a variety of structural changes in the socio-economic system.

The current theories lay excessive reliance on the manufacture of exports for regional growth. This is also proved empirically. In manufacturing we include here the processing activities too. The theories, however, do not say much about what sustains economic development once it has been initiated by export industries. According to Perloff, 'the occurrence of rapid self-sustaining growth involves a shift in the relative importance of growth factors away from the dominance of the export sector and in the direction of the internal organisation of production–which makes it possible for the region to play a more elaborate role in the national economy'. Some empirical evidences, however, indicate that it is the tertiary sector which really supports and promotes growth. Specially after the first flash of growth generated by the export sector.

Not every element of the tertiary sector, however, appears to support and promote growth. This sector can be classified into two sub-sectors–production oriented (POT) and consumption oriented (COT). It is the POT which supports and promotes regional development. The POT includes these tertiary activities which are linked directly to productive sector—agriculture, mining, etc. In this category comes repair services, agricultural marketing, agricultural extension, agricultural education, training in agriculture, industry, etc. While the COT activities play their own important service roles, it is really the POTs which support development.

To think that all manufacturing activities have the same impact on development has no empirical support. Manufacturing including processing based on local resources and labour producing enough surplus for export (to the markets outside the region) are the ones which are most conducive to regional development. Very sophisticated capital intensive plants located in backward areas fail to generate regional development partly because of the non-involvement of the local population in the plant's activities and partly because the income generated in the region is subjected to so many leakages that very little finally remains for regional investment. Labour and management for such plants are rarely drawn from the region. The commercial and service infrastructure are also alien to regional culture. All these forbid the plant and its associated activities to be integrated with the regional economy.

The typology of regions given above can help us to understand the potentialities of the district selected for planning and to identify activities which determine regional development.

Approaches to District Development

The approaches to district planning can be said to be (i) general, and (ii) specific. Specific approaches are designed to tackle certain specific or special problems of a district, while the general ones are applicable to all districts. We propose to discuss in this section the general approaches. The approaches are derived from the following propositions and considerations.

1. In a developing economy, regional differences in economic growth and social development cannot be avoided. The market conditions on the one hand and natural endowments on the other generate cyclical changes in regional growth rates. All that can be done through planned endeavours is to evolve methods of continuing adjustment so that the regional economy would not reach a point of no return. This continuing adjustment is, however, extremely difficult specially in a traditional society where the institutional structure is less responsive to change.
2. The capacity of a region to attract industries producing goods for export, is vital for regional development yet no region can sustain growth for a long enough time unless there exists substantial internal development both in economic and social sectors. It must develop the supporting activities specially the production oriented tertiaries and must make a bold attempt to distribute the new income as equitably as feasible. In the absence of these developments, internal market and infrastructure would not develop fast enough to support growth.
3. The concept of growth industries has to be modified and divorced from certain specific industries. For each region there is a different set of growth industries. For one region, the

growth industry may be agriculture, for another animal husbandry, for the third tourism and for the fourth steel. An industry which is on decline in the nation, can thrive in a region and pay large dividends. While it is obvious that certain industries are more conducive to regional growth than others, not all regions have the relative advantages as to input-output access enabling them to attract such industries (Perloff, 1963). Some regions, therefore, have to make do with whatever growth is feasible under the circumstances and perhaps wait for the technological changes which may offer better advantages. "In terms of such relative advantages as resources, markets, human skills, amenities, climate and transportation facilities, some areas can hope to grow only by attracting labour-intensive industries; others by attracting certain processing industries which exploit relatively untapped natural resources; some may have advantages for certain assembly operations; still others for relatively intensive recreation activities, etc. Attraction of industry is a competitive matter. A realistic appraisal of the region's relative advantages and disadvantages with regard to input-output access is an essential starting point for an understanding of its growth potential". (Perloff, 1963).

4. Regional development is very closely tied up with urbanisation, leading to the evolution of large and small urban centres. The regions having well distributed urban centres with efficient and attractive urban communities can attract capital from outside and stop capital outflow. A well-developed regional urban system supported by an efficient network of transportation and communication lines can be a great asset to a region.
5. Regional development has to be closely linked with population growth. Where the region's potentials do not allow growth at a desired rate and where the pressure of population on the available resources is too great, inter-regional planning designed to siphon off part of the population to adjoining regions having better prospects of development has to be attempted. This means that no region or district can be considered in isolation for development purposes. Its plan must be in harmony with the plans of the adjoining regions/districts.

This means that regional/district planning must form a part of the national planning effort and each government–national, State and local–must take responsibility for its implementation. The broader questions of locating national industries, providing power, extending national programmes touching various sectors have to be handled by the State and national governments.

6. Finally, regional/district development requires investments in four major sectors. It should not be considered to be a programme of economic development leading to increase in per capita income alone. In essence, district development attempts to achieve a higher level of welfare, elements of which cannot be measured in quantitative terms. The four major sectors are:

   (1) Human Resources,
   (2) Natural Resources,
   (3) Plant and Equipment, and
   (4) Social overhead.

The focus of all regional/district planning should be man and not the sectors. "In intensive effort to improve education, to prepare young persons for a life time of skilled, productive work is the keystone of any development programme. Compared with other government measures that have been proposed, public investment in education promises the greatest relative returns". (Perloff, 1963).

In the context of India, what we need today is a complete overhaul of our education system, greater emphasis on primary and secondary education based towards learning skill and under-privileged class of the society and relating education to indigenous, production processes.

In the initial stages of development, natural resources play a very significant role in accelerating growth. To some extent they work as substitutes to technology and as sources of external resources. The base for development can be broadened and strengthened through the intensive development of natural resources. Natural resources also attract industries and investment.

Investments in plants and equipments are important sources of development where the farms are not viable they must be made viable through supporting activities based on agriculture, etc. Similarly, modernisation in industry pays. Investment in social overhead–towns, villages, roads, railways, etc., has always paid dividends in terms of economic development.

Thus district planning has to be treated as an exercise in comprehensive planning for development of a district. It should not be an exercise in sectoral planning. It is here that the integration of economic and physical planning is required most.

4

The Planning Data Base

Data on Local Natural Resources and Environment

General Remarks and Concepts

LOCAL natural resources play a central role in development. Their availability on the spot can give rise to considerable advantages for the community or micro-region, among these being savings on transportation costs in the exploitation and marketing of the natural resource and its uniqueness to the locality, for example, limestone in the manufacture of cement or natural mineral water which is to be bottled and marketed.

It is, therefore, important to analyse local natural resources before any plans and projects for the future are formulated. For development planning purposes it is not enough for the local administrators and developers just to know that certain resources do exist in their micro-region. They should have clear knowledge of the quantities of the resource, its quality and associated features. Some of the information may be simple and easy to obtain, for example, the extent of fallow land. Other information may require considerable technical knowledge and sophisticated devices together the data needed, for example, coal or iron ore deposits. Data collection or renewable natural resources such as water or wild life would have to be organized systematically in order to obtain a time series in order to detect trends in natural processes. In case of others it is necessary to collect simultaneously data on correlated features or events, such as soil quality and yields or rainfall and vegetation.

Two kinds of information on natural resources are particularly important for development : the minimum level of a resource utilization required to start profitable operations, and the upper limits to resource exploitation beyond which the ecological balance of the environment could be endangered. In the first case it is necessary to ascertain if the available supply of the resource justifies undertaking an economic activity of a certain size. This is particularly crucial if the resource exploitation requires sizeable investment outlays such as mining of minerals.

The determination of the upper limits of resource exploitation is another crucial task. In the case of a renewable resource, the rate of renewal should be estimated before deciding on a certain economic activity or its expansion, for example, the recharge rate of underground water in relation to expansion schemes for irrigated crops. Sometimes it is not easy to determine the upper limits of feasible exploitation, and it may take many years before the over exploitation comes to light, such as in the Sahel region of Africa mentioned earlier or in the case of excess timber exploitation which later may result in irreparable soil erosion. Therefore, what is required here is a constant observation of all related facts connected with natural resource exploitation and conservation with due regard to all specific features of a particular resource.

Land

This is the most common natural resource for development found in every community and micro-region. How much of it is available for agricultural production? Is it used in accordance with its properties? How to improve it for higher yields? All these questions have to be answered by local and area planners at an early stage of their analytical work. A preliminary assessment can be made on the basis of direct observation of the existing conditions and a comparison of crops achieved from similar soils under the same conditions. However, a more profound analysis requires technical expertise which should be provided through the agricultural extension service.

Soils are classified according to various properties : the original material they come from, their composition, texture, horizontal structure, water absorption capacity and several others. All of them determine more or less the production capacity of the soil and the method of agricultural usage. In a number of countries special soil maps on scales ranging from 1:100,000 upto 1:5,000 are available on which most of the soil properties are indicated. The larger the scale the more detailed will be the information. On the small-scale maps, say 1:50,000 or 1:100,000, only the most generalized groupings of soil types can be determined, with little relevancy to a particular locality.[1]

Of particular practical relevance for development analysis are soil classifications, in which all important properties of the soil are summarized in terms of their values for agricultural production and the latter grouped in several classes indicating the best soil (Class I), the next best one (Class II) and so on. A comparison of soil classes of several areas with the corresponding production can give a good indication of the potential for further increase in output of some areas.

However, two areas with the same soil properties and values may still produce markedly different results, because a number of other natural factors, such as climate or the morphology of the terrain are co-determining the outcome. Various methods of analysis can be used to determine all relevant factors influencing field production in one index, thus enabling development analysts to directly compare localities and micro-regions among themselves. The weights attached to various factors are differentiated according to their role in the production process. For example, fields situated on flat land could have the higher value of two points, whereas those found in hilly terrain would be valued at one point. Naturally, such points in themselves do not have any meaning; they are needed only for summarizing different production factors and they serve such a purpose as long as they properly reflect the relative role of each factor in attaining overall production.

Water

Because of its crucial role in agriculture, settlements and industry, water supply and availability should be analysed very thoroughly. Data collection for this has to conform to certain requirements stemming from the specific features of water.

First, the data should be simultaneously gathered on every phase of the hydrological cycle, that is, precipitation, ground and surface water. Every phase is connected with the other, and one cannot properly assess the water potential of a community of micro-region without studying all the phases in their inter-dependency.

Secondly, the data collection on water should not be confined only to the locality or micro-region. The local supply of surface water is usually part of a wider water system and such events as drought upstream may seriously affect its availability on the spot. Similarly, ground water resources may be replenished from a wider catchment area and could be part of a wider underground water basin. Intensive exploitation of that basin elsewhere could considerably influence the local supply.

Finally, the data on water should be gathered systematically for a longer period, at least for several years, because fluctuations in rainfall, ground water level or river flow could be quite extensive, and only a time series can help detect consistent trends in water availability.

Turning to particular phases of the hydrological cycle, precipitation can be measured by simple devices such as any open vessel, as well as by such sophisticated ones as special radar equipment. Rain gauges are usually located in spots belonging to a national weather service network. However, it is useful to supplement this network with additional rain gauging devices in the locality that is being investigated. For development purposes it is necessary to know not only the average annual precipitation, but also the seasonal ones and even the daily amount of rainfall during the growing season of a particular field crop.

Easily accessible surface water is becoming progressively insufficient for the economy, and in some areas its availability is not constant. Man is, therefore, beginning to depend more and more on ground water. In arid zones of the world this dependence is total, and in such instances the need for gathering data on ground water becomes imperative. Among the methods for gathering such data at the level of the community or micro-region can be mentioned regular observation of the watertable in existing wells and of the quality of water in them. Natural recharge-discharge characteristic or aquifers, i.e., the ground levels, from which wells are being supplied, is another important method for data collection. The pumping out the wells gives some indication in this respect, but more advanced methods should be used to obtain more detailed and reliable data.

The need for more sophisticated evaluation methods increases with the scope of local and area development schemes, particularly with their water requirements. Specially trained experts have to be called in and more extensive studies of ground water resources made. Among others, they would have to explore the geological framework of the ground water system, reaching sometimes quite deep under the surface. If the geology of the area is not sufficiently known, surface and subsurface geological surveys would have to be initiated–these could also be of great value for mineral explorations. Such surveys and studies may be rather costly, but they would help to avoid serious losses and disappointments in the course of future development.

Minerals

At the local and area levels the knowledge about mineral resources is usually restricted to those appearing on the surface or close to it, being mostly used locally for such activities as housing construction or road building, for example, clay or stones. The need for these minerals will grow with the expansion of investment activities and, therefore, efforts should be made to acquire a full assessment of the resources available. However, acquiring more extensive knowledge about such minerals requires the services of experts : mining engineers or geologists. The fullest and most reliable information can be acquired only on the basis of mineral exploration organized on a wider scale, preferably for all regions of the country.

National mineral surveys are still uncommon in developing countries. Comprehensive nation-wide mineral surveys are costly and require experts with sophisticated equipment. In view of this, the current practice in most developing countries is to restrict mineral resource evaluation programmes to a basic minimum–to the development of an inventory of information on one or two minerals and their distribution. These programmes involve, among others, sampling procedures concentrated particularly on stream gravel, laboratory studies of samples and broader geological evaluation of areas where minerals have been found.

The success of such minimum evaluation programmes depends heavily on close co-operation with local and area inhabitants. Field collectors recruited from local population are able to establish close contacts with residents. In the course of these contacts, local inhabitants would report on all mineral findings, indicating their location, so that field collectors with some basic survey training could follow up on them and report to the supervising geological staff.

Soil, water and minerals are not the only natural resources of importance for local and area development. In concrete situations a great variety of others can play a major role, such as timber, reed, many other kinds of vegetation, fish or various species of wild life, possibilities of water transport, etc. Places endowed with natural beauty or benefiting from favourable climate can become the basis of a profitable tourist industry.

Maps as Instruments of Locational Analysis

A major task of development analysis at local and area levels is to take into full consideration all locational advantages and disadvantages of particular localities or micro-regions in relation to the surrounding areas, the wider region and the whole country. Among the prime factors in such a relation are those of a topographical nature which impede or facilitate interaction between the place under analysis and the immediate surrounding area, for example, distance between other locations of human activity, mountains, rivers, artificial boundaries, cultural barriers, etc.; the proximity of a dynamic city, which provides a strong market for the products, offers attractive work opportunities and affords numerous social and cultural services; and access to sources of raw materials, water, good soil and other development factors. Short distance is usually a locational advantage but in particular cases may also turn into an obstacle to development. For instance, this is the case when a chemical plant in the vicinity pollutes the air and kills vegetation, or the nearby national frontier cuts off a natural hinterland of an agricultural settlement.

Such relationships and their consequences can best be measured and appraised on maps which can be used as analytical and planning tools. Two types of maps are particularly useful in development work : general ones with a scale ranging from 1:100,000 to 1:250,000, and topographical maps of a scale as large as 1:5,000.[2] The first depicts basic features of physical and economic geography–rivers, mountain ranges, roads, bridges and cities–situated in a wider area. Hence, such maps are well suited for general analysis of locational advantages or disadvantages in relation to the surrounding regions.

The large-scale topographical maps are much more detailed and, therefore, can be used for specific analysis and planning. It is on such maps that the detailed soil classifications or location of natural resources can be ascertained. They are also used for site selection for most construction projects. Because of their larger scale these maps supply a wider range of information and become an important tool to the local and area development planner.

The usefulness of the two kinds of maps will be fully enhanced if their content is broadened to include additional information which will transform them from pure outline maps into analytical ones. There are various methods of drawing additional information on the outline maps. The most common ones applicable to local analysis are :

(a) The non-quantitative areal distribution method applicable to spatial features, which is usually expressed in the form of a shaded area symbolizing, for instance, land under specific crops, or a zone of high precipitation;

(b) the choropleth method, which provides ready of shading of certain areas on the maps;

(c) the dot method, which supplies quantitative information on the distribution of various features, such as population distribution or agricultural production with each dot on the map standing for a certain number of people or quantity of production, respectively;

(d) the isogram method, in which points of equal values of a phenomenon such as equal travel time or transport costs from a given centre are connected by lines;

(e) the diagram method used for portraying structural features of individual spatial units, as for instance the social structure of population living in a city and the surrounding settlements.

From the above methods those best suited to the particular feature to be analysed should be chosen for application. When studying a complex problem several methods are combined in order to find a proper solution. This is normally the case when a comprehensive picture of the locational features of a settlement is being sought. On one outline map would be depicted the areas with high-yielding soils using the non-quantitative areal distribution method. Dots would show what, where and how much is being produced in agriculture, and the isogram method would trace points of equal transportation costs of agricultural produce to the settlement's market. A map with such elements would help in deciding what opportunities exist for locating a food processing industry in the settlement, and also what would be the most appropriate scale of a new plant.

Similar procedures could be applied in order to study other development issues, such as the water potential of an area, delimitation of the service area or zone influence or the direction and intensity of migration against the background of the socio-economic characteristics of particular micro-regions. Obviously, such analytical maps require much time, effort and expertise to prepare. They should not be undertaken on a wider scale if the statistical information is not available or reliable. Overloading the map with various symbols which could obscure its analytical picture should also be avoided. From a few, well-selected items on the map one may often gain more insight as to the development potential at the local and area levels than from sophisticated maps prepared at considerable cost.

Population Analysis at the Micro-Level

Estimating the Total Population

Data on population at the local and area levels are most basic for any development analysis. This pertains both to the total number of inhabitants as well as to its structure according to sex, age and other characteristics. To obtain such information is relatively easy in some countries, which have established a regular system of demographic statistics; in those without such a system it may prove to be quite difficult to gather the necessary information.

The main and most reliable source of data on population is usually the population census. Censuses supply information on the total number of population and its composition according to numerous criteria. However, some factors restrict the usefulness and availability of census information. First of all it must be remembered that in some developing countries no systematic census has yet been taken. Where it is held, a census takes place at rather long intervals (approximately every 10 years) and, therefore, census figures registered several years ago may considerably deviate from the present situation. Finally, obtaining census figures for particular localities or micro-regions may be difficult or even impossible owing to delays in their publication, sub-division of data according to larger territorial units or because the needed data have been destroyed. In all the above cases the planner of local and area development has to cope with the situation according to methods most appropriate in the given circumstances.

If no census data are available, the total population of an area has to be estimated. Such estimates are based on two elements: on some circumstantial information which could be related to population, such as the total area of a rural micro-region or the number of houses in a settlement and a multiplier which measures the relation of population to the circumstantial information. As multipliers one could use, for example, population density, the average size of a household, or the number of households for an average village. Multiplying such figures by the circumstantial data results in an estimate of the total population of the locality of micro-region under study. The reliability of such estimates depends greatly on the accuracy with which the multiplier reflects the actual average situation. If considerable uncertainty exists, then the best way is to make an alternative estimate for control purposes for which a different set of a multiplier and circumstantial data would be used.

Of greater usefulness than the above estimates are various non-census counts organized by the local, regional or central authorities. These include enumerations of all individuals by registration boards, registrations of persons with specific qualifications and enumerations of groups of people such as those living in particular villages or belonging to different tribes. The enumeration of persons with specific qualifications or of particular groups leads to an estimate of total population of a locality or area through the use of a multiplier which would express the relation of the above groups to the total population. Therefore, attention should be paid to determine such a multiplier as accurately as possible. The simplest way of checking the multiplier would be through a complete enumeration of all inhabitants in one or two typical settlements and a comparison with the group of persons of specific qualifications to whom the multiplier is applicable.

Ascertaining the total population of a locality or micro-region from population census is usually connected with the need for updating the census data. The same applies to the previously mentioned non-census counts if they are not performed every year or at least every second or third year. The task is facilitated if at least two comparable counts are available taken in the same manner at two different points in time, say five or ten years apart. Then one could apply an extrapolation method in order to estimate the total population for the current date (year). The simplest method would be to calculate the average number of persons by which the population has increased annually between the two counts, to multiply the average by the number of years since last count, and add the results to the last census number.

Apart from its simplicity, this approach is more realistic than some other extrapolation methods in cases where the rate of population increase is high and the period of time from the last count relatively long. If this is not the case, an extrapolation by means of a geometric growth rate might be more appropriate. Such a rate can be found by utilizing the formula for calculating a compound interest and applying it to a comparison of two censuses' results :

$$(1+r) = {}^{t_1}\sqrt{\frac{P_2}{P_1}}$$

Where P_1 and P_2 are the population numbers from the first and second census counts, respectively, r is the annual rate of population increase and t_1 is the time interval in years between the two censuses. A multiplication of the population number from the last census by this growth rate would give the population of a year later. Repeating this procedure as many times as the number of years which had elapsed since the last census would bring the population totals up-to-date.[3]

The extrapolation by the use of geometric growth rates results in higher population estimates than by the arithmetic approach. For its computation it requires some calculating aids (logarithms, a compound interest table). One should take this into account and remember the above assumption of a constant proportion of population change, before deciding to use this method for estimating current population totals at the local and area levels.

Composition of Population

Development analysis at the local and area levels cannot be confined to population totals only. It is important to determine the composition of the total population according to sex and age, number and categories of households, the proportion of economically active people, income groups and other socio-economic characteristics. While some aspects can be determined on the basis of existing statistical reports, others will require special surveys in order to obtain the desired information.

Estimation of the sex and age structure of an area's population is a crucial analytical step both for evaluating the current situation as well as for projecting future population growth. With respect to the present situation, knowledge of the sex and age structure helps among others to evaluate the need for mother and child care services, the level of school attendance, the intensity with which the local labour force is gainfully employed, or the extent of assistance necessary for the aged.

The most detailed information on age and sex structure of the population is provided by census data or non-census registrations of similar scope. They can be used without any adjustment if the count has been organized most recently; if not, some updating method should be applied in order to obtain insight into the current sex and age structure of inhabitants. Prorating is the simplest method in this respect; it suffices here to have the population total estimated to the current date, calculate the ratio of increase (or decrease) between the census and the present total, and then to multiply each age and sex group by the same ratio. For most analytical purposes, it is not necessary to deal with each age group separately; they may be combined into five-year age groups: 0-4, 5-9, 10-14, 15-19 years and so on. The prorating method described here works under the assumption that the age structure of the census figures was normal, i.e., not distorted by war which heavily affects some age groups; furthermore, the birth rates, mortality conditions in particular age groups and migratory movements had not changed substantially since the last census. All these assumptions cannot be defended for a longer period of time, and, therefore, some other approaches must be taken in order to calculate sex and age structure for the current data from data of more than two to three years old.

Wherever information on births and deaths according to age is available, it should be used by adding births and subtracting deaths from corresponding age groups. In this manner the population structure by age and sex can be carried forward to the present date without the former assumptions made for prorating except the one on the relatively stable migratory movements (or lack of them). If birth and death data are available, they are particularly useful in the youngest age groups of zero to four years, where the mortality rate is the highest in the zero age group, i.e., among children less than one year old, and decreases rather rapidly in the subsequent single-year age groups between one to four. However, this is the age group where errors stemming from incomplete census figures and birth or death reporting are the highest.

While such errors appearing in older age groups could be eliminated through smoothing procedures,[4] adjustments based on independent assumptions should be made with respect to the youngest groups. One such assumption could be that another micro-region in the country, or an entire region for which sex-age data are available, could be regarded as representative also for the area in question and, therefore, its sex-age structure could be prorated to the area under study.

The sex and age composition of inhabitants in particular localities and micro-regions is part of a comprehensive population characteristic which should be obtained in the analytical phase of development planning. Another important feature of that characteristic is the number of households and their qualitative features. The grouping of people into households is particularly crucial when analysing the standard of living and personal expenditures. The main determining factors in this respect are, on the one hand, the income in money and kind at the household's disposal, and, on the other, the total number of persons included in the household. It is by comparing these two sides of the household characteristics that the real income level of people can be correctly ascertained. Household composition and total income determine also the amount and structure of consumption and the value of nutrition. Households which sometimes may not be identical with families are units of reference to housing conditions, purchases of various household appliances such as kitchen utensils or furniture, and to the supply of numerous services.

An important characteristic of the population is yielded by data on the economically active persons, on the structure of employment, or on size of the total labour force* of emigration and immigration and the pattern of commuting as indicators of supply and demand on the local labour market. Another crucial area of analysis is the plight of the under-privileged or marginal groups of inhabitants. Information is needed on their numbers, location in the micro-region and the reasons for their insufficient sharing in the fruits of development.

Data on the above population characteristics are rarely obtainable from a census. Their calculation in an indirect way, similar to the estimation of the sex-age composition, can also be seldom done with full reliance. On the other hand, someone who claims to know a certain locality or micro-region should not rely solely on his subjective perceptions of the situation in the above problem areas. What remains is to acquire the needed information through special investigations in the field. If the locality is small it might be possible to organize a complete population survey. However, in most cases this will not be possible because of the enormous amount of work needed to reach all inhabitants. In such cases sampling methods can be substituted for a complete survey.

Sampling allows drawing more or less precise conclusions on the needed characteristics of the total population by surveying only a small portion of it. However, certain strictly defined rules must be observed in sampling before its results can be extended to the entire population. In particular, these rules pertain to the procedure of selecting the individuals, households, or any other units for the sample and to the accuracy with which its results may be applied to the total population depending on the size of the sample. The execution of a sampling survey and the interpretation of its results require the knowledge of certain statistical concepts and methods. Therefore, it is advisable to ar-

---

* Unemployed or under-employed. One should also seek information on the size.

range the sampling survey with the help of persons with proper expertise.

Techniques for Population Projection

Future development at the local and area levels has to be oriented towards the population which will live there in three, five ten or more years. Therefore, population projections are an important part of the development planner's work. Basically, population projections are extrapolations of past trends and present conditions into the future and, therefore, are usually performed at the first analytical phase of planning. The planner has at his disposal numerous methods applicable to population projections, ranging from very simple ones, such as those using the arithmetic or geometric rates, to quite complicated ones, such as those based on the component method, which include the construction of life tables or elaborate econometric models. The selection of the most appropriate method depends on the available demographic information, the purpose of the projection and the unit it refers to.

Generally, the smaller the unit for which a projection is being made, the greater the influence of distorting factors, among which migration plays a major role. As distorting factors are difficult to predict, it is not worth using too elaborate methods of population projections at the local and area levels. Thus, in numerous situations the above-described methods of using arithmetic or geometric growth rates would suffice. In addition, in cases in which one expects population to increase at an accelerated pace, harmonic rates could be used. They are based on the difference of the reciprocals of the two subsequent census figures. If three or more censuses or other reliable population counts are available, extrapolations could be made by means of parabolas, that is, geometric curves, which can reflect both average growth rates as well as gradual increases of the latter. The parabola of the second degree has this formula: $Px = a + bx + cx^2$, where Px is the population to be attained after x years from the basic year, which could be the year of the first census, and a, b and c are parameters of the curve to be calculated from the simultaneous equations. Parabolas have one weakness: they lose precision with the length of the time-span they are suppose to cover. Population projections for longer periods, say 25 to 50 years, should be based on logistic curves, which in turn are unsuitable for short-term periods. However, practical application of such curves is rather limited at local levels.

The main drawback of the extrapolation methods is the fact that they do not produce figures on the future sex and age-structure of the area's population. Such structure can be ascertained in a relatively precise way only on the basis of dealing separately with each component of the demographic growth, namely, with fertility and mortality rates by age in addition to detailed sex-age characteristics of the population at the present time.

The component method projects separately future numbers of each age group of males and females, reducing them according to the mortality rates differentiated by age and sex and adding to the totals the newly born, calculated on the basis of fertility rates. The key element of the method is the life table which contains survival ratios for each age group of people called the 'cohort', that is, the probability of each number of the age group to survive to the next year. Such tables are normally constructed on the basis of detailed death by age statistics operating in the country, sometimes as to the expected changes in the mortality rates in the future.[5] This pertains, in particular to the mortality rates of children, especially to those newly born. Infant mortality rates, usually very high in a developing country with a poor health service, change rather quickly with the improvement of the latter and this cannot be ignored in the construction of life tables used for projections.

The calculation of the newly born rests on fertility rates observed through the birth statistics and also corrected according to assumed future changes. Fertility rates are usually calculated in relation to the number of women of child-bearing age. If uncertainty exists as to the future rates, alternative assumptions may be used resulting in two or more versions of the future population to be born in the years ahead.

It follows from the description of the component method that a good deal of expertise in the subject is required. Reliable demographic data and life tables, although available at national levels, and sometimes also at the regional one, are rarely available at the local and micro-regional levels. At the latter levels life tables constructed on a broader basis may considerably deviate from the survival probabilities existing locally and even if they do not, the ever-present danger of distortions caused by migration may render the elaborate calculations according to the component method fruitless.

Migrational Patterns and their Projections

At the sub-national level, and in particular at the local and micro-regional level, migratory movements constitute a major aspect of demographic analysis. Migration caused by various economic and social factors results in an increase of population above the natural growth or a decrease below it. Very often it is a two-way stream of out-migration and in-migration resulting in a positive or negative balance. The additional gain of population is usually noticeable in bigger cities and the loss affects the rural areas of the country. The study of migration and its causes can give a good insight into the socio-economic processes of the area in question. Migration influences in many ways the demographic characteristics of the area under study and, therefore, should also be dealt with when projecting future population.

Despite their importance for analysis and projections, data on migration are often very difficult to obtain. The main sources of information on migratory movements are the censuses, population registrations and surveys. The most detailed data can usually be obtained from the censuses, if they contain questions directly related to migration: about the place of birth, or place of former residence (last residence, the residence on a specific date, or the duration of residence in the place of census registration). The summaries of answers to these questions for a particular settlement or area give an indication of the number of in-migrants and, depending on the form of the question, also the place of their origin. If all persons who originated from the same place or area but registered at the time of the census in different places are summed-up they represent the total out-migration from the original place or area (with exclusion of persons who died before the census date). In this manner we obtain a pattern of in-migration and out-migration to and from particular settlements or areas which indicates both the geographical direction of population movements as well as their intensity in relation to the number of inhabitants in the original places or to those of present residence. A clear picture of this comes out on maps with appropriate symbols. Such maps enriched with additional information about various socio-economic characteristics of particular areas greatly help to draw inferences as to the causes of migration.

If census data do not contain questions directly related to migration or cannot be obtained for smaller areas, then some indirect methods must be employed in order to learn about this phenomenon. The direct methods applied most often rely on population data, the settlement or area at two different points in time which can be two census dates or non-census population registrations. Firstly, we calculate the natural increase of the population for the period between the two counts. Secondly, we compare the total population registered at the latter date with that which one would expect on the basis of natural increase only. The resulting positive or negative difference can be interpreted as the net balance of migratory movements to and from the settlement or area in question.

Depending on the way the natural population increase between the two time-points is computed, we differentiate several alternative methods of the indirect measurement of migration. The vital statistics method relies on registration of birth and death occurring among the inhabitants of the unit of study. Another method, the survival ratio method, uses the probability of survival of each age-group and, therefore, requires detailed data as to the sex-age structure of the inhabitants at the time of the two population counts. Survival probabilities can be substituted by data from life tables, provided that the latter could be assumed for the mortality conditions of the settlement or micro-region. Finally, when the use of life tables is impossible or not appropriate, survival ratios can be calculated for the whole country directly from the two census data by age- and sex groups and then applied to the area under study.

The advantage of indirect methods is their relative simplicity, their disadvantages being the lack of information as to the origin of migration, its two-way intensity and the danger of carrying forward all the errors of existing vital statistics or census counts. If migration is a particularly crucial issue of a locality or micro-region, then it would be necessary to organize a special survey on migration. In many cases the most efficient way to arrange such a survey would be through applying the above-mentioned sampling methods. The sample survey could be based either on the place of residence or on the place of work. Naturally, a survey would not be necessary if the local and area development planner had at his disposal regular registration data on migration which do exist in some of the more advanced countries. Such registration, if properly executed, constitutes the most detailed and reliable source on migration.

The projection of migration can be a most difficult task to a planner. That task is considerably facilitated if data on past migration trends are available. Assuming that factors which caused migration in the past would operate without major change also in the future, one could use one of the extrapolation methods in order to estimate the size of future migration and its contribution to the total number of inhabitants in a locality or micro-region.

Where data for the above extrapolation are missing or the assumptions underlying it cannot be defended, migration projections have to be based on other premises. The most appropriate ones for the local level are those which link migration movements to relevant features of economic development. If, for instance, a micro-region is expected to considerably expand industrially, the new work opportunities to be created should be confronted with estimates of the future potential of local labour supply, the latter representing the result of multiplication of the area's individual sex and age-groups by current or assumed activity rates appropriate for each group of them. If the local labour potential does not suffice to cover the future demand of industry (and other needs created by the multiplier effect) the missing amount of the labour could be supplied through migration, provided the work opportunities offered by industry are sufficiently attractive in comparison to employment possibilities in other areas. A similar indication as to future migration can be drawn from large schemes of housing construction in a particular place or area which go far beyond the local needs. However, in this as well as the previous approaches, one should always bear in mind that the estimates show only the potential for migration and not the most likely one. Besides the economic factors, there are many others–political, sociological, cultural, psychological–which co-determine the size and direction of migration. To measure the impact of each of them is beyond the possibilities at the local and area levels.

Characteristics of the Local Economy

Collecting Data on the Economy

The economy of a particular locality is closely interwoven with that of the region in which it is located and through it with the national economy. The major share of its outputs finds markets outside the locality, and many of the inputs have to come from outside. However, when it comes to planning for future development of the locality, the main characteristics of the local economy are of prime importance and have to be identified, their inter-dependence has to be analysed and their relationships with the outside economy have to be determined.

Many questions can be asked about the local economy. Is it predominantly agricultural? If so, what is the pattern of production—a mono-crop or is it diversified? Is the crop being produced on small farms? What is the level of mechanization? What is the state of technology? What are the markets for the produce of the locality?

Other questions can relate to labour utilization, the degree of investment in production enterprises, the services available, the level of education of the residents, their state of health, etc. In reality, there are many facts and figures about the local economy which have to be gathered in considerable detail, if any viable plans are to be made for its future development. When gathering such information, it is usual to ask two basic questions which hold good for any development sector, whether economic or social: (i) To what extent does the local economy provide a satisfactory level of living for the people? (ii) What is the potential for its future expansion?

The first question requires a good knowledge of the present level of production and consumption and the supply of services as well as an awareness of the needs of the local population. Improvements in the level of living in terms of higher consumption of goods and services can be sought through more efficient use of the existing resources--capital, land, equipment and labour--and through specialization of production. One implication is that in some outputs there might be more production than the local inhabitants can consume, and the excess will have to be marketed outside the locality. Another implication is that production of certain other outputs might have to be reduced, because other localities can produce them at lower costs. Such changes in the pattern of production will require changes in other sectors contributing to development, for example, land consolidation, credit facilities, marketing services, institutional arrangements, vocational training, etc.

The second question requires an understanding of unutilized and under-utilized resources in the locality, both natural and human. They may range from cultivable land, water resources, raw materials and local crafts to unemployed and under-employed labour, tourist attractions, local institutions and behaviour patterns conducive to development. These will have to be examined in relation to the wider economy in order to determine their potential for future development.

It is around these questions and problems that planners and developers at the local and area levels have to organize data and information collection. Existing data and information often prove to be insufficient or may not be suitable, as they might have been collected and presented for some other purpose. The bulk of the data on the local economy has to originate from field work and surveys on the spot, a task that should not be too difficult to perform considering the dimensions of the local and area levels. Yet, field work and surveys, in order to produce the desired information for the local planner and reports for the higher authorities, have to be organized and performed according to certain methodologies.

Such investigations have to be carefully designed. The first step would be to state clearly and precisely the objectives of the data collection or to have a clear understanding of the objectives of the exercise as required by the regional or central authorities. The objectives then have to be translated into operational terms, that is, into questions that could be asked in the course of the investigation. For this purpose an appropriate data sheet should be designed (if already not prepared by the higher authorities), which is very important, and if more persons than one are to co-operate in the investigation clear instructions should be attached explaining the terms used on the data sheet and the technical details of their collection. A very important next step is to test the data sheet on several examples in order to remove any misinterpretations and to adapt it to the real situations. If it has not been decided before, one should at this stage determine whether the investigation should be a comprehensive one, covering all units concerned, or only a sample would suffice. In general, at the local level, exhaustive investigations would be appropriate with respect to all sectors of the economy, except perhaps agriculture. In the latter case the procedures for sample surveys already mentioned should be followed.

The execution of a field investigation is also governed by detailed procedures, most of them strictly related to the kind and subject of investigation. Some of them may sound trivial, such as those pertaining to the order of asking questions or to the selection of the hour of investigation, but in concrete cases their observance may determine the outcome of the entire endeavour. One general rule applies to most kinds of field investigation, namely, that of checking recorded information. In order to eliminate errors which may occur during the investigation a double-check of the records should be made, if possible, on the spot. If the data sheets contain provision for cross-checking, they should be utilized as long as the possibility of making corrections exists. Only after such checking of records has been made and the data sheets completely filled out, should they be used for further processing at the local level or sent to higher levels for analysis.

REFERENCES

1. For example, an area of 100 metres diameter on a map of 1:100,000 is represented only by a spot of 1 mm diameter, whereas on a map of the scale 1:500 it would be 2 cm in diameter.
2. Despite considerable progress in mapping, among others through the use of aerial photography, there are still many areas for which such maps are not available. Where they are not available, the local and area planner can only use simple situation sketches drawn on the basis of his knowledge of the area in question.
3. There is a simple short-cut to this procedure it we multiply the last census figure by the growth rate raised to the power equal to the number of years from the last census (t_2), i.e. $(1+r)^{t_2}$.
4. Among these the statistical concept of moving averages is the simplest one. In the case of one particular five-year age group it implies that data on the preceding two five-year groups as well as on the two following groups must be added to the group in question in order to calculate the average. For the age group between 10 to 75 years, the formula reads:

   $$\bar{S} = 1/16\,(-S_{-2} + 4S_{-1} + 10S + 4S_1 - S_2)$$

   Where $\bar{S}$ symbolizes the adjusted number of persons in one five-year group, S is the reported number of persons in the same group, S_{-2} and S_{-1} are reported number in the two preceding five-year groups, and S_1 and S_2 are the reported numbers for the two subsequent groups.
5. If the information on mortality is incomplete one can use model life tables constructed on the basis of data from countries with similar conditions.

5

Statistical Methods of Data Analysis

B.S. BHOOSHAN*

DEVELOPMENT Planning is an exercise in space. Any development must ultimately come to the land. And it is for the benefit of man. In a sense, area planning could be understood as a control process of the man-nature system. Effective control needs proper understanding of the system and its behaviour. In short planning process consists of the following analytic and synthetic phases :

(1) Situation analysis–Systems study or analysis,
(2) Forecast and Projection–Systems projection,
(3) Plan Formulations and Evolution–goal setting, System Synthesis and System Evaluation,
(4) Implementation and Review.

In this chapter survey of the analytic tools available for the planner for the first three stages is made emphasis would be laid on the statistical techniques of quantitative data analysis which specially are useful for the two crucial stages of systems study and systems projection.

The system synthesis or plan formulation still largely is an initiative exercise and analytic techniques can only improve the perception of the planner. Earlier days of development planning the whole process has been based on the intuitive assumptions and now slowly the analytic techniques are making their way. By and large, it still continues to be an amalgam of both, though many planners do not admit

* B.S. Bhooshan is an architect planner in the Institute of Development Studies, University of Mysore, Mysore.

this. And it is a fact that there are people who do not believe in the excessive use of analytic techniques, and believe that people are better than machines. To certain extent it is true that whether we should train and make use of initiative and imaginative planners or depend on analytical techniques, is a question of debate. Nonetheless, the society should not be held for the penalty of planners' mistake.

It is a fact that statistics and statistical and mathematical models have failed at times in revealing the true picture. Their failures are attributable to the following reasons :

(1) Models are models and not real. They are based on certain assumptions which themselves could be wrong.
(2) Statistical techniques rely largely on averages. There are chances that things could happen very well outside the averages.
(3) Statistic is a kind of generalization and does not apply to individual items. Such a trial will yield unrealistic results.
(4) As statistic is generalization, it requires a substantial sample to predict or bring out the characteristic of a particular phenomenon accurately. Sometimes, it so happens that either sample may be so small or the data are unreliable, due to errors in enumeration or obsolescence, that it may vitiate the results altogether.

Data Analysis

The system under study viz. the man-nature system or the area for development consists of several components or elements. Broadly they consists of man, society, nature and man-made nature. In another way these elements may fall under the physical, economical and social headings. Under the caption of nature we may come across elements like soil, water, minerals, climate, rainfall, topography, etc. and among the economic groups are the elements like man's activities over space such as agriculture, capital, industries, marketing system, etc., under special groups we may have to study social groups, communities, social habits and even social resistance or acceptance to innovations all equated to fundamental needs of man.

Analysis means the understanding of the characteristics of each one of these components or elements, and also the understanding of the inter-relationships between these components or elements that makes the whole into a balanced or unbalanced system.

Data or informations will pour in a planning office about all these components, which may consists of primary as well as secondary information. This clumsy mass of data cannot be fruitfully used unless some order is put into it. Further analytic techniques vary with the type of data and type of results needed. It is a statisticians job, but the planner or the man-in-charge be able to guide them. For that matter he must be able to understand the statisticians technical slang also.

Statistics and its Use in Planning

The term statistics is used plurally as well as singularly. In a plural sense, it means the whole body of data pertaining to a particular phenomenon and in a singular sense, it means the whole body of techniques available to analyse these data.

In the planning process, statistical techniques have the following specific functions :

System Description – Situation Analysis

(a) *Descriptive Functions*: Statistics present facts in a definitive form. Numerical facts give more precise information than facts expressed in general terms. It is the quality of definiteness which is responsible for the growing popularity and applications of statistics in various sciences. Because of the same nature, statistics should be used continuously and discriminately. It could be used to prove fallacy and its indiscriminative use may make wrong impressions.

(b) *In Areal Analysis:* Statistics would be used to identify backward regions with respect to any particular phenomenon, and also for the comparison of different sub-regions and identification of homogeneous sub-regions.

(c) For the study of characteristic behaviour of certain periodic events like rainfall.

(d) Establishing relationships between different variables for understanding the nature of the whole system–Correlation such as rainfall and agricultural production, run off and slope etc.

System Projection

Statistic is the main tool for the projection of the events into the future and make forecasts such as population, cattle, crop production etc. to make estimates of future requirements.

System Evaluation

For comparison of projected and desired targets with the capacity of the designed system.

The Methods

Let us make a brief survey of the statistical methods and basic concepts:

Classification and Tabulation

Data in loose form will not reveal anything. It is very difficult to interpret raw data. Some order has to be put into it. Classification and tabulation is the first job to be done to reduce the bulk of data and to simplify the details into such a form so that the salient features may become explicit for analysis.

Classification is the process of arranging things (either actually or nationally) in groups or classes according to their resemblance and affinities and gives expression to the unity of attributes that may subsist amongst a density of individuals. In other words classification is grouping of raw data into homogeneous classes.

When any collection of figures, representing some quantitative values of any given phenomenon, is to be processed it will be found that although all such figures represent the same phenomenon they are not all of exactly the same value. Example, rainfall over years or area under-cultivation in different regions, etc. This highly variable nature of numerical data is common to all sets of data, and this quantity which varies is known as the *Variate or Variable.*

There are Two Kinds of Variables:

(a) *Continuous Variable:* Such that there are no clear cut or sharp breaks.between the values that are possible. Examples, land under cultivation, rainfall crop production, etc.

(b) *Discrete Variables:* Which can take only whole numbers and cannot vary continuously. Example, number of towns in a region, number of population, cattle etc. Special care must be taken when deriving conclusions from the analysis of such discrete varieties.

The data are first grouped into 'Classes' so that it is known how many occurrences fall into each of a series of quantitatively different set of conditions. Classification could be based on qualitative characteristics (for items such as sex and literacy in population data, types of soil, or types of irrigation etc.) or quantitative characteristics (such as production of rice, irrigated area income, etc.).

Class Interval

When quantitative characteristics are used for grouping of data, the usual method is to group them in class intervals, by arranging arbitrary limits.

The rainfall data over a set of regions could be grouped as :

Below 400 m/Year	2 Taluks
Below 400 - 600 m/Year	3 "
Below 600 - 1000 m/Year	2 "
Above 1000 - m/Year	4 "

The income of families could be grouped as :

Below Rs. 100	100 families
Rs. 100 -250	400 "
Rs. 250 - 400	250 "

Care should be taken in the fixing up of class interval so that all or most of the occurrences or none or too small a number of occurrences fall into a class interval. Further for data analysis purposes it is better to keep the class intervals equal. Classes should be mutually exclusive.

In general all classifications fall under three sets of statistical series:

1. Time series – relating to the chronological order
2. Spatial series – relating to area or spatial units
3. Conditional series – relating to changes in some conditions such as income, rainfall, etc.

Tabulation

A table is a systematic arrangement of statistical data in columns and rows. This could be an inter-section of two sets of classification and as such has the property to contain a large mass of information in compact form. A table is easy to be understood and remembered than a running statement containing the same information. The following example explains this:

*The Descriptive Statistics**

According to a pamphlet 'Agricultural Development Problems and Perspective' published by the Department of Agriculture (Ministry of Food and Agriculture) Government of India, April, 1965, efforts to step up the physical Programmes of agricultural development have gained momentum. The additional acreage under minor irrigation steadily increased from 1.5 million acres in 1960-61 to 2.8 million acres in 1963-64. The anticipated acreage for minor irrigation for 1964-65 is 3.3 million. The fertilizer consumption increased from about two lakh tonnes (nitrogen) in 1960-61 to about 3.9 lakh tonnes in 1963-64. In 1964-65, it is expected to show a further increase to 5.9 lakh tonnes (nitrogen). The consumption of phosphatic fertilizers (P_2O_5) increased from 70 thousand tonnes in 1960-61 to 140 thousand tonnes in 1963-64 and estimated to have risen to 180 thousand tonnes in 1964-65. The production and utilization of compost is estimated to have risen from about 69.4 million tonnes in 1960-61 to about 96 million tonnes in 1963-64. The anticipated level for 1964-65 is about 114 million tonnes. The coverage under improved seeds of foodgrains has increased from the level of about 49 million acres in 1960-61 to about 82.9 million acres in 1963-64 and about 101.5 million acres in 1964-65, (Table 5.1).

Frequency Distribution

Frequency is the number of times at which a particular event occurs in a selected sample of values. For example, if we select a sample of 50 villages and assess their population and if 30 villages happen to be of

* D.S. Mithani, Elementary Statistics for Economics.

the size between 3000-4000 then we say that the frequency of occurrence of that particular event (i.e. a village falling in the class interval of 3000-4000) among 50 is 30. The frequency distribution indicates the frequency is the number of times each individual item occurs. (Table 5.2).

Table 5.1: Progress of the Physical Programmes of Agricultural Development

Year	Minor irrigation '000,000 acres	Consumption of Fertiliser: Nitrogen '00000 tonnes	Phosphatic (P_2O_5) '000 tonnes	Compost '000,000 tonnes	Improved seeds of foodgrains '000,000 acres
1960-61	1.5	2.0	70	69.4	49.0
1963-64	2.8	3.9	140	96.0	82.9
1964-65	3.3	5.9	180	114.0	101.5

Note: All figures relating to the year 1964-65 are estimates only.
Source: "Agricultural Development Problems and Perspective", published by the Department of Agriculture (Ministry of Food and Agriculture) Government of India, April 1965.

Cumulative Frequency

For certain problems, the statistician may like to know not only how many items fall in a specified class, but also how many lie above or below the limits of class. Such a type of information is found in 'cumulative frequency' distribution.

Table 5.2: Frequency distribution

Size of village	No. of villages
Below 1000	4
1000 - 2000	2
2000 - 3000	6
3000 - 4000	30
4000 - 5000	8

For the above example the cumulative frequency distribution will be as per Table 5.3.

Table 5.3: Cumulative Frequency

Size of village	Cumulative Frequency	
	Less than	More than
0	0	50
1000	4	46
2000	6	44
3000	12	38
4000	42	8
5000	50	0

Behaviour of the frequency distribution could be studied by drawing a histogram or graph.

On the other hand, there were an even number of occurrences, then the median would be midway between two of these values.

Median is the reading on the scale of the variable such that there are equal number of entries above it and below it.

Mode: When data are grouped into classes, then the class containing the most occurrence is referred as the mode. It means the most likely value, one which occurs most often. By definition the mode is the value of the class within a statistical group in which there are most incidences.

There are advantages and disadvantages in the use of these three types of means. The mode by its very definition indicates that which is most common or frequent. Very often, however, there is some difficulty in deciding exactly where the mode occurs. This difficulty can arise for two reasons. First, the distribution may not be unimodel, or it may well have two or more model groups of roughly equal importance. The second difficulty arises from the selection of the classes which are to be adopted. No algebraic treatment is possible in mode. On the other hand, mean is capable of algebraic manipulation. But they are always influenced by the extreme values and have an upward bias. Moreover it is not a representative figure. Median is not affected by extreme value. It is not difficult to calculate also except for long series of data. Again it is not capable of algebraic manipulation.

Mean is the one most commonly used. But in some cases like certain attributes, like income, median could be preferred.

Measures of Dispersion or Deviation

For true and worthwhile understanding of the mean value of a set of data it must be possible to associate that mean easily and readily with some measure of the degree of variations about the number. There are several measures of dispersion of data arround mean or deviation of values from the mean. The most commonly used form is *standard deviation.*

Standard deviation or sometimes known as 'root mean square deviation', is the square root of the average of squares of the deviations from the arithmetic average. This parameter is signified by the Greek letter Sigma(σ).

While σ^2 is called variance

Standard deviation $(\sigma) = \sqrt{\frac{(x-\bar{x})^2}{n}}$

In fact it roughly represents the average of the amount of deviations of the values from the average of the whole set of values either positively or negatively. Deviation when expressed in percentage of the mean is known as Index of Variability.

$$\text{Index of Variability} = \frac{\text{Standard Deviation}}{\text{Mean}} \times 100$$

This parameter is a good index to understand the erratic behaviour of certain natural phenomena such as rainfall.

The Problem of Correlation

In many problems, there is the need to compare sets of data in terms of the extent to which a change in one is or is not rejected in the other. For such problems the technique or correlation is used. This technique is used for establishing relationships between two sets of data, such as, rainfall and production. Permeability of soil and crop production of a particular crop, rainfall and run off etc. This necessarily implies that the individual item of the two sets of data co-exist either in time or space, such that inter-relate changes can be considered. In such a problem an index is required that reflects the degree to which changes in one direction (+ or –) and magnitude in one set of data are associated with comparable changes in the other set.

The index is provided by what is called 'product moment correlation coefficient' or simple correlation coefficient.

The correlation coefficient (ϒ) is represented by the simple formula:

$$r = \frac{\frac{1}{n}\Sigma(a-\bar{a})(b-\bar{b})}{\sigma a - \sigma b}$$

Where n = total number of values
a = individual values of one set
b = individual values of the other set
$\bar{a}$ = mean of set (1)
$\bar{b}$ = mean of set (2)
σa = Standard deviation of values of a
σb = Standard deviation of values of b

This formula gives the simplest way of calculation of ϒ. There are still complex methods for more accurate calculation when data is large.

When ϒ is + 1 there is perfect positive correlation

When ϒ is – 1 there is perfect negative correlation and when ϒ is 0 there is no correlation. P is positive means when one value increased other also increases. P is negative means when one value increases other decreases.

A rough assessment of the correlation of the two variables could be made by graphic method or by drawing a scattered diagram.

Regression Lines

Regression lines are graphic representations of the correlations between two sets of values. Regression line of *a* on *b* will give a graph point around which *b* may take a value for a corresponding value of *a*. Similarly Regression line of *b* on *a* will give points around which *a* may take a value for corresponding value of *b*. The angle of intersection between these lines gives their relative correlation when there is perfect correlation both lines merge and become one (ϒ = + 1 or – 1) and when there is no correlation they intersect at 90° (when ϒ = 0)

Regression lines could be used for prediction of values of either *a* or *b* given the value of other set. For example, if we construct regression lines of two sets of variables like rainfall during sowing season and production of a particular crop, it would be possible to predict the production if we know the rainfall during the sowing season. Also *vice versa* we can calculate the rainfall required for the production of a desired amount of crop. However, there is no guarantee that the predicted value found from the graph will be exact. The assumption is that the true value will occur around this value. It is possible to calculate *Confidence Limits* also for these regression lines so that the chance is that in 95 per cent cases the value will lie within these limits (range).

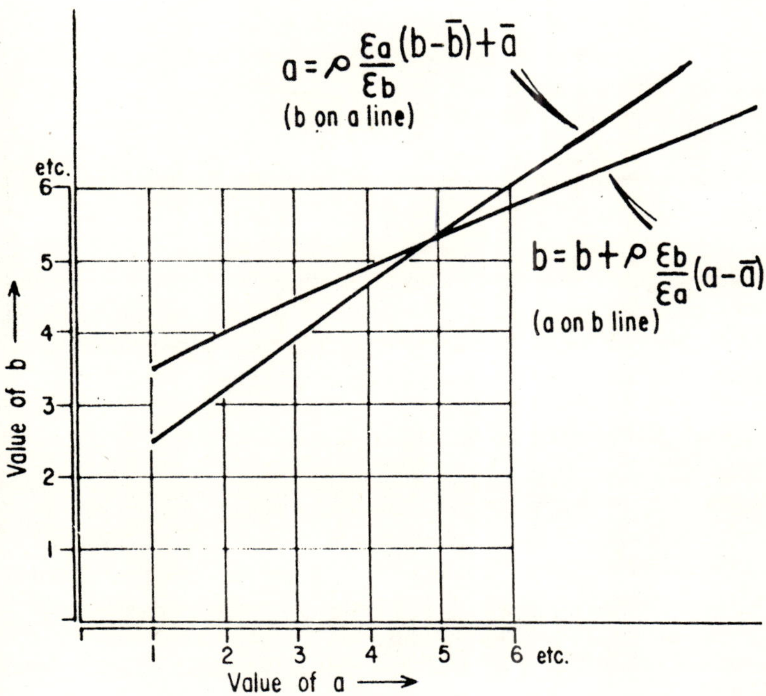

Fig. 5.1: Regression Lines

What have been given in the previous pages are some fundamental concepts of statistics and some basic methods of analysis of establishing relationships. Still there are much complex and sophisticated methods which could be effectively used for analytical purposes in integrated area development. The most important and crucial stage where statistical help would be needed most is the projection or forecasts stage. It would be beyond our scope to go into these techniques but it would not be fair to leave them untouched.

System Projection

Various projections may have to be used in the planning process to assess the future requirements. The most important one is population projection or to assess the future content of the population in the area. This could be done either by simple projection of past trends into the future or by making a systematic analysis of various factors affecting the population growth, such as birth rate, mortality, migration, etc.

For the forecasts of any relevant data for the future value, the following methods could be used:

Projection by Extrapolation

Graph Technique

Plotting a graph of the past trends of the phenomenon, such as population, soil erosion or per capita income and sketching a line which, in the judgment of the forecast appears to fit in the past data; and extending this line into the future to obtain the future values.

Extrapolation by Mathematical Functions

On the light of the past trends a mathematical function or equation is established which relate the phenomenon (number of population or per capita income etc.) to the distance from a base year. This mathematical function will approximately define the graph or curve should we plot the past trends. The solution of this function for a future year give the predicted value. This method is known as curve fitting. Straight lines, exponential curves, parabola or hyperbola curves or logistic curve used is to suit the curves are solved.

Correlation Methods

(a) Once established a correlation between two variables the values of one could be predicted from the value of other by simple regression (see Graph 5.1)

(b) *Multiple regression method:* Frequently in regional study it is found that growth of one phenomenon such as population is simultaneously associated with more than one independent variable. Here a multiple regression analysis is pursued. Multiple linear regression equation provides for the relative effects of several phenomena on a particular phenomenon.

Example: Crop production is a regression function of, rainfall, slope, fertilizer, temperature variation, etc. This could be used for population projection also.

Developments and Advanced Techniques

During the past few decades several analytical tools were developed by economists, planners and mathematician which have come to be known generally as operations analysis, many of these techniques have been evolved first for military purposes. Development of Cyberneties, theory of random search and statistical thermodynamics, and above all the computer and general system theory have provided adequate analytical tools for the planners to deal with complex situations. Of the many techniques used at present for regional analysis, are:

1. The linear programming techniques
2. Input-output analysis
3. Game theory, risk theory and decision theory, could be rated as the most powerful analytical tools.

Linear programming is particularly useful for underdeveloped conditions, since it is tool used for identifying optimum levels of human activity under limited resource conditions to maximize profits or, social gains, or total income.

Input-output analysis gives a clear picture of inter-sectoral relations in a region and could be used for the estimation of the level of activity needed in different sectors to promote the activities of a particular sector or the total activities to a desired level.

Game theory and decisions theory can be used by selectors to promote the activities of a particular sector or the total activities to a desired level.

Game theory and decision theory can be used for selection of optimum strategies of development of different rival sectors or rival industries.

However, all these techniques are only decision-making aids and plan formulations or system synthesis much depending on the innovative ability of the planning team. There is no guarantee that use of a most sophisticated analytical tool will yield good results.

Sampling Technique for Socio-economic Surveys*

Many development projects are intended to reach considerable number of people. Obtaining information on project results by observing or questioning the entire group of people potentially affected would be wasteful. By observing or questioning only a fraction ('sample') of the group the desired information can be obtained more quickly, and very often more accurately than by questioning the entire group.

It is essential, however, that the sample be selected properly, that is, by relying on the laws of chance in the selection process. Otherwise, biased or erroneous conclusions may be drawn.

The two major characteristics of a sample are:

Its size : Large sample (over one hundred) are needed relatively infrequently in studying development projects. Many useful kinds of data can be obtained from samples of ten persons known to be well-informed or twenty (cross-section of a whole community or region).
Its representativeness: A sample cannot fairly represent the whole if the persons in the sample differ substantially from those not in the sample, and if these differences are related to the kinds of data being collected.

---

* Reproduced from: *Evaluating Development Projects:* A manual for the use of field workers. Prepared for UNESCO by Samuel P. Hayes, Jr. UNESCO, Paris, 1959. 2nd edition, revised 1966. Sales no. A. 2103, pp. 95-102.

Size of Sample

Sample must, of course, be large enough. The fallacies that can emerge from anecdotes of a single instance or from study of a very small group are well known. It is very difficult to avoid bias of some sort in a very small sample. On the other hand, because a development project usually affects a limited area or a limited class of people (for example, teachers in technical schools), and because the persons affected are thus a good deal more homogeneous than when a national survey is undertaken, a sample of twenty individuals (if effort is made to avoid bias in the sample) will provide a good deal of useful information, particularly if one is interested only in fairly marked changes. A hundred individuals, again with efforts to avoid bias in selecting them, will usually be enough to indicate fairly precisely the direct effects of a development project. After all, great precision in the measurement of such effects is unnecessary, because changes to be socially significant must be sufficiently marked to show up under even quite crude measurement.

The size of sample needed is obviously related to the variability of data obtained. If, in interviewing a representative sample of families, all the first twenty said that they spent between 10 per cent and 30 per cent of their income for rent (see Table 5.4), one could accept this as indicating the range of rent income ratio for the whole community.

Similarly, if all, or all but one, members of a representative sample of twenty said that they were in favour of building a school, it would hardly be necessary to inquire further.

Where substantially identical or unanimous results are obtained from representative samples, therefore, the samples used can be quite small.

On the other hand, if there is great variation in replies, or if a large measure of disagreement exists, then substantially larger samples are required. Even here, however, the samples need not be very large unless it is important (which is rarely the case in studying development projects) to get precise measurements or to identify or measure small differences between one group and another. Usually, findings that might be utilized in planning projects, and the project results themselves, are either large enough to show up in small samples, or are not important enough to justify the time and expense of using large samples.

For example, consider the results, of a survey of working class households in New York, United Kingdom. The income of each family was determined, and then the rent each family paid was expressed as a percentage of income. Dividing the whole group into five income classes, Table 5.4 shows the percentage of income spent for rent by all households in each class. It also shows the percentage obtained from a sample comprising only one out of fifty households in each income class.

While the results from the sample differ in each income class by up to 2 per cent from the results of the complete survey, still the same factual conclusions can be derived from the sample as from the whole, to the effect that, in this community, the percentage of income spent on rent has a consistent and important relationship to income level, being more than twice as large in the highest income group as in the lowest. This finding was obtained by using a sample from the thirty-four to seventy-seven households in each income class.

Table 5.4: Percentage of income spent for rent

Income class	Complete survey		Sample 1 in 50	
	Total number of households	Percentage	Number in sample	Percentage
A (Highest)	1,748	26.5	34	27.1
B	2,477	22.7	67	22.6
C	2,514	19.8	46	18.0
D	1,676	15.8	35	16.9
E (Lowest)	3,740	11.3	77	11.5

Another important point is illustrated in this table. If the whole sample (in this case 259) is broken down into sub-samples, it is the size of each sub-sample which is at issue. Many survey samples in the United States and Europe are quite large (2,000 to 3,000) partly so that numerous sub-groups can be studied separately, and partly to permit identification of relatively minor differences among sub-groups, or between these sub-groups and similar sub-groups studied in other surveys.

The size required for samples under certain conditions is indicated in Table 5.5.

To use this table, one may first 'guesstimate' the percentage to be used in entering the first column or, much better, one may actually obtain responses from a first sample of twenty-five or so. If this sample is representative, their responses will often provide enough indication of homogeneity to permit planning the size of the final sample. These plans may, however, have to be altered later if it is found that the first sample was not representative.

There are no rules for entering the second column. This is simply a decision one must take in the light of the importance attached to accuracy of results and the cost of getting enough interviews to reduce the margin of error.

Table 5.5 shows that 70 per cent of a representative first sample drawn from a village of several thousand can, when asked, give the name of the local village extension worker. Even if the sample contains only twenty persons, one can be 'reasonably sure' (nineteen chances in twenty) that at least 50 per cent of the total population (which may be several thousand) know his name and perhaps 90 per cent know it. (50 per cent is 70 per cent minus 20 per cent; 90 per cent is 70 per cent plust 20 per cent the true answer for the whole village is indicated to lie within 20 per cent above or 20 per cent below the 70 per cent figure obtained).

Table 5.5: Sample size required when 'margin of error' of specified size is tolerable (calculated for questions requiring only 'Yes' - 'No' or 'Favour' - 'Oppose' reply)

If approximately the following percentage say 'Yes'	And if it is satisfactory to have a 19 out of 20 assurance that the 'margin of error' percentage is not larger than	An adequate sample is
50	20	25
	10	100
	5	400*
	2	2,400*
70 or more, or 30 or less	20	20
	10	80
	5	300*
	2	2,000*
90 or more, or 10 or less	10	35
	5	140*
	2	900*

* This precision and therefore this sample size is ordinarily not needed in guiding the administration of development projects.

Conversely, if it is desirable to establish the fact that at least 60 per cent of the whole village know the village worker's name, the sample size should be increased to eighty. If 70 per cent of this sample of eighty knows the village worker's name, one can be 'reasonably sure' that this is not in error by more than 10 per cent.

If in the process of getting these additional responses, the proportion of the sample knowing the name climbs from 70 per cent to 90 per cent, one can stop with a sample of thirty-five or less. With a sample of thirty-five and a response of 90 per cent knowing the name, one can be 'reasonably sure' that at least 80 per cent of the whole village knows the worker's name (90 per cent with 'margin of error' of 10 per cent).

As indicated in the example above, the required sample can be small when the results obtained do not differ greatly from person to person. The data on percentage of income spent for rent showed relatively little variation. Answers to a 'Yes' - 'No' question very much more widely, as an individual can really only answer 100 per cent 'Yes' or 0 per cent 'Yes', with no gradations between. Samples used for such questions generally need to be larger than where intermediate gradations of response are possible, although groups giving very high (90 per cent or more) responses in one category can be represented adequately by quite small samples. As indicated earlier the general principle is that the more homogeneous the population the smaller the sample needed.

One way of reducing the size of the sample needed is to stratify the sample, i.e., breaking it up into groups, each of which is internally more homogeneous than is the group as a whole. A relatively small sample can then be taken from each sub-group, and the results are then weighted by the reciprocal of the fraction comprising the sub-sample before being added together. This method avoids unnecessarily large representation of particularly numerous sub-groups in the total sample.

Sample size does not have to be finally determined before undertaking a survey. A series of small samples (if each is representative) can be studied, and the results examined. If great homogeneity is present, or if successive samples give results which do not vary too greatly to be useful for evaluation purposes, the collection of data can be terminated at an early stage. Even if not terminated, the study of early small samples to provide a basis for the designing of subsequent samples will result in saving the total time and money necessary to obtain results of a prescribed precision.

Representativeness

How to avoid bias? To avoid the mistake is allowing to use a selection method that depends on factors related to the operations being performed or to the effects desired. If, for example, one is measuring the impact of a fertilizer demonstration programme, one should not limit his sample to the farmers who were already buying fertilizer from a dealer at the beginning of the programme. A later survey of the same farmers would miss all the newly converted fertilizer buyers. Similarly, one would not limit his sample of malarial patients to those who come to the clinic for treatment, ignoring those who were to ill or not ill enough, or too poor, or too afraid, to come to the clinic. In both examples, 'self-selection' would be an important biasing factor.

Representativeness, or freedom from bias, in a sample depends mainly on proper procedure in the drawing and collecting of the sample. The objectives here is to give every person in the whole group, or in each sub-group if the sample is stratified, a known chance of selection. This usually means an equal chance of selection, at least within each sub-sample.

This objective is most important if precise results are sought from a sample of a large and heterogeneous population. When one is seeking only rather obvious results, in limited and fairly homogeneous groups, not as much attention needs to be given to refined methods of getting a representative sample; but, of course, any action that is feasible to take to improve representativeness will add conviction to the conclusions reached.

The following are the chief methods by which an equal chance of selection can be attained:

Simple Random Sampling

One can write on a separate slip of paper the name and address of every person or family who might be selected, mix all the slips together, and then draw the requisite number of slips at random. However, sometimes the mix is poor.

Systematic Random Sampling

One can file all the slips prepared above or use lists already prepared for other purposes (if believed to be complete lists), and then count the number of names and decide on the size of the samples. If there are 5,000 names and one wishes a sample of 100, one can simply choose every fiftieth name from the file or list.

If there is any reason to suspect that a list has some repetitive pattern, such as one based on multiples of five, one should of course avoid intervals which are related to the pattern. In the example just cited, if one suspected a pattern based on a multiple of five, the whole list might be divided into 10 sections of 500 each, and within the first section one might take every fiftieth name, starting with the first; in the second every fiftieth name, starting with the second, and so on.

Stratified Random Sampling

As indicated above in discussing the size of the sample, substantial economies can be obtained by dividing the whole group being studied into sub-groups, each of which is internally more homogeneous than the whole. For example, families living in high income areas may be put into one group or stratum, those in middle income areas may be put into another, those in low income areas may be put into another. Or different communities located near a development project may constitute separate strata. Or the persons known to be favourable to an expert may be one stratum, and those critical of him another.

If the different strata differ in their responses to the questions asked, the results from a stratified sample will be more reliable than those from an unstratified sample. Within each stratum of course, every person must have as much chance of being selected as any other person.

For many studies, particular groups or strata are more important than others. The whole population of a community might well be stratified; and then 100 per cent of the leaders might be interviewed, along with 50 per cent of the storekeepers, 25 per cent of the other urban dwellers and 10 per cent of the farmers (assuming that the farmers were the most numerous group). The sample of each group to be studied must meet the tests for size indicated above but it is not necessary for each sample to include the same percentage in its group. Of course, if the results are to be combined to give single percentages or averages applying to the whole community, appropriate weights have to be given to the results from each sample when calculating the combined figures.

Cluster Sampling

The foregoing three methods limit the number likely to come from any one family to one or two persons. In studies in which it is desirable to interview the whole family, or the head of the family in every case, lists of families can be used (or other natural groupings) and then one or more individuals can be selected from each family. Lists of villages may be similarly used. This method requires expert statistical guidance, and is mentioned here only to indicate its availability and pertinence.

Area Sampling

This is another technique that requires expert statistical guidance. If enough is known about the geography of the area primarily affected by the development project, it may be possible to lay out the area in a substantial number of separate sub-areas, preferably of approximately equal population size. If areas are unequal in population size, attempts should be made to estimate the relative population size of each. Samples can then be drawn from each sub-area, in proportion to its size. Within each sub-area, however, some rigid techniques must be used so that the sample is not made unrepresentative by containing just those people living on main roads, or just those on the first floor of apartment buildings, etc. Blindly sticking pins at random into an aerial map of sub-area is one technique sometimes used to force representation of less accessible families. Travelling specified distances in specified directions within each sub-area is another.

Judgment Sampling

Sampling which do not rely on the principles of chance are usually called 'judgment samples' The person drawing the sample may consider that official X or community leader Y should certainly be included in the sample. If each selected person is considered to be a separate stratum, of course, and is given his appropriate stratum weight in the final result, this introduces no bias. If, however, such judgements result in certain persons being represented and certain others excluded without appropriate adjustment in the weighting process, the results will not be representative.

Moreover, if judgements are made that, for example, 25 per cent of the sample should be entrepreneurs, and if it is not known and cannot be reasonably estimated what proportion of the whole group are entrepreneurs, then the results for the group as a whole may be biased by a figure which it is not possible to measure.

If, moreover, quotas are thus established and are allowed to relieve interviewers of the necessity of getting representative persons (by some form of random selection) within each quota group, further bias, of unmeasured amount, may result.

On the other hand, such 'quota sampling' (really a form of judgement sampling) is usually better than no stratification at all, for it helps to ensure representation of different important groups and permits separate study to be made of each such group.

Panels versus Successive Samples

In studying changes over a period of time, one may select successive samples of comparable composition, or in certain circumstances one may re-interview the same sample. In studying consumer behaviour, for example, as was done by the Central Bank of Ceylon, it may be desirable to select a sample of households and then interview them several times. In the United States, 'consumer panels' of this kind are often used, and are asked to keep diaries of purchases, reading, radio listening, etc., and to take stock (or allow an interviewer to take stock) of the kinds and amounts of goods on hand at periodic intervals.

In some areas, the most feasible way of obtaining desired data on income, expenditures, employment, illness, etc., is by periodic re-interviews of the same sample. Some families themselves can and will keep the daily records required. In many situations, however, it is best to employ a local person to make the entries in consultation with the family.

When a panel is used, relatively small changes over time are often statistically significant, whereas changes of the same size might be ascribed to chance variation from one sample to the next when successive but different samples are interviewed. Thus, for trend studies, results based on relatively few interviews repeated several times with a constant panel can be as reliable as results based on interviews with many more people who are contacted only once. Moreover, more information can often be secured by a series of interviews with the same group, because the results of successive interviews can be cumulated, and because panel members become more articulate over time (partly because they get to know the interviewer, and partly because, between interviews, they think about the subjects studied). It may even be possible to get panel members to co-operate in a development project, for example, by keeping literature available in the house or by turning on certain radio programmes. The exposed families thus become the most likely ones to show changes.

The major disadvantages of repeat interviews are : (a) the considerable 'drop out' of respondents from one round of interviews to the next (this is called 'panel mortality'), resulting from people moving, becoming ill, dying or becoming uncooperative; (b) panel members may develop a 'critical set'; and thus cease to be representative of the journal public; (c) panel members may try to be consistent in actions or opinions, from one interview to the next thus submerging the very changes the development project is intended to produce and the study to uncover; (d) village workers may concentrate their efforts on the sample villages or panel families they know are being surveyed, thus making them progressively more unrepresentative of the whole area.

Time Slice Samples

Where either the behaviour to be observed or the process of collecting data is continuous, a different kind of sample is often taken. This is the 'time slice sample', made up of periods of time of specified length, during which data are gathered.

For example, in time and motion studies in factories, an observer (perhaps with a motion picture camera) may select five-minute periods at random throughout the day, each period providing adequate data for a single worker. Care must, of course, be used to ensure that the choice of periods does not introduce a bias. This may be done by random selection (for example, drawing all possible periods out of a hat), or by systematic selection (for example, selecting one period every half-hour throughout the day).

The Dun and Bradstreet surveys of expectations of American businessmen, for example, use a systematic time slice sample of business concerns having a net worth of $ 75,000 or more. Dun and Bradstreet analytical reporters call on a number of business concerns every business day (the selection reflecting a periodic need for new data, not personal choice) to obtain financial information for credit rating purposes. During two weeks at the beginning of each quarter, each analytical reporter asks certain additional questions about the expectations (of sales, profits, inventories, etc.) of all businessmen called on. The sample thus comprises not every fiftieth businessman, but all businessmen called on during a particular period, or 'time slice'.

6

Theories and Models Useful in Integrated Area Development Planning

AFTER having discussed some of the basic principles and concepts underlying integrated rural area development, let us now proceed to examine some of the relevant theories and models useful to us. These are examined here, with two objectives in view. First, every planner should have some idea of these theories and models for they are generally referred to in planning and development literature; and second, every planner must attempt to evolve new models by modifying or adapting the existing ones to suit his specific planning situation.

Economic Growth Models

Theoretical models of regional growth (development) are essentially by-products of general economic theory and, therefore, cover only certain aspects of regional development process.

Myrdal Model

Gunner Myrdal, a Swedish economist, has stressed that economic market forces tend to increase, rather than decrease, regional differentiation. In his model the build up of activities in prosperous growing regions influences the less prosperous regions through two types of induced effects :

(1) Spread effects, and
(2) Backwash effects.

The first refers to the positive impact on all other regions of growth in the thriving region. This growth comes from the stimulation of increased demand for raw materials and agricultural products and the diffusion of advanced technology. The second refers to the adverse effects of agglomerated (concentrated) growth leading to net movement of population, capital and goods in favour of the growing area. The classic backwash effect works through selective migration which has harmful effects on both the age and skill structure of the sending region.

The two opposing forces do not imply the existence of an equilibrium situation. Indeed, Myrdal maintains that the balance of the two effects occurs only rarely. A more likely situation is a cumulative upward or downward movement over a considerable time that leads to long periods of increasing regional contrasts. This situation as applied to a growing region called cumulative upward causation is given in Fig. 6.1. The reverse is true for lagging regions.

Myrdal model is qualitative. There are some more precise econometric models, a summary of which is given below :

Neo-classical Models

These models of growth are supply oriented, i.e., if the supply of inputs is assured, growth will also be assured. The rate of growth in income, is determined by three elements: capital accumulation, an increase in labour supply and technical progress. The latter is assumed to be a constant function of time. For the sake of brevity, let us put this as per Fig 6.1

$$Y_i = F_i(K, L, t)$$

Where Y = real regional income; K = capital stock; i = region, L = supply of labour and t = time subsuming technological progress.* The model requires that there is continuous full employment of the capital stock, a demand that calls for some mechanism to equate investment with full employment and savings. In the neo-classical theory, this mechanism is none other than rate of interest (r). The model also prescribes that output and capital accumulation must expand at the same rate. Ultimately, it is the capital output ratio that determines growth.

* F_i denotes that Y_i is a function of K, L and t with unspecified relationship.

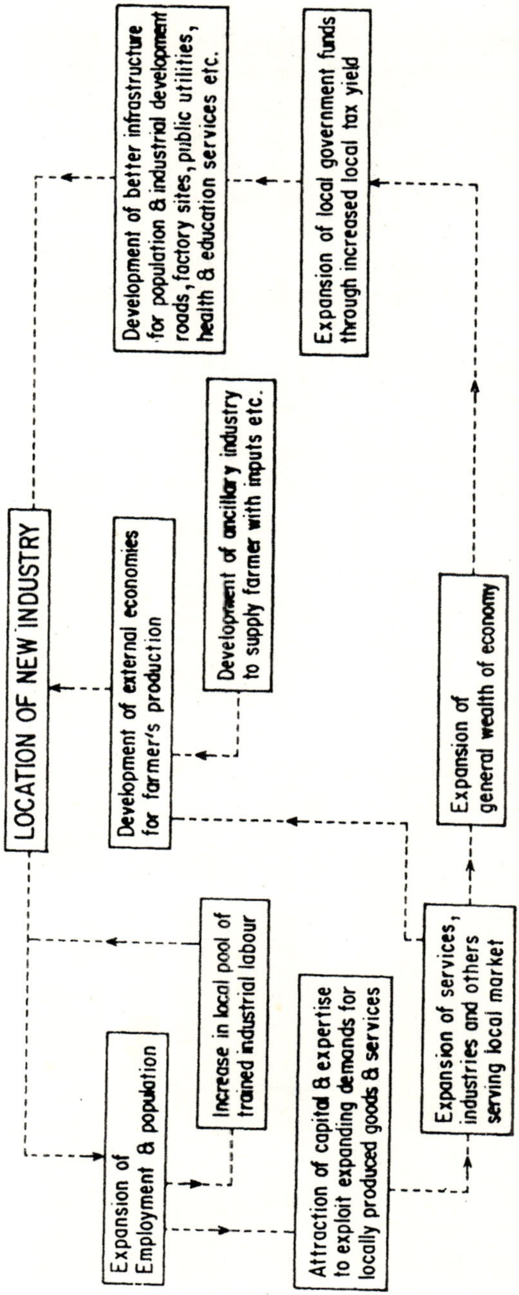
LOCATION OF NEW INDUSTRY
Expansion of Employment & population
Increase in local pool of trained industrial labour
Attraction of capital & expertise to exploit expanding demands for locally produced goods & services
Expansion of services, industries and others serving local market
Development of external economies for farmer's production
Development of ancillary industry to supply farmer with inputs etc.
Expansion of general wealth of economy
Development of better infrastructure for population & industrial development roads, factory sites, public utilities, health & education services etc.
Expansion of local government funds through increased local tax yield

Fig. 6.1

From the above we can derive another equation which is indicative of the rate of growth:

$$Y_i = a_i k_i + (1-a_i) n_i + T_i$$

Where Y_i = rate of growth of output or income, k and n the rates of growth of capital and labour, respectively, T the rate of technical progress (i.e., the annual rate of growth of output due to technical progress alone), a = capital's income share (marginal product of capital, ∠ Y/Δ K, multiplied by K/Y), and because of constant returns (1–a) = labour's income share (ΔY/ΔL multiplied by L/Y), all referring to region i.

Harrod-Domar Model

Unlike the neo-classical equilibrium growth model, the Harrod-Domar model is demand oriented, i.e., the backwardness is because of the lack of effective demand rather than because of shortages of factors of production. The available resources such as labour, are not fully utilized and hence the demand for the goods is lagging and hence low production and hence under-development. This model differs from the neo-classical model in another sense. It postulates cyclical growth as against steady growth.

The equilibrium growth (i.e., adjustment of growth rates of various regions to a common growth rate) requires labour to migrate from low income to high income regions and capital to flow in the reverse direction. While the first could happen, the flow of capital from high income to low income region is doubtful. The regions with higher propensities to save and lower capital-output ratio should grow rather rapidly. Thus, regions with net import surpluses [$m_i-(X_i/Y_i) > 0$, where m_i=marginal propensity to import in region i, X_i= export of region i, Y_i=output of region i] should grow faster than other regions. Similarly, regions experiencing net immigration should tend to grow faster than regions affected by net emigration.

Export Based Theory of Growth

According to this theory, the growth of a region depends upon the growth of its export industries implying that expansion of demand, external to the region, is the crucial initiating determinant of growth of the region. Thus, an increase in the export base, a concept denoting collectively all the exportable goods and services of a region, set off a multiplier process (where the multiplier is equal to total regional output divided by total export). The presumption is that all economic activities are not for export, especially the region's trade and service activities. Nevertheless they are induced by the expansion or decline of export industries. This theory thus emphasizes the earlier explained view that the growth of a region is not likely to be decided within its own borders.

The limitations of this theory are quite obvious. It is too simplistic, non-predictive and insensitive to the realities of a multi-commodity, inter-regional economy, Expansion in different components of the export-base could have widely diverse results for regional growth. Secondly, the theory ignores the fact that internal growth impulses may be vital factors in regional growth. This is more so in the case of a macro-region.

Other Models

There are a few other hypotheses which contain the seeds of a theory or model. We propose to list them below, for they do not appear to be of much significance for our present discussion. Sector theory proposed by Clark Fisher suggests that rise in the per capita income would be accompanied by a decline in the proportion of resources employed in agriculture and rise in manufacturing (secondary) and later in service (tertiary) industries. Perloff, Dunn, Lampard and Muth contend that the growth of a region is more likely to be determined by the structure of the industrial economy rather than by income. A region may grow because it has industries which are growing fast nationally or because it is gaining an increasing proportion of a given industry or industries, regardless of whether these industries are growing or not.

Comparison and Review

We can now compare the major theories and models of regional growth. The above models are not so very relevant to integrated rural area development. Yet one can easily get some insights from them. In the first place, it is clear that diversification of activities with accent on those products which have markets outside is important for rural development. Secondly, it is also important that the consumption pattern of people must change, which is possible only if their income increases and is better distributed.

Table 6.1: Characteristics of fast growing regions

Economic Model	Income Level	Direction of labour flows	Direction of capital flows	Direction of inter-regional growth
Model 1 (Neo-classical)	Low	Outward	Inward	Convergence
Model 2 (Harrod-Domar)	High	Inward	Inward	Divergence
Model 3 (Expert base)	Unspecified	Inward	Outward	Unspecified

Along with these models which were not constructed in the light of the problems of the developing countries and regions, we must keep in view the indigenous models suggested by Mahatma Gandhi and social development model, which de-emphasize the pre-eminent role of income as a measure of welfare.

Theories of Spatial Development

Having discussed some of the models of economic growth, we now proceed to discuss the theories which are pertinent to the spatial (horizontal) arrangement and location of various human activities including population centres. Knowledge of these theories helps us in taking a more rational decision with regard to location of various production and consumption-oriented activities.

Von Thunen's Isolated State

Perhaps the earliest attempt to explain the land-use in relation to a central place (village or town) was made by Von Thunen in his book *De Isolierte Slaat in Bezlehung and Landwirtschaft* first published in 1826. In 1810, Thunen, at the age of 27, acquired an agricultural estate, Tellow, near the town of Rostock in Mecklengurg, on the Baltic coast of Germany, and accumulated data during the subsequent 40 years which provided the basis for his theory.

Thunen postulated a concentric pattern of land-use with a number of bands. ranging from narrow bands of intensive farming zone and forest zone to a broad band of extensive agricultural zone and ranching zone to the waste that lies beyond. His model is given in Figure 6.2.

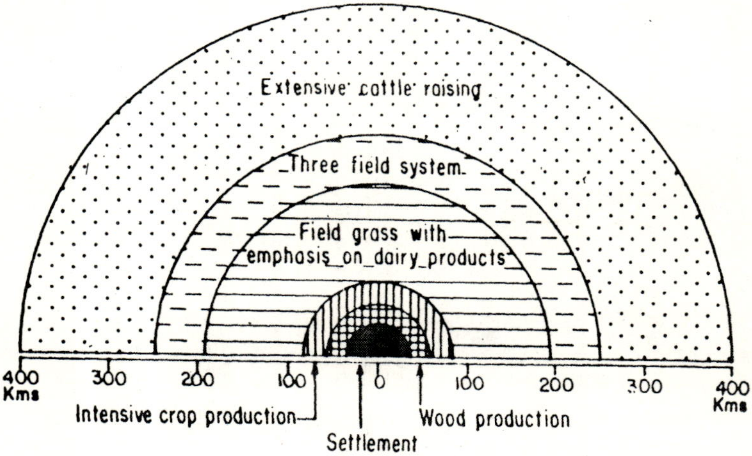

Fig. 6.2

Thunen's model was an idealized form of land-use pattern valid only under following conditions.

1. The existence of an isolated State cut off from the rest of the world.
2. The domination of this State by a single large city that served as the sole urban market.
3. The setting of the city in a broad, featureless plain that was everywhere equal in fertility and ease of movement so that production and transport costs were everywhere the same.
4. The suppliers of the city are farmers who shipped agricultural goods there in return for industrial produce.
5. Transport of farm produce by the farmer himself, who hauled his own produce to the central market along a close, dense trail of converging roads of equal standard with costs directly proportional to distance.
6. Maximizing of profits by farmers in terms of automatic adjustment of crops to the needs of the central market.

The above assumptions were made by Thunen to simplify the problem and to provide a model. If we relax the assumptions, the shape of the rings would change in the same way as a circle drawn on rubber sheet would change its shapes depending on the force with and directions from which it is pulled.

Thunen regarded the operation of locational rent as the key factor in sorting the uniform area of his isolated State into distinct land-use zones. Locational rent for any crop at any location is given by :

$$L = Y\,(P-C) - YD\,(F)$$

Where, L = Locational rent (Rs/km²)
Y = Yield of crop (tons/km²)
P = Market price of the crop (Rs/ton)
C = Production cost of the crop (Rs/ton)
D = Distance to the central market (km)
F = Transport rate (Rs/ton/km)

Thus, for a crop yielding 1,000 tons/km² fetching Rs. 100/ton at the central market, costing Rs. 50/ton to produce, and Re. 1/ton/km to haul, the locational rent at the city centre would be Rs. 50,000/km², at 10 km distance only Rs. 40,000/km² and at 20 km distance down to Rs. 30,000/km². Beyond 50 km production would be at a loss. The competition of two crops (i and j) for the same area depends on their yield (Y) and relative profitability (P–C). When the condition :

$$1 < \frac{Y\,(P-C)i}{Y\,(P-C)j} < \frac{Y_i}{Y_j}$$

obtain for crops i and j, they form two distinct spatial zones; crop i dominates a circular area adjacent to the city, and crop j occupies a ring-shaped zone immediately outside it. Symbol < means 'less than'.

Central place theory of Walter Christaller

Christaller (1893—1969), a German Scholar, wrote dissertation on the settlement structure of Southern Germany in 1932. Partly because of his association with Nazis and partly because of the language barrier, the concept evolved by him did not catch the attention of scholars until late 1940s.

The terminology of Christaller's model is straight forward central places are broadly synonymous with towns that serve as the centres for regional communities by providing them with central goods and central services. Central places vary in importance. Higher order centre stock a wide array of goods and services; lower order centres stock a smaller range of goods and services, that is, some limited part of the range offered by the higher centre. Complementary regions describe the areas served by each central place. They exist for both higher and lower order centres and are defined by town-country relationships. The regions for higher order goods are large and those for lower order goods are small.

Christaller defined the centrality of an urban centre as the ratio between the services provided and the local needs of its inhabitants. Town with high centrality would supply many services per inhabitant and *vice versa*. In recent years, two more terms have been added to Christaller's theory. Threshold refers to the minimum size of market below which a place will be unable to supply a market good. That is, below the Threshold's lower limit sales will be too small for firms to earn acceptable profits, Range of central goods delineates the market area of a central place for the goods. The market area's lower limit is determined by the Threshold limit, and its upper limit is defined by the distance beyond which the central place no longer is able to sell the goods. If we assume that travel is equally easy in all directions, the range of a goods will be a perfect circle which is the outer limit of a demand cone in which the quantity of a central goods consumed decreases with distance from the central place because of increased transport cost. (Figure 6.3).

Given the circular demand cone, Christaller demonstrated that the final solution for a group of central places of similar order is a set of hexagonal complementary regions, where the central places are arranged in a regular isometric lattice. The circle was replaced by hexagon because the latter, when arranged together does not leave any space uncovered. He suggested three organizations of central places to optimize marketing, transportation and administration. In all the three cases Christaller assumed that the relationship established for one level, e.g., between village and small town will also apply to other levels, e.g., between city and metropolis; he called it fixed K-hierarchies. For the three cases, the K values would be 3, 4 and 7, respectively. This means that, in the first case, each higher level centre will serve three next level centres including itself; in the second case, each higher level centre would serve four next level centres including itself, and so on. The pattern of location of centres would be as given in Figure 6.4.

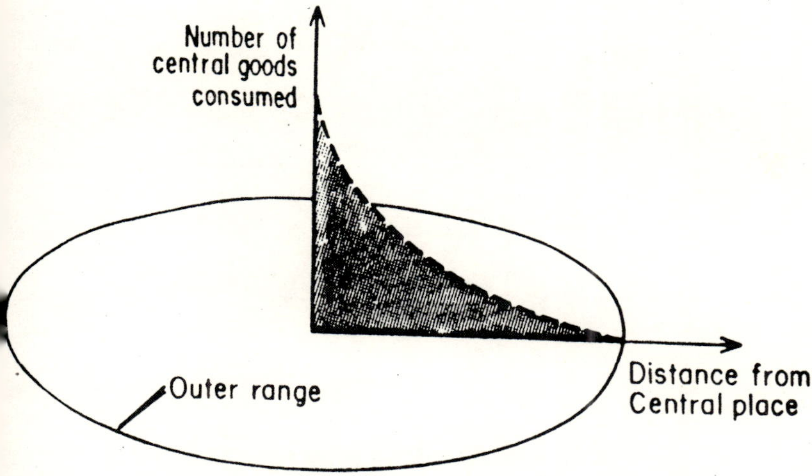

Fig. 6.3

Christaller's model takes into account only the tertiary activities, i.e., commerce, trade, transport, administration and services. It is a useful theory for optimal location of these activities. Losch, a fellow German, used the hexagonal frame of Christaller and brought the secondary activities (manufacturing) also into the model. In his scheme, settlements of the same size need not have the same function, and larger places need not have all the functions of the smaller central places.

Growth Centre Theory

Francis Perroux, a French regional economist, developed the concept of growth pole which in essence means that to develop a lagging in a major city to set off a chain reaction of minor expansions throughout the hinterland. Thus a growth pole policy in regional development is the deliberate selection of one or a few potential poles within a

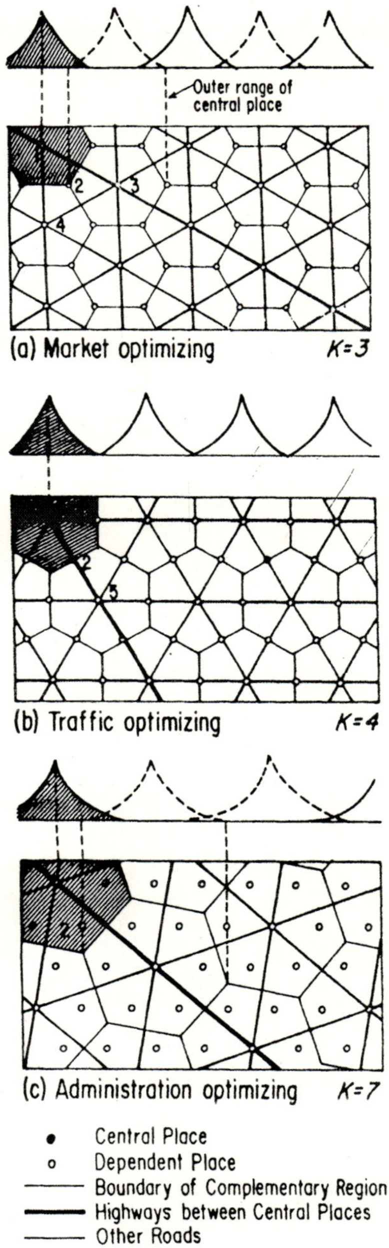
Outer range of central place
(a) Market optimizing K=3
(b) Traffic optimizing K=4
(c) Administration optimizing K=7
Central Place
Dependent Place
Boundary of Complementary Region
Highways between Central Places
Other Roads

Fig. 6.4

problem area. New investment is concentrated in these poles, rather than being spread thinly over the whole area. The arguments in favour of this policy are that public expenditure is more effective when concentrated in a few clearly defined areas and that the new industries there will stand a better chance of building up enough external economies to achieve some degree of self-generating growth.

In practice the growth pole policy faces three problems: a technical one of selecting the best potential pole; a political one of convincing the unsuccessful candidates of the wisdom of the policy; and a strategic one of making a choice between centralized and decentralized development. This theory suffers from urban and industrial fundamentalism and does not appear to be so useful in areas which are essentially rural. In such areas Christaller becomes more relevant.

To get over these problems associated with the growth pole theory and make the concept applicable to Indian rural condition, R.P. Misra evolved the concept of system of growth foci popularly known as RPM model. In this model, the growth foci consist of a hierarchy of central places. Higher the level of a centre in the hierarchy, more the activities of secondary and tertiary type. Lower the level, more agro-based the activities. They have suggested a five-tier hierarchy :

1. Growth pole
2. Growth centre
3. Growth point
4. Service centre
5. Central village

This size and spatial distribution of these would be determined by the level of socio-economic development of the area/region.

Stages of Development

Several social scientists have postulated the characteristic changes which take place in economic system as development proceeds. The changes are such that different stages of development could be noted. The proof for these is provided by economic and social history, more importantly the former. A summary of these postulations is given as per Table 6.2.

The first two are now fairly old and descriptive. They cannot be said to be models. Rostow's model is the one which is most debated. It has been criticized on many counts but the most important criticism points to the lack of empirical evidence and regularity. In fact, many developing countries have reached the stage of take off in some sectors but still remain traditional in others. Further, the stages through which western countries passed in their road to economic development, in a given historical context, may not be so relevant to the developing countries of mid 1970s. It is not only possible but also feasible for a developing country to leap-frog some stages by taking the benefit of modern divisible technology.

Notwithstanding the criticism of the model, its terminology is repeatedly used in the developing countries.

Table 6.2: Postulation Summary

No.	Author	Stages
1.	Hildebrant	Barter — money — credit
2.	List	Savage — pastoral — agricultural — agricultural and manufacturing — agricultural — manufacturing and commercial
3.	W.W. Rostow	The traditional society — the pre-conditions for take off — take off — the drive to maturity the age of high mass consumption

Social Models

According to Johnson, the main elements in the structure of a social system are :

1. Sub-groups of various kinds, normatively related.
2. Roles within the larger system and within sub-groups each role system being normatively related with each of the others.
3. Regulative norms governing sub-groups and roles.
4. Cultural values.

Every social system must solve four functional problems.

1. Pattern maintenance and tension management;
2. Adaption;
3. Goal attainment; and
4. Integration.

In very broad terms, the family schools, religious groups and so on deal with the first problem, the economy deals with the adaptive sub-system of society, the polity or government deals with the society's goals and the integrative sub-system is maintained by the legal profession, opinion formers of the mass media, religious leaders and so on. Each of these functional sub-systems of a society can, in itself, be analyzed as a social system and the other systems are then seen as part of the 'environment' to which the sub-group must adapt if it is to survive and achieve its goals. It, however, so happens that the cost of meeting societal problems is borne unequally by the sub-groups of the society. The major burden falls on those who are the least protected. To understand the social system, we must, therefore, analyse and study the various sub-groups, the mechanism through which inequalities develop among them, and the planning implications of these inequalities.

The analogue model of social systems explains the social structural problems in the context of development planning. This model divides human societies into three main types. These are :

1. Porous.
2. Permeable.
3. Impermeable.

Porous societies are those ideal types whose members are equal in social, economic and other status and which possess mechanism for quick percolatory, capillary and lateral spread of new energy in the whole system. Permeable ones are those which have developed well-defined channels for energy movement from one direction to another, leaving a sizable part of the society unaffected or affected only marginally. The impervious societies are those which do not permit the energy to pass down the various strata; it is absorbed by the upper crust and radiated in the form of conspicuous consumption etc.

The above terminology is more expressive of the social processes than the usual terms like feudal, semi-feudal, etc.

The main objective of social development is to move the society towards porosity. The present day Indian society is pervious (or semi-feudal). It is controlled by middle strata of society through a series of networks of middle men down to the lowest stratum.

7

Methods and Techniques Useful in Integrated Area Development Planning

THIS chapter aims at illustrating some of the methods and techniques of data analysis which are often used by area development planners. No attempt is made to cover all possible methods and techniques. Only the ones used more frequently have been selected.

Population Analysis

It is now a well recognized fact that 'people' constitute the most powerful resource of a country. A country with large reserve of quality people can transform the potentials and resources into realities. At the same time, a country with a huge population of illiterates, unhealthy and poverty-stricken people, can do precious little with its known resources.

Developing countries the world over are attempting hard to control their population for they know that poor quality people eat more than they produce. Since the growth of their economy is almost equally matched by the growth of population, they fail to invest enough in activities which can improve the quality of people.

A planner must know the quantity and quality of the people at the time of plan formulation; he should also know the expected growth of population in years to come because planning is done more for the future than for the present. The planner must know the human resources, to identify the activities which can use the available talent and which can fill the gaps in training and expertise. He has another reason to know the facts. He must estimate the amount and type of food, clothing and shelter and plan ahead. So that the people are better fed, better clad and better sheltered.

The total population of any country or area represents a balance between two sets of forces – natural change (birth-death) and migration change (immigrants-emigrants) (Fig. 7.1)

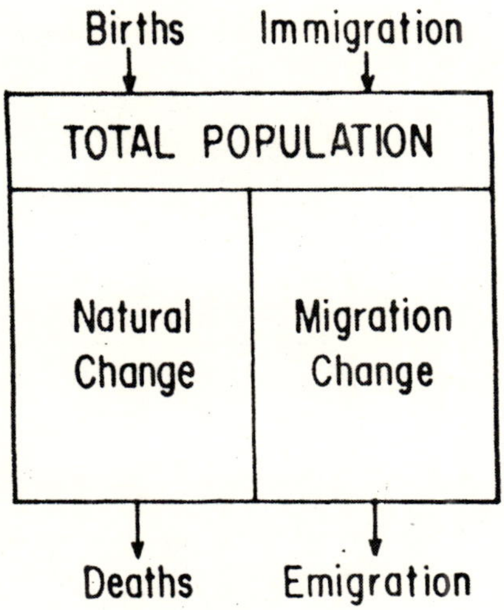

Fig. 7.1

Population Forecast

Birth and death rates together with migration can provide us data for forecasting future population. There are some limitations of these data but we can ignore these as they are of no major consequence to rural areas. If we subtract the crude death rate from the crude birth rate, we have a rough measure of the rate of natural increase (or decrease) in a population. We should remember here that the rate is calculated per 1,000 population. Supposing the differences between the two = eight. It means that we add eight new individuals to every 1000 living, i.e., it would take 125 years to double that population ($125 \times 8= 1000$). But this calculation ignores the fact that the people added to the population would also increase at the rate of eight per thousand. This means that population growth follows an exponential form just like that of money earning compound interest in a bank. The doubling time is therefore shortened from 125 to only 87 years. The mathematical expression for the exponential rate of growth is :

$$\frac{dn}{dt} = rN$$

Where N = number of people;

r = rate of natural increase (a constant) and

$\frac{d}{dt}$ = calculus method of stating rate of change per unit of time.

The expression states that the amount of growth is related to the size of the population; the larger it is, the faster it grows. It may also be written as

$$N_t = N_o (1 - r)^t$$

For easier compilation, we can write the formula as;

$$N_t = N_o e^{rt}$$

Where N_t = number of people at time t;

N_o = number of people at time 0;

e = 2.71828 (natural log); and

r = rate of natural increase.

If we start with 1000 people (N_o) and assume a growth rate of 1 per cent per annum (r = 0.01), then we can show by substituting those values in the equation that after 70 years (t = 70) the original population will be double (N_t=2000). We should note here that this method does not take note of migration. Moreover, it assumes that the present trends of growth would continue in future too.

The above method of population projection is useful only for short-run projections because it refers only to biotic potential of the population, i.e., its theoretical rate of growth without environmental limits. We know that a number of checks – a natural and/or cultural – start operating so that the population increase remains adjusted to carrying capacity of the area.

We can introduce the environmental resistance into our model by the term :

$$1 - \frac{K - N}{K}$$

Where K = maximum number of individuals allowed by the carrying capacity and;
combine this with our exponential growth model to obtain the equation

$$\frac{dN}{dt} = rN - \frac{K - N}{K}$$

Where r = rate of growth per individual;
N = total population or density of population

The growth curve that we get when we use the above formula is of S shape and is called Logistic growth curve where in the rate of increase is modified as numbers approach the critical level. Such a solution does, however, imply more knowledge about environmental limits and more social control over births than presently existing in human groups.

There are several other methods to project population. We do not propose to discuss them all here. For rural area development planning, the exponential method is adequate, provided that migration is also taken into account.

Migration is

$$M_t = (P_t - P_o) - N_t$$

Where M_t = migration during t year;
P_t = population in t year;
P_o = population in base year;
N_t = net natural increase during t years.

Stages of Population Growth

It would not be out of place to mention here the hypothesis of demographic transition which is so relevant to developing countries. While forecasting the population this hypotheses should be kept in view.

Demographic transition is an idealized sequence of changes over time in vital rates. We can recognize four connected phases in this sequence.

(i) High-stationary phase,
(ii) Early expanding phase,
(iii) Late expanding phase, and
(iv) Low stationary phase.

Graphically, it can be presented in the form given in Figure 7.2. In high stationary phase, birth and death rates are high, while in the low stationary phase they both are low. During the second phase death rates decline fast but birth rates remain stationary, while in the third phase, the death rates become stabilized at a low rates and the birth rates come down drastically. The junction of phases two and three records the highest rate of population growth.

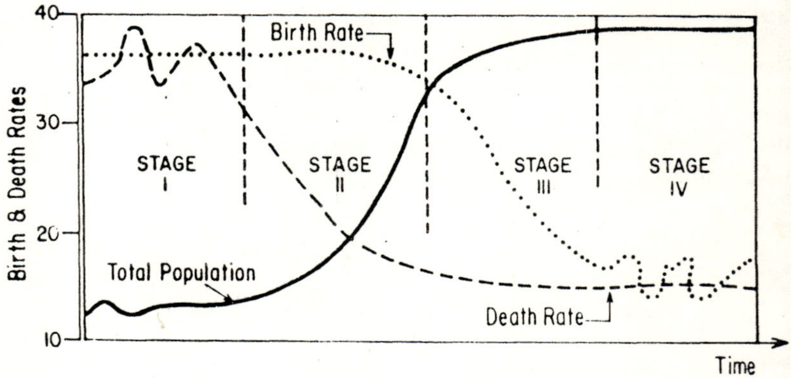

Fig. 7.2

Pressure of Population

Carrying capacity of an agricultural area depends largely on the man: land ratio, i.e., the number of people per unit of land. But we know that every piece of land is not equally productive. An acre of land in Rajasthan desert cannot be equated with an acre in Mandya district.

Similarly, the dry land cannot be equated with wet land. Methods have been devised, therefore, to classify lands in different categories. We would look into this in a later section. Here our problem is how to measure the pressure of population on land.

Density of population per unit of land is one indicator of pressure. But we encounter two conceptual problems here. First, as noted earlier, the quality of land is not the same everywhere, and second, the pressure will differ depending upon the standard of living we have in view. For example, 100 persons per sq. km. may be low if the expectations of the people are low, but it may turn out to be high, if the expectations are high.

Another factor that intervenes is the income generated outside agriculture. That part of the income which comes to the area of planning should be added to the income derived from land to get a realistic pressure of population on land.

We have yet to perfect a method which can give dependable results. The best that we have at our disposal is :

$$I = \frac{P - P_1}{A}$$

Where I = Index of population pressure;

P = Actual rural population;

A = Rural area in sq. km.

P_1 = Areawise derived rural population capable of being supported by the utilized land resources = $\frac{X}{K}$

Where X = gross value of output of the area from primary sector at current prices;

K = constant income per head from the primary sector desired for a slight improvement in the standard of living of rural population.

This formula can be further improved by (a) converting rural area into standard hectares; (b) adding to X the area income derived from other sources.

Food Requirement Estimation

One of the main objectives of integrated rural area development is increased production of food. For proper planning we should know how much the area consumes, how much it produces and what is the surplus or deficit. For estimating the local requirements of food, we can use the following formula:

$$TR_e \; \frac{TP \times R_{ph} \times 86}{100}$$

Where TR_e = Total requirements of cereals in the area;
TP = Total population of the area;
R_{ph} = Cereal requirement per head = 190 kg per annum; and

$\frac{86}{100}$ = Conversion factor for adult units.

Standard deductions are :

Seeds = 68 per cent (3.5 to 14 per cent)
Wastage = 10 per cent.

It is estimated that with about 200 kg. of cereals per head per year (about 20 ounces per head per day), we can maintain a fairly high level of nutrition in the country.

Interaction Analysis

Different areas and places interact with each other leading to movement of people, goods and information. Area planner should know something of the interaction models so that he can appreciate the implications of implementing various projects in his area. Let us take the case of project to establish agricultural market yard in an area. There are yards in surrounding areas. He has to find out the catchment area of the new yard before he can implement this project because unless he knows the marketable surplus, he cannot know definitely whether the project would pay. We can use the following variation of the gravity model to get the boundary of the area of influence.

$$B_2 = \frac{D_{12}}{1+\sqrt{\frac{M_1}{M_2}}}$$

Where, B_2 = Break point in distance units from market yard 2;
D_{12} = Distance between yards 1 and 2;
M_1 = Market size of yard 1;
M_2 = Market size of yard 2.

The above model is derived from the basic Newtonian gravity model which states that two bodies in the universe attract each other in proportion to the product of their masses and inversely as the square of their distance. This concept was introduced by W.J. Reilly in 1929 to the study of trade areas. We can estimate the spatial interaction between two regions or areas by multiplying together the mass of two regions and dividing it by some function of the distance separating them. Mass has usually been equated with population.

Population as a mass can be further refined by multiplying it by per capita income or some other weight. Similarly, the distance could be measured in terms of costs or travel time. The formula to measure the interaction is :

$$F_{ij} = a\frac{M_i M_j}{Dij^b}$$

Where F_{ij} = Flows between regions i and j;
M_i M_j = Mass of regions i and j;
D_{ij} = Distance between regions i and j;
a = Empirical constant; and
b = Distance exponent.

Natural Resource Analysis

Plant Productivity

The Swedish geographer, Sten Paterson, determined that productivity of plants increases with the length of growing season, the average temperature of the warmest month, the annual precipitation and the amount of solar radiation and it decreases with temperature range. By combining these values into a single index, we can give numbers to stations indicating their potential for plant growth. The formula is :

$$I = \frac{T_m PGS}{120 (T_r)}$$

Where I = Index of plant productivity;

- T_m = Average temperature of the warmest month in degrees Centigrade;
- T_r = Annual range of temperature between the averages of the coldest and warmest months in degrees Centigrade;
- P = Precipitation in centimeters;
- G = Growing season in months; and
- S = Solar radiation expressed as a proportion of radiation at the poles.

This formula gives only the potential plant productivity; it only measures what plant life a particular environment can support in terms of climate. The actual plant cover reflects other factors such as the vegetational history of an area and the degree of human interference.

Rainfall Variability

While planning for a rural area, one problem that we always encounter is the rainfall variations and their implications for land utilization. Some areas get too much rainfall, while some get too little in a year. But the total rainfall in a year is not that useful an indicator of climatic potential of land-use. We must know also the variations in rainfall in time and space. Temporal (time) variation means how the rainfall is distributed throughout the year, month or week. If there is adequate rainfall during the months or weeks which constitute the growing season, crops can be raised well, even though the other months may be dry. So a total rainfall of 30" distributed almost equally among 4 months is more useful for agriculture than one distributed equally among 9 months. But if much of it falls in one month alone, it may not be of much direct use – in fact, it may prove injurious to soils.

One method of estimating the usefulness of rainfall is the index of de Mortonne/Lauer :

$$i = \frac{12n}{t + 10}$$

Where n =average monthly precipitation amount in millimeters;
t = average monthly temperature in centigrade; and
i = aridity index.

The boundary between aridity and humidity is reached when i = 20; a higher index indicates humidity, a lower aridity. It should be noted here that for agro-climatological purposes, an effective dry period is a period of three consecutive months during which precipitation is less than 4" (102 mm) per month. This is the minimum amount of rain needed for cultivation of crops and hence to maintain agricultural land-use.

Variability of climate can also be measured statistically. Standard deviation (σ = Sigma) is the more widely used measure of variability. It is calculated by summing the square of the deviation of each value from the average, dividing by the number of cases and then taking the square root.

$$\sigma = \frac{(xi - \bar{x})^2}{n}$$

Where $\bar{x}$ = an individual value;
x = xi/n (the mean or average)
n = number of cases
Σ = sum of values for i = 1 to n

Variability of rainfall may be compared between stations is the standard deviation is expressed as a percentage of the mean (co-efficient of variation, CV).

$$CV = \frac{\sigma}{\bar{x}} \times 100$$

Water Resource Assessment

In 1945-46, Khosla evolved the following relationship describing run off as a function of rainfall and temperature. The method is useful for assessing water resources for large river basins. But it is less useful for small watersheds where topography plays a significant role in run off.

Khosla formula is :

$$R_m = P_m - L_m$$

Where R_m = monthly run off in cm;
P_m = monthly rainfall in cm;
L_m = monthly evaporation losses in cm = 0.481 T_m
T_m' = mean monthly temperature in °C

Water Requirements for Agriculture

Blaney and Criddle derived an equation in 1962 which is widely used for estimating the water requirement of crops. It is written as :

$$U = KF$$

Where U = monthly evapotranspiration in inches referred to as consumptive use.
K = Crop constant
f = monthly evapotranspiration factor = $\frac{t \times p;}{100}$
t = mean monthly temperature in degrees Fahrenheit; and
p = monthly per cent of day time hours of year.

The consumptive use coefficient (k) varies from month to month and has to be derived empirically.

Ground Requirements for Agriculture

The amount of ground water available in a particular area can be expressed by the formula :

$$G = P - (E + R)$$

Where G = recharge of ground water

P =average precipitation multiplied by the area of the basin.

R = run off

E = evapotranspiration..

Economic Base Analysis

Productive activities, as we know, differ among themselves in many ways. We know the differences among agriculture, manufacturing etc. All these activities are therefore classified in three classes.

1. *Primary* : Agriculture and related activities,
2. *Secondary* : Manufacturing, and
3. *Tertiary* : Transport, commerce, education health etc.

There is another way of classifying these human activities. The criterion for this classification is, whether the products of the activity are sent outside the producing region or they are used within the region. The exporting activities are classified as basic and the non-exporting ones as non-basic.

The Location Quotient

Frequently, the study of region's export-import relations begins with a simple analysis employing location quotient. This quotient does not require extensive data collection and processing. It is a device for comparing a region's percentage share of a particular activity with its percentage share of some basic aggregates. If region A, for instance, accounts for 10 per cent of the national total of steel manufacturing, and the region's total income is 20 per cent of the nation's total, the region's location quotient (with income as base) for steel making would be 0.5.

A more elaborate way of calculating location quotient for an industry (i) in the given region is :

$$\frac{S_i/N_i}{S/N}$$

Where S_i = Number of wage earners in industry i in a given region;

S = Number of wage earners in all industries in i region;

N_i = Number of wage earners in industry i in the nation; and
N = Number of wage earners in all industries in the nation.

Instead of number of workers, one may take income, value added, population or area as the base for calculating location quotient.

Localization Curve

Another device to assess the position of a region in a system of regions is localization curve. It is constructed from a set of regional percentage figures by plotting on the vertical axis the cumulative percentage figures for the given industry's employment and on the horizontal axis the corresponding cumulative percentage figures for the base magnitude. The procedure involves (1) ranking regions by location quotients along the relevant row; and (2) plotting regions by rank on a cumulative percentage basis. Suppose that we have a four region country – A,B,C,D. Location quotient for each region for a particular industry is : 1.33, 1.5, 1.17, and 0.43.

Since, region B has the highest location quotient, its percentage in Figure 7.3 is plotted point 1. We then add A's percentage to B's and plot point 2 and add the two percentage to C's and plot point 3. Joining the points gives the localization curve. If the distribution is the same as in the nation as a whole, the curve would be closer to 45° line. Farther away from 45° line it is, more is the distribution (Fig. 7.3)

Inter-Regional Flow Analysis

The location quotient and localization curve are indicative of the extent to which a region's activities are in balance. Additional data can be acquired about region's strengths or weaknesses in relation to other regions by resorting to inter-regional flow analysis. There are three types of flow analysis which are often used by area planners.

1. Commodity flow analysis;
2. Money flow analysis; and
3. Analysis or regional balance of payments.

The commodity flow analysis deals with the physical movement of individual commodities and groups of commodities from and to the region. This analysis immediately points out the importance of imports as well as exports in a regional economy. If possible, a planner should collect historical data giving details of the amount and value of commodities of different types moving in and out of the planning area. Destination of the outgoing and origin of the incoming commodities should also be noted.

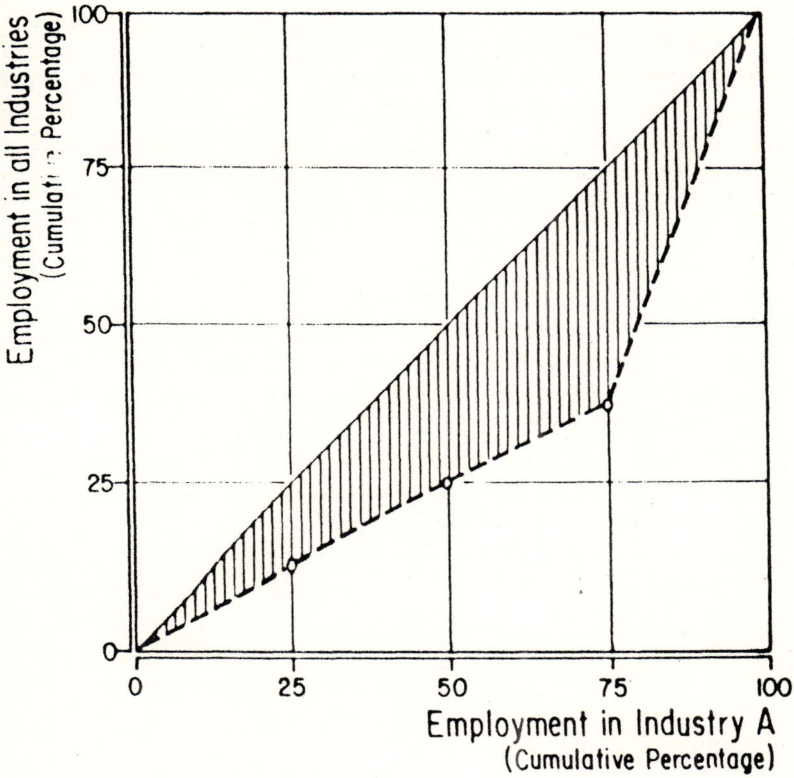

Fig. 7.3

Apart from commodity flows, there are money flows, communication flows, human flows, etc., which also should be studied and analyzed. To some extent, the money flow is nothing but monetarily evaluated commodity flows. But money flow is also in response to flow of services. People of region A, working in region B, send money-orders and cheques from B to A. In a sub-national planning situation, savings of one region can be spent in another region through the national banking system.

Closely related to commodity and money flow analysis is balance of payment analysis. The latter, however, considers a single region *vis-a-vis* the rest of the world and thus precludes the general inter-regional perspective captured by the commodity/money flow analysis.

The balance of payment statement gives all transactions between the planning region and the rest of the country and equates total in-flows and total outflows. A typical statement may be as per Table 7.1.

Under the current account would come only those transactions which are completed in a particular year. Those which spill over longer periods are covered by capital account. For example, if Rs. 1,000 worth of wheat is exported, money has come in and so it is recorded under current account export as plus. But supposing, it has gone as loan, then it would be entered under capital account as plus.

Regional Multiplier

It is the rate of the spread of impulses originating in any sector of the regional economy to other sectors. Such spreading in essence has a multiplying result. It thus tells how growth in one sector induces growth in other sectors.

The concept of regional multiplier is a derivative of the concept of basic and non-basic activities. Basic activities are those which produce goods/services for export; and non-basic are those which produce goods/services for local consumption/use. The non-basic activities are also known as service or local activities; and the basic as export activities. The regional multiplier is equal to total (or increase in) employment in both basic and service activities divided by total (or increase in) basic employment. The unit of measurement may be employment, production, value added or any other convenient unit like income.

The formula for the calculation of multiplier is :

$$Ke = 1 + \frac{Se}{Be} \quad \text{or} \quad 1 + \frac{Se_{t+\theta} - Se_t}{Be_{t+\theta} - Be_t}$$

Where Ke = Employment multiplier;

Be and Se = Employment in basic and service sectors;

t = time (base)
θ = Period

For example:

If total employment in basic sector = 1,000 in 1950 and 1,200 in 1970.

Total employment in service sector 3,000 in 1950 and 2,400 in 1970.

$$\text{Multiplier for 1950} = 1 + \frac{3000}{1000} = 4$$

$$\text{for 1970} = 1 + \frac{2400}{1200} = 3$$

$$\text{for 1950-70} = 1 + \frac{1200}{200} = 7$$

Table 7.1: Payment Statement

Item	Export	Import	Net
A. **Current Account**			
1. *Commodity trade*			
(a) Wheat	+ 100	– 10	+ 90
(b) Ore	+	0 – 50	– 50
.....			
(n) Others	–	–	–
2. *Service trade*			
(a) Freight	+ 200	– 300	– 100
(b) Education	+ 250	– 100	+ 150
....			
(n) Others	–	–	–
3. *Gifts and unilateral transfers*			
Total	+ 2,250	– 1,500	+ 750
B. **Capital Account**			
Net Capital Movement			
C. **Errors and Omissions**	–	–	–

While the concept of multiplier is simple, the data for it are difficult to find. In the first place, it is very difficult to identify in clear terms, basic and service components of an economy. Most firms produce goods both for export and for internal use. Adequate data to allocate export and import component of each firm are not available in India. Another issue often raised is the dependability of past data for prediction. The technology may change in the future Nevertheless, it is a useful tool of analysis in area planning.

Indicators of Development

Several attempts have been made in the past to work out indicators of development. The idea is to find quantitative measures for determining the relative poverty or richness of an area. Quite often per capita income is taken as an indicator of development. But, we do not have income data for areas smaller than a district. Moreover, income as the sole indicator of development is also questionable. There are many other factors which determine development and quality of life.

The average per capita income may be so distributed among groups of people, and areas, that a few may enjoy luxuries while a majority may fail to get even basic necessities. Availability of education, health, communication and other services is an equally important indicator of development. Other indicators are sectoral employment and output, use of modern technology in productive and service sectors. Keeping all these in view, a number of people have developed indices of development. The indicators which are commonly included in the test consist of :

1. Per capita income,
2. Working population as per cent of total population,
3. Urban population as per cent of total population,
4. Factory employment (daily) per 1000 population,
5. Per capita factory output,
6. Irrigation area as per cent of cropped area,
7. Per cent of area under crops,
8. Fertilizer consumption per hectare of cropped area,
9. Per capita electricity consumption,
10. Length of surfaced roads per 100 km of all roads,
11. Motor vehicles per 100,000 population,
12. Percentage of children in school,
13. Daily newspaper circulation per 1000 population.

There are cases of more than 100 indicators being used. The values of the indicators are added together and placed in descending order area-wise. The total of all indicators is often called composite indicator or index of development. In a particular year, the area getting highest index will be counted as best developed.

Several analysts use factors analysis to identify one to three major factors which account for development. We would not elaborate the methodology of factor analysis, as it is too sophisticated to be of much use in rural planning activities. Further, it suffers from many limitations and hence should be used only if one knows fully well the drawbacks of this technique.

The index method also suffers from many drawbacks. In the first place, all indicators of development are treated equal. In real life, it is not so. Secondly, what appears to be a set of indicators is in reality nothing but the consequence of something which is yet to be understood, or it may be the inter-relationships among various indicators which is the real cause of development, not the indicators themselves.

Notwithstanding the above drawbacks and shortcomings, the index method of determining the degree of development of an area (in comparative terms) is the best and the simplest which field workers and micro-level planners with limited facilities can fruitfully use.

Industrial Complex Analysis

Industrial complex is a set of activities occurring at a given location and belonging to a group of activities which are subject to important production, marketing or other interrelations. Complexes may be of three types:

1. Comprising of successive stages in the production of an end product;
2. Joint production of two or more commodities from a single class of raw materials; and
3. Two or more of basic raw materials and intermediate products combine to form two or more products.

Figure 7.4 shows the links in an industrial complex. It gives a simplified example in which fertilizer and synthetic fibre production is linked to the basic oil refinery.

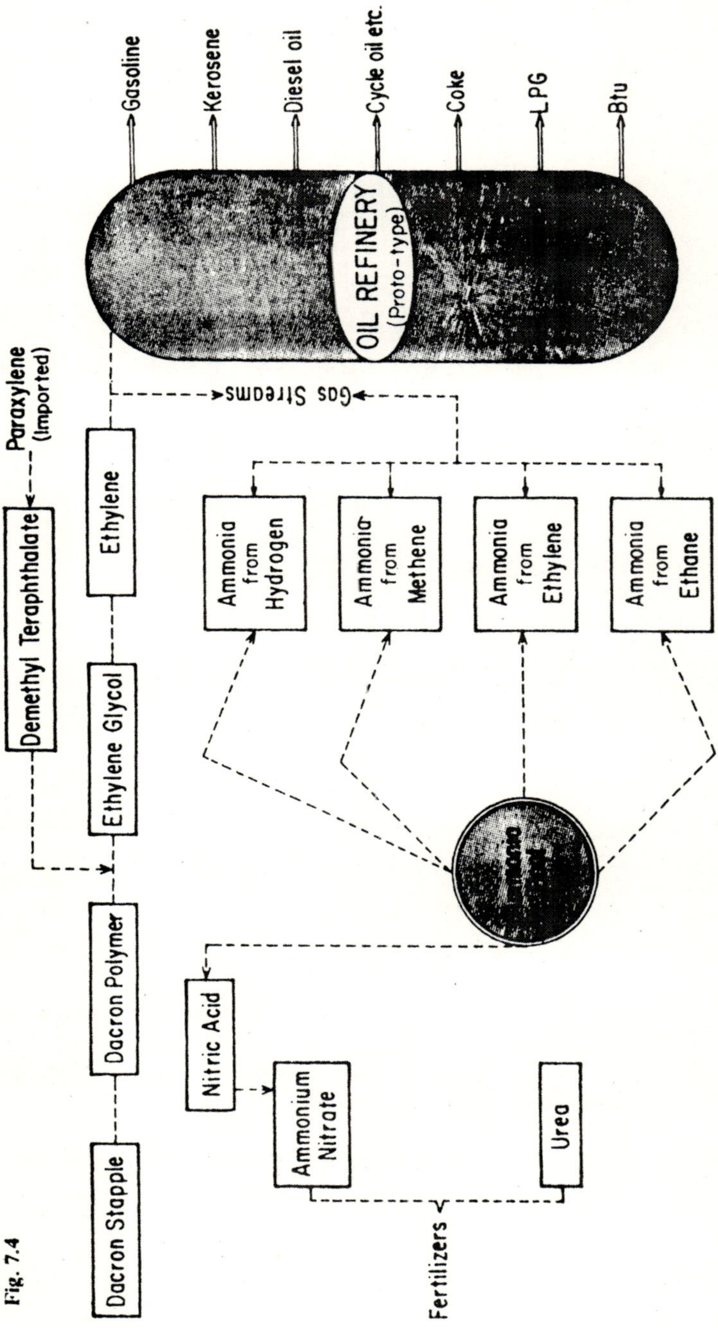
OIL REFINERY
(Proto-type)
Gasoline
Kerosene
Diesel oil
Cycle oil etc.
Coke
LPG
Btu
Gas Streams
Paraxylene
(Imported)
Demethyl Teraphthalate
Ethylene
Ethylene Glycol
Dacron Polymer
Dacron Stapple
Ammonia from Hydrogen
Ammonia from Methene
Ammonia from Ethylene
Ammonia from Ethane
Nitric Acid
Ammonium Nitrate
Urea
Fertilizers

Fig. 7.4

Industrial complex analysis can become a very useful tool in rural area development. If the main activities of an area are confined to agriculture, one can think of an agro-industrial complex. As explained through Fig. 7.4 there are two types of link activities which can be built around a basic product/activities: (i) final products for consumption and (ii) raw materials for other industries. The whole concept can be further extended to cover marketing, servicing, etc., also.

While planning for rural area development, it would be useful to identify a few products around which agricultural or agro-industrial complexes could be developed. Even if one such complex is developed in the area of operation, It would provide enough incentives for more integrated ventures. The role of co-operatives and the public sector agencies is quite important in this regard. A case of dairy complex is given in Fig. 7.5.

Input-Output Analysis

As apparent from industrial complex analysis, various human activities are mutually inter-connected. The output of one activity is used as input by many others. It means that we cannot develop a selected activity without taking care of the other products which go as raw material or other activities which use the final product. Input-output analysis, also known as inter-industry analysis, is a fruitful approach to depict and investigate the inter-linkages, among various activities.

Input-output technique tells us how the output of a particular sector of activity is used by other sectors of activity. It does so with the help of a flow table (Table 7.2).

The Table 7.2 reveals how the gross output of agriculture (row 1) is used by various sectors. Similarly, it also tells how much agriculture buys from other sectors (column 1). The total input in agriculture is equal to total output. In other words, it tells that to produce 100 rupees worth of agricultural products, the inputs required are : Rs. 13 from agriculture, Rs. 20 from manufacture, Rs. 12 from transport, etc. If the other sectors are not developed enough to contribute these inputs, agriculture cannot produce Rs. 100 worth of goods. So planning of agricultural development cannot be done in isolation. Same is the case with all other sectors.

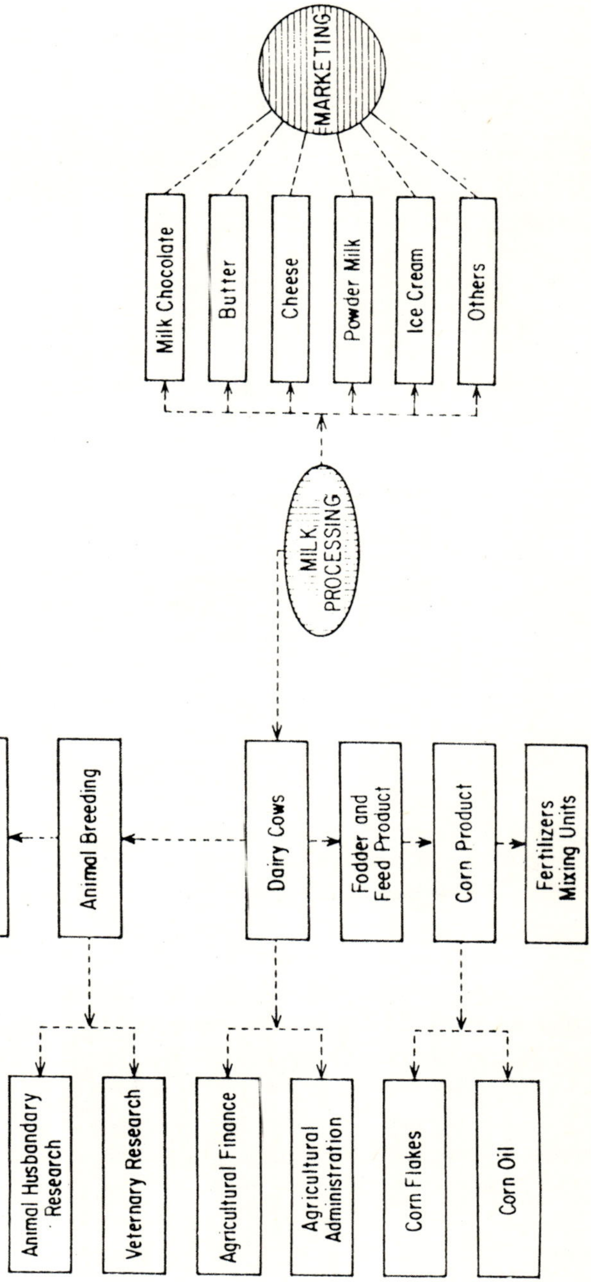

MARKETING
Milk Chocolate
Butter
Cheese
Powder Milk
Ice Cream
Others
MILK PROCESSING
Farmer's Training
Animal Breeding
Dairy Cows
Fodder and Feed Product
Corn Product
Fertilizers Mixing Units
Animal Husbandary Research
Veternary Research
Agricultural Finance
Agricultural Administration
Corn Flakes
Corn Oil

Fig. 7.5

Table 7.2: Input-output flow

Producing industry	Purchasing Sector'						
	Agricul-ture	Manu-facturing	Trans-portation	Trade	House-hold	All others	Total gross output
1. Agriculture	13	15	10	20	22	20	100
2. Manufacturing	20						
3. Transportation	12						
4. Trade	5						
5. Households	40						
6. All others	10						
Total inputs	100						

In Table 7.2 we have shown only six sectors. But this is not a realistic model of the economy. One can have as many sectors as the data constraints permit. Input-output tables with more than fifty sectors are quite common. No effort has so far been made to prepare input-output tables for villages, groups of villages or districts.

The concept of input-output may be further expanded to develop inter-regional input-output tables which would show which sector of which region buys the products of a region and supplies and inputs of various products of a region.

8

Watersheds as Units of Planning*

STREAM watersheds form a convenient areal unit of planning because they can be simply and unambiguously defined from a topographic map. They are independent of scale in that large river basins like the Cauvery can be broken into a hierarchic system of smaller basins; each smaller basin fits exactly within the next larger one.

The hierarchy of stream segments can be ordered in several different ways to designate the order of the watershed. Strahler's system designates the fingertip tributaries as order one. The channels formed by the junction of two first order channels are designated as order two and the channels formed by the junction of two second order channels are designated order three, and so on (see Figure 8.1).

Watershed is an area which drains into a river. Thus there is a hierarchy of watersheds as there is a hierarchy of rivers. The smallest watershed is formed by the fingertip tributaries. In figure 8.1 the largest watershed is formed by the third level tributary within which the second and first level watersheds fit. There would be as many watersheds of a particular hierarchic level as the number of tributaries of that level. For example, in Figure 8.2 there are three streams of first order and one stream of second order. There are, therefore, three watersheds (I, II and III) of first order and one watershed of the second order.

Watersheds as units of planning have several advantages. Edaphic changes in soil and vegetation reflect location within the watershed as the physical features of basin directly affect the hydrologic characteristics of the streams draining it. A rainstorm falling on a long, narrow basin is likely to produce a lower discharge in the stream draining it than a similar storm falling on a rather broad, almost circular basin.

---

* Partly drawn from Peter Haggett: *Geography: A Modern Synthesis.*

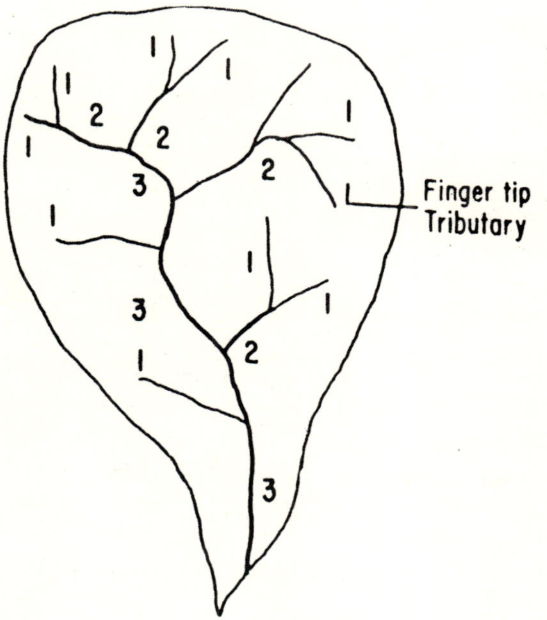

Fig. 8.1

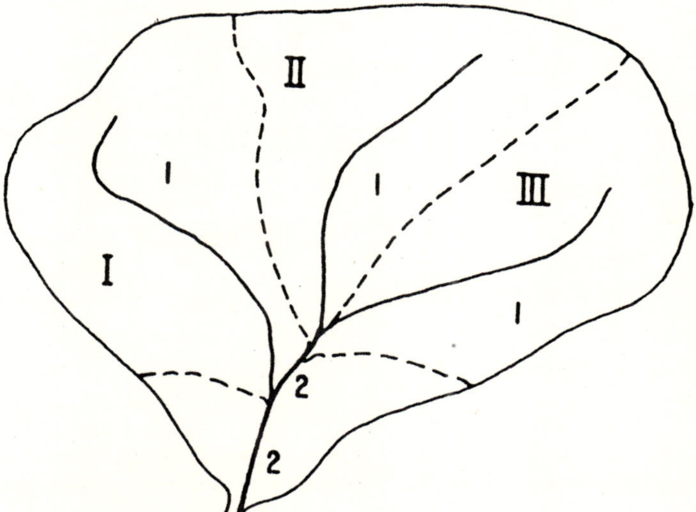

Fig. 8.2

Watersheds, therefore, form the appropriate units for intervention in flood control, navigation, hydro-electric power production, soil conservation, water management, crop planning, etc. It constitutes an ideal areal ecosystem for planned development of natural resources.

Watersheds in Humid Areas

Humid areas with profuse rainfall often suffer from recurrent floods in flat lands and soil erosion in the steeply sloping lands. In its natural state, a watershed offers a complete ecosystematic balance between topography, rainfall, vegetation and animal life. Because of the vegetative cover of the area, the rain water moves down the stream only slowly. Considerable amount of it is absorbed as soil moisture and percolates underground.

Man's intervention by way of agricultural use of the land and exploitation of vegetation for commercial purposes, often renders the ecosystem unbalanced. It has to be remembered that watershed also constitutes a spatial ecosystem in which the smallest watershed is organically linked to larger watersheds. Any disturbance in a small watershed would have repercussions in the larger area. The *vice versa* would also be equally true. If the watershed resources are used without keeping this ecosystematic integration in view, the system is rendered unbalanced and several negative forces do not allow the rebuilding of the resources like soils, vegetation, etc.

In the humid areas, the felling of the forests and indiscriminate use of land for various purposes can lead to the following major problems.

1. Floods;
2. Soil erosion and soil depletion;
3. Irregularity in rainfall; and
4. Lower carrying capacity of land.

Watersheds in Semi-arid Areas

In areas with scanty rainfall, watersheds are important controlling factors. In such areas, the rains come seasonally and in large quantity. In the absence of any vegetation on the slopes, the water carries the upper mantle of the soil downstream leading to intense sheet and gully erosion. A side effect of this is the unpredictable and sudden flooding of the lower stretches of the stream and lack of soil moisture. The second problem is more serious in undulating topographic areas like that in peninsular India. In the desert areas, the flooding of the usually undefined streams and removal or burial of good soil by sand constitute a serious problem.

The scanty vegetation found on the slopes of these watersheds is often used up by domestic animals. The bigger trees fall prey to human ignorance, and soon the slopes are left without grasses even. In due course, the capacity of land to sustain human activities declines and poverty and pestilences result. One of the most important objectives of watershed planning in these areas is to bring back the ecological balance through scientific use of the land so that soil erosion is minimised, rainfall is more regular, rain water percolates in the soil and the carrying capacity of the land increases.

Identification of Watersheds for Micro-planning

As noted earlier, watersheds can be of different sizes depending upon the order of the stream we select for the purpose. Thus the Cauvery basin forms one watershed. Within the Cauvery basin, we have Kabini watershed, and still smaller ones. The question is: which size of the watershed should be used in integrated rural area planning?

The optimum size of a micro-watershed largely depends on the specific emphasis of the development programme. If the programme aims at integrated area development, as is the case with DPAP, the emphasis is clearly on optimal utilization and conservation of land and water resources. Water being the most precious element in drought prone areas, the desired watershed function of the land is primarily to receive precipitation and to utilise it in the most efficient way. Even in areas of deficient rainfall, watersheds convert large amounts of rainfall to stream flow. For example, in places where the rainfall is only 60 cm annually (and this is the situation over larger part of the drought prone areas in India), only a 10 feet square plot receives and disposes of about 6.25 tonnes of water each year. One acre receives 2,718 tonnes; and 10,000 acres, not a very large watershed, receives and disposes of more than 27,180,000 tonnes.

The concentration and time distribution of run off from a watershed is mainly governed by the size and shape of the watershed. Surface run off in some watersheds is quickly assembled and discharged. In some others, the surface drainage is delayed longer and the discharge released more slowly. Part of this influence is due to soil characteristics and part due to vegetative cover. As watersheds increase in size, they become more complex with regard to slope, topography, soil and the vegetative cover conditions.

Watershed management is thus primarily concerned with planning the land-use to suit the landscape. Land-use planning, in turn, is closely linked with the farming activity. As it has already been discussed earlier, the basic unit for a micro-region or rural area for planning should be a farming locality with a radius of no more than five kms.

The optimum size of a micro-watershed for integrated rural development should, therefore, be no more than 10,000 hectares. A size between 5,000 and 10,000 hectares would possibly be the optimum size. The actual size of the micro-watershed should, however, be determined in accordance with the topographic characteristics of soil texture and composition, vegetative cover and the existing land-use.

There are several practical reasons for limiting the watershed areas to 10,000 hectares. In the first place, funds available for micro-level planning are limited, and hence can be better utilized if the investments are made in a small area to restore the ecological balance. If they are spread over too large an area, nothing substantial could perhaps be achieved to make any major impact on the existing situation. Secondly, the projects identified for implementation at the micro-level are small. And thirdly, the administrative and technical infrastructure available at the micro-level cannot undertake large projects.

As the ultimate purpose of watershed management is to improve the quality of human life in the area, the size of human population should also be taken into account while determining the optimum size of a micro-watershed. The methodology of determining a planning unit and grouping settlements/villages into micro units has already been discussed earlier. It will be seen that a grouping of 5 villages with 200 farming families each will form an optimum micro-unit for development purposes. In administrative terms, a micro-watershed could conform to the size of a village group panchayat.

To sum up, an area of 5,000 to 10,000 hectares and a population of 5,000 to 10,000 persons (or 1,000 to 2,000 households) would make an optimum micro-watershed for integrated rural development. In areas of high population density, the higher population limit and in areas of sparse population, the higher area limit should be the deciding criteria.

Watershed Planning

After a watershed has been identified, the next step is to prepare a land-use plan for the area using the principles laid down. It is important to note that agricultural use of the land is not necessarily the best use of it. For a good land-use plan, we should have the following maps :

1. Contour map with contour intervals of at least 5 metres. In case, such a map is not available, as is usually the case, a map with 50 feet interval can be used. It may be recalled that one inch to a mile topographic sheets of Survey of India give this contour interval.
2. A map showing the existing land-use should also be prepared. This map should show the land under forests, pastures, field crops, other crops like plantation, fruits, etc.
3. A map showing the soil types.
4. A map showing all streams within the watershed, all tanks, all canals and their distributaries, etc.
5. A map showing the areas irrigated by various irrigation methods – wells, canals, tanks, etc.
6. A map showing all human settlements–rural and urban with important economic and social facilities such as health centre, schools, veterinary hospital, drinking water facilities, communication facilities like posts and telegraph offices and other public institutions like co-operative, banks, police stations, etc., and
7. A map showing the road network with bus facilities.

The land of the area should be classified into eight categories and each category should be assigned a particular type of land-use. But, if detailed data pertaining to soils are not available, a slope map should be prepared using the contour map as a base. Distance between two contour lines in kilometres, and the difference between contour values should form the basic data to prepare a slope map. For example, if the distance between two contours along a given line is 20 kilometres and the contour value difference is 300 metres, then the slope is 15 metres per kilometre or 1.5 per cent.

To facilitate this work, the whole area may be divided into squares of 1 kilometre and then each square may be assigned the slope so calculated. When the whole area is marked with squares of different slopes, we can use the principles (already discussed) to assign land for various purposes.

The funds available for various sectors such as agriculture, forestry, animal husbandry, etc., should be used within the framework of the land-use plan prepared for the watershed. Within the constraints of this plan animal husbandry and other such industries should also be developed. The settlement, road network and other maps can be fruitfully used to locate and create facilities which would strengthen the economy of the watershed. For example, if there is enough land for pasture development, the scope of dairy industry could be studied. But this industry would need marketing facilities, suitable road-network, veterinary hospitals, artificial insemination centres, feed manufacturing or mixing centres, finances, etc. All these have to be planned in advance before launching the dairy development project.

9

Land-use Analysis*

To make a sound and comprehensive land-use plan, two sets of facts are needed. One is an inventory of the land, which is best recorded on a map. The other has to do with facts about the farm business –available facilities, etc. It is necessary to know the carrying capacity of each hectare of land.

Land Capability

Soil conservation technicians have discovered that the land inventory, in order to meet the needs for planning conservation farming, must be more than a soil map, erosion map, or a slope map; and yet it must be simple. It must show clearly the adjustments that are needed. It must be sufficiently detailed to allow separate treatments field by field or acre by acre if necessary. It was in response to these needs that the method of classifying land capability was developed.

Land capability refers to the suitability of land for specified uses. Farmland as a rule is used either for the production of crops requiring tillage or for some form of permanent vegetation (usually grass, other forage plants, or timber) requiring little or no tillage. In classifying land capability, answers to these questions are first sought. Is the land suited for the production of crops? Can it be cultivated without soil erosion? Is it safe and permanent use limited to the production of perennial vegetation?

Probably most farmers have made at one time or another in their own minds some kind of classification of the capability of their lands.

---

* An extract from *A Manual on Conservation of Soil and Water*, United States Department of Agriculture, Soil Conservation Service Agriculture Handbook No. 61.

They know that some fields can be used for cultivated crops and that others are too steep, too stony, too thin, or too wet for cropping. They know that some of their fields which are unsuited to cultivation make good pasture, and that still others are most productive if trees are planted. In a general way they know these outstanding facts about their lands although probably they have never made a map of their farms nor even expressed all of these ideas in words.

Many farmers, however, have failed to realise fully that steeply sloping land cannot be farmed safely with level-land methods. They have plowed straight furrows and planted straight rows rather than change their farming to fit the land. This makes some of the rows run uphill and downhill, and every rain falling on an unprotected slope removes part of the soil. A few farmers, watching muddy water flow from their fields, have appreciated how valuable and how irreplacable their thin layer or topsoil really is and have taken steps to check this kind of waste. But losses of soil for the most part come about so gradually that they are not fully realised. Farming habits, like any others, are difficult to change; moreover, precise recommendations for soil-saving measures have not been generally available to farmers. Therefore, it is not surprising that in the past, farmers in classifying their lands for use more often than once have neglected to consider the full significance of soil erosion.

Use and conservation of land are influenced by the nature of the soil, the degree to which it has been affected by erosion, the slope, the wetness of the soil or its droughtiness, and the climate. The climate must be considered because it affects the crops that can be grown and the density of vegetation, both of which help to determine the need for and the possibility of erosion control and water conservation.

Any one of these factors, or several of them together, may limit the possible use of land. The rate of soil erosion depends on several properties, as soil, vegetative cover, climate and steepness of slope. On some soils erodibility on critical slopes is the deciding factor in setting up classes of land suited for cultivation. On others, the combined influence of a high watertable and low fertility may be dominant.

Facts obtained in the Field

The only dependable way of determining the capability of land is to make a careful examination of it in the field. This is done by soil scientists who walk over the ground, bore or dig holes in the soil, and determine its depth, texture, permeability, available moisture capacity, characteristics that affect the use, management and treatment of the land. They measure the slope, determine the degree of soil loss by erosion, the overflow hazards, the wetness of the land and other significant characteristics. They note also the present use of the land. These facts are recorded on aerial photographs for later use by farmers and others.

The factors used in mapping land are characterized by differences that significantly affect conservation practices, use suitability, crop yields and management requirements. In interpreting what the land can do and what it needs, each of these land characteristics is considered in relation to all others.

The land characteristics and those significant ranges of each that have been found most generally to be meaningful are given below:

1. *Effective depth of soil* (as depth over rock, tough clay, or hardpan);

Very deep	...	60 inches or more
Deep	...	36 – 60
Moderately deep	...	20 – 36
Shallow	...	10 – 20
Very shallow	...	0 – 10

2. *Texture of surface soil* (fineness of constituent particles):

Very heavy	...	(heavy clay; 60 per cent or more 2-micron clay particles)
Heavy	...	(clay, silty clay, sandy clay)
Moderately heavy	...	(silty clay loam, clay loam, sandy clay loam)
Medium	...	(silty loam, loam, very fine sandy loam)
Moderately light	...	(sandy loam, fine sandy loam)
Light	...	(loamy fine sand, loamy sand)
Very light	...	(sand, coarse sand)

3. *Permeability of subsoil*

Very slow	...	(less than 0.05 inch of water percolation per hour)
Slow	...	(0.05 – 0.20)
Moderately slow	...	(0.20 – 0.80)
Moderate	...	(0.80 – 2.50)
Moderately rapid	...	(2.50 – 5.00)
Rapid	...	(5.00 – 10.00)
Very rapid	...	(10.00 or more)

4. *Permeability of sub-stratum*

Very slow	...	(less than 0.05 inch of water percolation per hour)
Slow	...	(0.05 – 0.20)
Moderately slow	...	(0.20 – 0.80)
Moderate	...	(0.80 – 2.50)
Moderately rapid	...	(2.50 – 5.00)
Rapid	...	(5.00 – 10.00)
Very rapid	...	(10.00 or more)

5. *Thickness of surface soil*

Thin	...	(0 – 6 inches)
Moderately thick	...	(6 – 12)
Thick	...	(12 – 24)
Very thick	...	(24 – 36)

6. *Available moisture capacity* (inches of absorbed water per 60 inches of soil depth):

Very high	...	(12 inches or more)
High	...	(9 – 12)
Moderate	...	(6 – 9)
Low	...	(3 – 6)
Very low	...	(less than 3)

7. *Reaction*

Acid	...	(6.5 pH or less)
Neutral	...	(6.6 - 7.3 pH)
Alkaline	...	(7.4 pH or more)

8.	*Natural soil drainage*		
	Well drained	...	(well oxidized and free from mottling of colours in surface and sub-soil)
	Moderately well Drained	...	(well oxidized and free from mottling except in lower part of sub-soil)
	Imperfectly drained or somewhat poorly drained	...	(well oxidized surface, sub-soil mottled)
	Poorly drained	...	(gray colour, mottling in surface and sub-soil)
	Very poorly drained	...	(dark surface soil and gray or mottled sub-soil)
9.	*Inherent fertility*	...	High; moderate; low; very low
10.	*Organic content*	...	High, medium, low
11.	*Slope*	...	Nearly level, gently sloping, moderately sloping, strongly sloping, steep, very steep.
12.	*Erosion*	...	Not apparent or slight, moderate, severe, very severe, very severely gullied land
13.	*Wetness*	...	Slightly wet (growth of crops slightly affected or planting dates delayed for brief periods, less than a week) Moderately wet (growth of crops moderately affected or planting dates delayed by a week or so)

	Very wet (growth of crops seriously affected or planting delayed as much as a month or more) Extremely wet (swamp, marsh, too wet for cultivated crops or improved pastures)
14. *Salinity*	Slight (crop yields slighdy affected or range of crops slightly limited) Moderate (crop yields moderately affected, or range of crops moderately limited) Severe (crop yields seriously affected, or range of crops severely restricted) Very severe (growth of useful vegetation prohibited except some salt-tolerant forms)
15. *Frequency of overflow*	Occasional overflows, or overflows of short duration (crops occasionally damaged, or planting dates delayed) Frequent damaging overflows, or overflows of long duration (crops frequently damaged, or range of crops limited) Very frequent overflows, or overflows of very long duration (not feasible for cultivated crops).

With these facts and a knowledge of the climate of the area, the land can be classified according to its capability–its ability to produce permanently under specified uses and treatments.

For each area, one or more soil conservationists, combining the techniques of soil science, plant technology, engineering, biology and working with local farmers together determine how the land should be used and the practices needed for each kind of land. The facts recorded on the land map, research findings and all technical information are joined with practical farm experience in classifying the land and in working out the right combination of practices to make full use, without waste, of the land resources.

The Classification Scheme

The land-capability classification is a systematic arrangement of different kinds of land according to those properties that determine the ability of the land to produce on a virtually permanent basis. Suitability for cultivation is assumed to include the use of machinery–at least of plows, tillage implements and harvesting equipment–and the capacity for at least a moderate yield of one or more crops with suitable treatment and protective measures. The restrictions imposed by natural land characteristics necessarily affects (a) the number and complexity of the corrective practices to be used; (b) the productivity of the land; and (c) the intensity and manner of land-use--for example, the choice of crops on cropland or the amount and season of use on grazing land.

The classification is made and used for practical purposes, which is the selection and application of land used and treatments that will, while using the land, keep it in condition for long time production. The latter will involve control of erosion, conservation of rainfall and maintenance.

The classification is arranged according to a number of categories.

The first category covers land suited for cultivation and land not suited for cultivation.

The second category covers the eight land-capability classes. Four are suited for cultivation and four are not. The classes under this category are differentiated according to the degree of limitations in land-use imposed by the nature of the land itself.

The eight land-capability classes range from the best and most easily farmed land (class I) to land which has no value for cultivation, grazing, or forestry, but may be suited for wild life, recreation or for watershed protection (class VIII). They all fall into the two broad groups of land, one suited for cultivation, the other not suited for cultivation.

Classes I, II and III include land suited for regular cultivation. Class I land is very good nearly level land, with deep, easily worked soils that can be cultivated safely with ordinary good farming methods. Class II land is good but it has some limitations. It needs moderately intensive treatment if it is to be cultivated safely. Such treatment, for example, may be contouring and cover-cropping to control erosion, or simple water-management operations to conserve rainfall. Class III land is moderately good and can be used for cultivated crops regularly in a good rotation, if plowed on the contour on sloping fields. It has limitations of such degree that intensive treatment is necessary. The treatment may be terracing or strip-cropping to control erosion, or intensive water management on flat, wet areas.

Class IV is fairly good land, but its safe cropping use is very limited by natural features such as slope, erosion, adverse soil characteristics or adverse climate. As a rule its best use is for pasture or hay, but some of it may be cultivated occasionally with proper safeguards.

Classes V, VI and VII are not suited for any cultivation but may be used for grazing or forestry, according to adaptability. Class V land has few natural limitations for such uses and needs only good management. Class VI needs protective measures, usually because of slope or shallow soil. Class VII needs extreme care to overcome or cope with its major limitations, which usually are steep slope, very shallow soil or other very unfavourable features.

Class VIII land is suited for wildlife, recreation or watershed protection. It is usually characterized by such features as extreme steepness, roughness, stoniness, wetness, sandiness or erodibility. These characteristics make it unfit for any safe or economical cultivation, grazing or forestry.

An outline of the land-capability classification is shown in Table 9.1.

The eight land-capability classes cover a simple land classification useful for many purposes. They are not detailed enough, however, for many specific recommendations about management and treatment of land. These eight classes are distinguished from each other by inherent, durable land characteristics. Each of the eight classes is determined by the degree to which the land characteristics represent long time limitations on land-use. Each land-capability class includes a specified range in degree of its natural limitations with respect to use.

The sub-classes represent convenient groupings of subordinate characteristics. A land-capability class is determined by the degree of limitations in land-use, together with the hazards involved. Within a given land-capability class the sub-classes are determined by the kind of limitation. For example, within class III land, suited for cultivation but subject to severe hazards, most frequently we have sloping land subject to water erosion, but we also have smooth land subject to wind erosion and wet land that produces crops only if drains are installed and maintained.

Within each sub-class the land that is suited for essentially the same kind of management and the same kind of conservation treatment is designated as a land-capability unit. A land-capability unit is essentially uniform in all major characteristics that affect its management and conservation. It is the smallest unit recognized in the land-capability classification, although greater detail may be recognized for some local purposes in mapping.

Table 9.1 shows the relation of the different categories to each other. It gives the eight land-capability classes and examples of the sub-classes and units.

The eight land-capability classes are indicated on maps by Roman numerals I to VIII, or by standard colour or by both. The Roman numerals and the standard colours are uniform on a nationwide basis. Sub-classes are designated by lower-case letters, and land-capability units by ordinary numericals, as IIe1 and IIe 2.

The eight land classes express degree of usefulness. The sub-classes express kinds of limitations within each class; and the units, divisions of the sub-classes, are practical groupings for use and treatment of the land.

The four sub-classes, which may be recognized in most of the land-capability classes, except class I, are:

e. Land dominantly subject to wind or water erosion, or both,
w. Land subject to presence of excess wetness or to overflow,
s. Land limited chiefly by soil conditions, such as excessive sandy texture, excess of gravel or stones, or shallow depth,
c. Land limited chiefly by climate, either inadequate precipitation or low temperature.

Land-capability maps show the eight land-capability classes in colours and the physical land factors of soil, slope and erosion by boundary lines and symbols. Class I land is shown in green, class II in yellow, class III in red, class IV in blue, class V in dark green, class VI in orange, class VII in brown, and class VIII in purple on coloured maps.

Land Suited for Cultivation

Class I Land : Class I is very good land that can be cultivated safely with ordinary good farming methods. It is nearly level land, has deep, productive, easily worked soils, and is not subject to more than slight water or wind erosion. It is well drained and is not subject to damaging overflows. It is suited for intensive cropping, such as production of corn and other inter-tilled crops.

Class I land may be recognized under irrigation where under natural conditions it was essentially valueless for crop production. Class I irrigated land ordinarily has a slope of less than 1 per cent and deep, medium-textured moderately permeable soil of good water-holding capacity. Some Class I irrigated land requires initial conditioning, such as levelling to the desired grade, leaching to remove salts, or the lowering of a seasonal water table. If limitations are likely to recur and require periodic attention, however, the land is subject to continuing limitations in use, and is not Class I. Class I land may also be recognized in artificially drained areas where the soil is moderately to rapidly permeable. On certain lands that meet the ordinary requirements for Class I, drainage is sometimes worthwhile as a practical method for greater production or ease of operation.

Class I land for crop use may, in some places, require the use of fertilizer and lime, cover and green manure crops, crop residues, and crop rotations.

Class II Land : Class II is good land that can be cultivated with easily applied special practices. Some of its variations are: gentle slopes, moderate susceptibility to erosion, soils of only moderate depth, occasional moderate overflow and moderate wetness easily correctible. These are examples–the list is not complete. Each of these limitations requires attention on the part of the land operator. The limitation sometimes gives the farmer less latitude in choice of crops or of management methods or requires special practices such as soil-conserving rotations, water-control devices and tillage methods, to name only a few.

Table 9.1: Outline of the Land-capability Classification

Land-use suitability (broad grouping)	Land capability class (degree of limitations for use)	Land capability sub-class (grouped according to kind of limitation; shows examples only)	Land-capability unit (land-management groups based on physical characteristics; shows examples only)
Suited for cultivation	I. Few limitations. Wide latitude for use. Very good land. (Green on coloured map) II. Moderate limitations in use. Good land. (yellow) III. Severe limitations in use. Regular cultivation possible if hazards are provided against. Moderately good land. (Red) IV. Very severe limitations in use. Suited for occasional cultivation or for some kind of limited cultivation. (Blue)	e. Use is limited by moderate hazards of water or wind erosion. c. Climate. w. Use is limited by excess water-drainage needed for cultivation s. Use is limited by low water-holding by capacity or by low plant-nutrient content.	Moderately sloping slightly acid soils on limestone. Moderately sloping, highly acid soils on sandstone or shale. Imperfectly drained acid soils. Poorly drained neutral soils. Sandy rapidly permeable soils.
Not suited for cultivation	V. Not suited for cultivation because of wetness, stoniness, overflows, etc. Few limitations on use for grazing or forestry. (dark green) VI. Too steep, stony, dry wet, etc., for cultivation. Moderate limitations on use for grazing or forestry (Orange) VII. Very steep, rough, dry, wet, etc. Severe limitations on use for grazing or forestry (Brown) VIII. Extremely rough, dry, swampy, etc. Not suited for cultivation, grazing or forestry, suited for wildlife, watershed protection or recreation (Purple)	Grouping of sites according to kind of limitation	Sites significant in management of ranges, pastures, forests, etc.

Generally its safe use calls for a combination of mutually supporting practices. For example, the Class II gently sloping land having deep soils subject to moderate erosion needs several of the following practices: Terracing, strip cropping, contour tillage, crop rotations that include grasses or legumes, vegetated water-disposal areas, cover or green-manure crops, stubble mulching, fertilizers, manure, and lime. The exact combination of measures will differ from place to place. It depends on the characteristics of the land, including climate, and the system of farming the farmer wants to follow.

Class III Land : Class III is moderately good land that can be used regularly for crops in a good rotation, with intensive treatment. Some of the characteristics of this kind of land are: Moderately steep slope, high susceptibility to erosion, moderate overflow, slow or very slow sub-soil permeability, excessive wetness, shallow depth to bedrock, hardpan, or clay-pan, sandy, very sandy, or gravelly soil with low moisture capacity and low inherent fertility.

Class III land is more limited in use by its natural characteristics than Class II land. Limitations of some Class III land restrict the choice of crops or the timing of such operations as planting and tillage. An adequate soil-conserving rotation includes enough ground cover to reduce losses of soil through erosion, minimize losses of plant nutrients through leaching, maintain good soil structure so that it will absorb water readily, increase and maintain organic matter and nitrogen supply of the soil and promote high yields of cultivated crops grown in the rotation. On moderately steep slopes of some Class III land, the rotations should be longer than on level land and must include more years of hay or other sod crops to prevent excessive soil losses.

On much of the nearly level wet land of this class, having heavy, slowly permeable soil, a drainage system along with a cropping plan including deep-rooted legumes grown in rotation is needed. To maintain good soil structure and prevent puddling and resultant reduced permeability on such soils, it usually is necessary, also, to supply organic matter and to be careful not to work the soil when it is too wet or too dry. Class III land in some irrigated areas is limited in use by a high watertable, slow permeability and danger of salt accumulations.

Class III land which is subject to wind erosion, the practices for controlling this erosion are the same as those recommended for Class II land–contour farming strip cropping, stubble mulching, rough tillage and terracing where it can be used effectively.

Class IV Land : Class IV is fairly good land that is best maintained in perennial vegetation but can be cultivated occasionally or in a limited way if handled with great care. Its cropping use is restricted by natural features, such as slope, erosion, unfavourable soil characteristics, or adverse climate. Much Class IV land in the humid regions is suited for occasional cultivation. On it the farmer can safely use a long rotation such as a grain crop every 5 or 6 years, followed by several years of hay or pasture. Some of the nearly level, imperfectly drained land, classified as IV is not subject to erosion but is unsuited for intertilled crops because of the time required for the soil to dry out in the spring and because of its low productivity when in these crops. Also choice of crops is often limited. Some Class IV land is suited only for certain specialized crops.

In sub-humid regions some of the Class IV land is shallow or only moderately deep, moderately or strongly sloping, low in fertility, extremely sandy, or sometimes moderately saline. Long time rotations including soil-building legumes and grasses are in some places difficult to follow in a semi-arid climate. Periods of weather suitable for getting a stand of grasses or legumes occur at irregular intervals. Whenever a stand is obtained the land should remain in these protective crops at least long enough to restore soil structure and fertility.

In some semi-arid regions, on the other hand, the best land is in Class IV. All cultivation is subject to very severe limitations because of wind erosion. Special and intensively applied cropping systems and practices are needed during the time of cultivation to conserve soil moisture and reduce erosion.

Class IV semi-arid land often produces high yields of adaptable crops during years of above-average rainfall. But during years of average or below average rainfall it produces low yields. During bad years the land must be protected from blowing. It needs special treatments, special cropping systems, or special practices to protect it against erosion and to conserve moisture. These treatments must be applied with greater regularity in dry years. Sometimes protective crops must be planted primarily to hold the soil. Perennial vegetation is needed to protect the land during severe drought and to rebuild soil structure and fertility.

Most of the Class IV land in humid regions is well suited for woodland. Unless needed for pasture, it is not as a rule desirable to clear areas now covered with trees.

Land Not Suited for Cultivation

Class V Land : Class V is the land not suited for cultivation but is suited for perennial vegetation (grazing and forestry) with few or no limitations. Cultivation is not feasible because of one or more factors, such as wetness, stoniness, or some other limitation. The land is nearly level and not subject to more than slight wind or water erosion. Grazing use or forestry is governed by the requirements for a good cover of vegetation. Certain range-management or woodland-management practices, such as stocking within the range's carrying capacity and the control of burning, are always needed for satisfactory production. Class V land on which vegetation has become temporarily depleted through misuse may require moderate or even severe restrictions in grazing or woodland use for a period in order to improve the vegetation. The land, however, is not damaged easily.

Class V land also occurs in many of the swampy areas where drainage is not feasible.

Class VI Land : Class VI is the land subject to moderate limitations under grazing or forestry use. It is too steep, subject to erosion, shallow, wet, dry, or otherwise not suited to cultivation, but with careful management is suited to either grazing or forestry. Some Class VI land can be tilled just enough to establish pastures; some can be used safely for tree crops. The restrictions commonly needed on Class VI range land are chiefly adjustment of grazing to the carrying capacity, deferred grazing to permit growth of grass in the spring and rotation of grazing to permit the grass to recover enough to form seed. Fencing, careful location of watering places, salting and harding are some of the practices necessary to use the land properly. Gullies should be controlled by diversion of water, planting, or other adaptable measures. Contour furrows, ridges, diversions, or water spreaders are useful on some sites to store in the soil more of the runoff by checking or diverting the water.

Class VI land is capable of producing forage or wood-land products under moderate restrictions. If the vegetation has been depleted by mismanagement, severe restrictions in use for a few years probably are needed to permit recovery of vegetation. An example of such temporary severe restrictions would be exclusion of livestock from overgrazed Class VI range-land until desirable vegetation is restored.

Pastures in humid regions on Class VI land generally need liberal fertilization and careful adjusting of grazing. Many of them need liming and reseeding.

Class VII Land : Class VII is the land that is subject to severe limitations or severe hazards under either grazing or forestry use; it is not suited for cultivation. It is very steep eroded, stony, rough, shallow, dry, swampy, or otherwise unfavourable, but can be used for grazing or forestry if carefully handled. Owing to these adverse land characteristics that severely limit the growth or utilization of vegetation, the land is generally only fair or poor for grazing or forestry. Depletion of cover on rough, erodible Class VII land leads to more rapid damage than on Class VI land that has similar but less extreme limitations. Structures such as contour furrows, ridges and water spreaders for the most part cannot be used on Class VII range-land because of steep slopes, shallow soils, or other unfavourable factors.

Most Class VII land in humid regions is recommended for woodland rather than for pasture. Practices recommended for woodland usually include exclusion of livestock, prevention of fire, selection of trees for cutting, and careful harvesting methods. Most of the severely gullied land in humid areas consists of Class VII that should be planted to trees.

Land Not Suited for Cultivation, Grazing or Woodland

Class VIII Land : Class VIII is the land of such unfavourable characteristics as to be unsuited for cultivation, grazing, or forestry. It is suited for wildlife, recreation, or water-shed-protection uses. It includes such areas as marshes, deserts, badlands, deep gullies of the caving type, high mountain land, and very steep, rough, stony, barren land. Class VIII land often occurs in small areas, such as roadsides or ditch-banks, that cannot be shown on the maps made for farm-conservation planning. Protection is necessary even for some of these areas.

10

A New System of Soil Appraisal in terms of Actual and Potential Productivity

Introduction

BECAUSE of the food shortages besetting mankind, it is urgent that an inventory be made of the world's soil resources to ascertain what uncultivated land can be brought into production and which cultivated soils could produce more than at present.

The task of compiling such an inventory has been entrusted to the FAO/UNESCO Soil Map of the World project. The procedure adopted is to interpret soil maps since these provide an indication of the types of soils and their geographic distribution.

Soil maps are usually used not to find what genetic soil type exists at a certain place, but rather to determine the agricultural value of the soil and its susceptibility to improvement. It is necessary for this to interpret the soil map for the users, and to state the suitability of a given soil, in relation to its properties, for agricultural use. Only a soil specialist is capable of making such an interpretation, but since other considerations–geographic and socio-economic–have a place in determining both the possible and the most appropriate agricultural uses of a given piece of land, he must call in the agronomist, the botanist, the economist and the sociologist to assist him on such things as :

1. Vegetation, rainfall, erosion and present land-use;
2. Response of soils to various management practices such as irrigation and fertilizer application;
3. Crops already grown and yields obtained;
4. Agricultural experiments conducted in the region.

The object of the interpretation and the use of the above data is to provide :

1. A classification of land in terms of its agricultural value, its specific capabilities and potential use;
2. Land resource maps showing the geographical distribution of soils, their most appropriate use, their agricultural value and their potentiality under specific management practices.

The maps may be small scale, sometimes covering an entire continent, or large scale, intended say, for a particular farm. Obviously, the classification will vary with the scale used.

Principal Land Classification Systems

A classification system depends on :

(a) The data available,
(b) The scale of the map,
(c) The purpose.

This explains the multiplicity of systems that have been evolved by individual researchers and government services.

In his *Aspects de pedologie applique*, Vink distinguishes seven main classification systems in use. These may be described as :

1. Land classification in terms of inherent characteristics (soil classification in the strict sense);
2. Land classification in terms of inherent qualities (soil quality, i.e., technical quality classification);
3. Land classification in terms of present use (land-use classification);
4. Soil-crop response (or response to management);
5. Land classification in terms of use capabilities (soil suitability classification);
6. Land classification in terms of recommended use;
7. Land classification in terms of programme realisation.

Classification system 3, based on present land-use requires special soil surveys. The soil scientist may sometimes explain present use by reference to the nature of the soil and check his assumptions regarding soil fertility, but the system offers no way of determining ideal or future use.

The last three systems have socio-economic and even political implications, for which the soil scientist should not normally accept full responsibility. Classification under system 5 nevertheless can, and should, be guided by the soil scientist who will indicate the suitability of the soil in question for different type of crops. The final decision, of course, rests with the economist, who will give due weight to such factors as distance from markets, dietary habits and standard of living of the population.

What follows is an attempt to reconcile these different systems as far as possible.

The Main Classification Systems Currently Employed

The principal classification systems currently in use and the reasons that we have discarded them are given below :

1. Storie's index for rating the agricultural value of soils. This was conceived especially for land appraisal for taxation purposes. It is highly appropriate for California and agricultural practices there, but does not allow assessment of improvements as a result of future management–the potential value of the soil.
   In this report we have kept Storie's basic procedure of establishing a "productivity index" expressing soil conditions as ascertained together with his ingenious method of calculation.
2. The land classification of the Bureau of Reclamation of the United States of America. This is not used here because it was conceived solely in terms of irrigability and, therefore, also takes economic factors into account.
3. The land-capability classification of Soil Conservation Service of the U.S.A. This is intended primarily as a means of determining the steps to take to control erosion. Its "capability classes" mainly reflect the extent and complexity of conservation problems; exaggerated importance is attached to slope, while other qualities indicative of soil fertility may be neglected. It is a classification in terms of the limitations of soils for agricultural use and the economic implications of such limitations. It is also an interpretive grouping according to capability. Moreover, the capabilities considered, such as suitability for the cultiva-

tion, range or woodland, introduce economic factors the significance of which can only be judged by an agricultural expert who is thoroughly acquainted with the region.

In its latest versions this classification has gone somewhat beyond considerations of soil conservation to become, more precisely, a classification according to limitation. The capability sub-classes are based on limitations due to climate, excess water, presence of salts, etc. The capability unit takes into account various criteria, among them "potential productivity", but without indicating the means used for appraising it. The limitations are, moreover, subjectively determined, the criteria utilised and the significance attributed to them by different soil scientists varying from one region to another. The resulting classification leads to rather vague definitions in such terms as: "Soil with few limitations that restrict their use". Class III, for instance, may include: a soil subject to erosion, a wet soil in need of drainage, a sandy soil limited by the low moisture-holding capacity, or a fertile soil in a region that is too arid. The authors themselves admit that their classification is not specifically intended for land-use planning and does not give sufficient information on land capability for growing individual plants, and that it does not classify the soils in terms of productivity. The potential value of a soil is neglected for a description of its limitations–a procedure that may be justified if the purpose is to determine the successive steps in conservation measures but not if it is to rate soil value. Moreover, it is inapplicable on a continent-wide scale where the primary purpose is to assess the value of virgin lands in terms of traditional agricultural practices.

4. The classification of Aubert and Fournier. Here soils are classified according to the type or magnitude of the conservation or development work required. The intrinsic value of the soil is excluded because, as the authors themselves recognise, the rating of agricultural soils as excellent, good average and poor is a delicate problem. The appraisal of soil response to cultivation is highly subjective, the assignation to one class or another after management being decided upon in a very arbitrary fashion (e.g., irrespective of the difficulty involved in, or the cost of, management). The possibility of several types of management being employed simultaneously is not considered.

This classification has one advantage that certain important soil characteristics are shown on the map and management practices can be indicated with a greater degree of precision than in the American system.

5. Christian's physiographic classification. Here land is classified from the standpoint of pedology, geology, relief and plant cover. Here again the soil characteristics, the only true criteria of productivity, are almost entirely neglected. However, unlike the other systems which are intended for large scale maps on which climatic variations are irrelevant, this one is suitable for small scale maps.

Limitations of the Systems Presently Used

Most of the classifications above discussed are concerned primarily with the extent, the difficulty and the cost of management, or even solely with limitations affecting crop growing or requiring development work. However, a number of objections may be raised against the use of limitations as criteria for classification.

The concept of limitation is extremely complex. The term may indicate that soil conditions are such that :

(a) Very difficult and costly work is required if a crop is to be obtained,
(b) Only very poor crop yields are possible with ordinary farming practices,
(c) Very few plant species can grow on the land in question, or
(d) Combinations of these.

Limitation is merely a *negative aspect* of a given soil property. Why not consider the good property rather than the bad one?

Again, the word limitation suggests a gradation in the property under discussion, and within that gradation a cross-over point between good and bad. Now that point, or dividing line, from the standpoint of general land-use, is not in fact clearly defined since it varies according to the crop and the requirements of the user.

For instance, a deep soil is looked on as good, a shallow soil as poor. Where does the dividing line between the two extremes lie? No absolute limit is determinable in the classification phase. It is only under actual use, when minimum yield figures are set for a given crop, that it is possible to draw a line between adequate and inadequate depth.

A soil is classified either according to its most significant limitation or by the number of its limitations, but the seriousness of the limitation (e.g. greater or lesser degree of stoniness or shallowness) is rarely considered. Accordingly the classification systems reviewed lack flexibility. Again, if a soil has several limitations this may affect the total *cost* of development and management, but it is not the ***number*** of limitations that affects yields as even a single limitation is capable of reducing these.

From limitations, such as excess water or erosion, an attempt is made to predict plant growth behaviour. This is a mistaken procedure, however, because it is the soil as a whole, with all its complex of characteristics, taken together with factors of the environment that determines growth rate. The usefulness of certain soils, like the alluvial soils of the Nile, is limited by several factors–dryness, salinity, excess water–yet they are highly productive when properly managed.

In under-developed countries it is much more important to consider productivity, the positive factor, rather than limitations, the negative factor. The latter merely indicates required management measures, which are costly undertakings and, therefore, often feasible only over small areas.

Evolving a New Classification System

In our view what best expresses present and future land capability is productivity rather than limitations. This avoids economic and sociological considerations which lie outside the province of the soil scientist. Soil productivity, or known yields, moreover, provides the best grounds for understanding between the soil scientist and the economist.

It is a somewhat theoretical concept but it does provide a basis of comparison between soils which is our object. And yet it is reasonable, since in the same climate soils cultivated in a similar way produce more or produce less according to their inherent properties; it is the soil type that determine yields.

Despite the fact that the concept of productivity is somewhat abstract and relative, it is still the best base of soil classification for the user who wishes to know before all else whether a piece of land is "good" or "bad", in other words whether he can cultivate it to advantage. Vink suggests that a good system in land development planning would be to take soil mapping units and establish productivity norms or average yield estimates at various management levels, even if these be no more than rough approximations. Yields standards cannot in themselves be considered classifications, yet they constitute a big step in the direction of a quantitative classification of land capability.

The underlying principle in this study is that if favourable conditions, extraneous to the soil are present (sound husbandry, good plant varieties adapted to the particular climate, freedom from pests, etc.) the productivity theoretically possible can be expressed by reference to the intrinsic soil characteristics (depth, base status, organic matter content, and the rest). We have thus been at pains to evolve a formula expressing soil productivity as a function of soil characteristics assuming an efficient farmer following normal practices is working the land. If, subsequently, soil management, land development, or intensive farming systems are introduced, these will improve soil properties, in which case, on the basis of the foreseeable improved characteristics, the same formula can be used to calculate "potentiality" or potential productivity. The indexes of productivity and of potentiality thus calculated are used to classify soils. The ratio of the two indexes gives a "coefficient of improvement"–either global, when every possible type of improvement has been introduced, or partial, if, say, only one of a number of possible improvements has been made.

Such a classification of soils in terms of productivity would necessitate compiling :

1. Maps showing present productivity (under prevailing farming practices) and hence the agricultural value of land, and
2. Maps showing potentiality or potential productivity resulting from new management practices.

Purpose and Value of the System Now Proposed

When this study was begun the purpose was ultimately to compile a soil resources map on the basis of an interpretation of small scale soil maps. The system, however, lands itself to other purposes as well. Thus, now, on any map, each type of soil shown possesses specific characteristics–its distinguishing properties. Overlooking, for the time being, factors extrinsic to the soil itself, such as climate, slope and farming practices, those characteristics enable us to calculate average theoretical productivity and classify soil types on the basis of quality. Since soil improvement measures will enhance that productivity, the soil resources map will accordingly indicate not only actual but also potential productivity.

The calculation of a productivity index is of interest to the surveyor as well as to the farmer. By taking soil profile samplings and making a few routine chemical analyses quite a clear idea of the soil value virtually mathematically accurate, can be obtained by amalgamating the different soil properties into a productivity index. Nevertheless, the formula used is empirical and leaves a great deal of room for improvement. The system proposed in the Annexes has been evolved for interpreting the 1:5,000,000 scale map of Africa.

It facilitates land classification for purposes of taxation, consolidation of land holding, etc., and may be combined with other classifications, in particular that of Aubert and Fournier or that of the United States Soil Conservation Service, in which soil quality and potential productivity are expressed at land-capability unit or sub-class levels.

It is possible to draw up large scale productivity or potentiality maps for a single holding, a large agricultural enterprise or a region where development is being planned.

It can, of course, also be used with small scale maps, since it was devised for that purpose. However, it should be emphasised that the formula suggested in the Annexes may be adapted, depending on the purpose and on the data available. For instance, on a small scale map it is not possible to include the slope factor (which would be included on a large scale map) for the purposes of indicating the erosion (factor K) or degradation hazard.

The purpose here is not to put forward a formula of universal application but to state a principle and to suggest a methodology that can be improved upon. To summarize, with the system it is possible :

(i) To determine the value or quality of a soil,
(ii) To set up a soil classification scale,
(iii) To compile large scale land-use maps, and
(iv) To compile small scale maps.

Maps

There is no need to enlarge upon the value of maps here. Maps answer the chief requirement of land users in that they show in such a region there is such and such type of soil, which can be improved in such and such manner and brought to a given potentiality.

Map usefulness depends greatly on scale. Small scale maps can help land-use planners and international organizations like FAO to estimate the area of arable land of a continent, while individual farmers, agricultural engineers and economists need large scale maps.

Large scale maps rate land according to :

(i) Inherent characteristics,
(ii) Technical properties,
(iii) Response to cropping and management methods, and
(iv) Potential utilization.

But they do more than that, because :

(a) Ecologists and agronomists can readily use them to compile maps indicating suitability of land for growing specific types of crop. If the soil requirements of individual plants are known, it suffices to refer to the tables attached to the map or to the map itself (if soil characteristics are indicated there) to determine which region offers soils with requisite properties (see Table 10.7 which illustrates an imaginary case);

(b) Economists knowing the selling price of a given commodity as well as the cost of land development or improvement can assess returns to be expected from farmland where management has been undertaken and from land where it has not been, and thus judge the advisability or otherwise of development in the case under review. Some idea of the type and magnitude of the necessary work may also be estimated from the number of letter-symbols (representing specific types of work) appearing on the map or in the table;

(c) The specific crop suitability of a soil is itself largely governed by the local economy and by such considerations as distance from markets. The soil capability distinctions of the classifications are subjective and very often amount to little more than classifying land without further ado as suitable for crop growing, pasture or forest bearing, with no clear reasons given for the choice.

Land Capability

In the classification system proposed here a first approximation suggests :

(a) The lands of Classes I and II (Table 10.4) are suitable for all agricultural crops,
(b) Class III is marginal, in particular where tree crops are concerned,
(c) Class IV is land best for range, reforestation* or recreation, or planted to special crops such as rice, and
(d) Class V is land which is not suitable at all for cultivation.

All these capabilities, however, are determined on considerations of economic returns.

By contrast, the calculation of each productivity index for crop growing, pasture or forest bearing (using the ratings as assigned to characteristics shown in Table 10.2) allows a comparison between the various indexes of a soil; and it is from these that suitability may be deduced: the highest index means the greatest suitability considering not the likely financial returns from the operation but the productive capacity. Finally, as has been said, the specific crop-suitability of a piece of land will be decided by the user, who will ensure that soil characteristics and the requirements of the proposed crop are in harmony.

Tree Crops and Forest

A distinction should be made between the two concepts. Tree crops must be considered more exacting, especially as regards depth and often in aeration of soil, than forest.

This way of thinking is justified because :

(a) The term "tree crops" is intended as grouping strictly all cash crops, where the aim is to obtain (1) a partial product from the

* It may appear strange to read that with Class III one is already at marginal level, in particular for tree crops followed immediately by a statement to the effect that Class IV refers primarily to land reserved for reforestation, etc., while tree crops and forest are lumped together.

plant, (2) a seasonal harvest, and (3) a product whose quality must be constant and adapted to a narrow range of well-defined uses (orchard or plantation crops, Hevea Latex or the like). In such cases account must be taken of the edaphic requirements of the plant.

(b) The term "forest" is more complex. The idea of returns in the economic sense is not the only reason for creating or maintaining a forest: the chief end in view may be the control of erosion or recreation, or purifying the atmosphere in industrial areas. Even where timber production is the main objective, it can only be on a long-term basis, and the various end-uses (joinery, pit props, paper, fuel) will be made of wood of widely differing kinds.

Accordingly, as governed by the purpose of a forest, edaphic requirements may or may not be taken into account, and afforestation may be recommended on soils of widely differing productivity.

The value of this method lies in the fact that it largely avoids the arbitrary and subjective elements by its appeal to scientific data that are measurable (texture, contents of various chemical elements) or are readily definable in unambiguous terms (structure, nature of mineral reserves, etc.). The findings based on such data are accordingly reproducible, which allows for comparing the interpretations of various researchers. This possibility of comparison is of vital importance to FAO's World Soil Resources Office and similar agencies concerned in correlating soil data on a worldwide scale because on this depends the further possibility of compiling productivity maps on a similar system and legend.

The Method Described

Definition of Terms

The concept of productivity is a complex one and requires definition. Obviously, only theoretical productivity is envisaged, i.e., optimum soil yields, not taking into consideration damage caused by insects or other pests, or choice of seed, unsound husbandry, and the rest. The concept is very close to that of "soil quality". The term "productivity" is preferred, however, because a comparison of our index with production figures (e.g., for peanuts on different soils in Madagascar, (Table

10.2) indicates that the concept is far from being a mere fiction and that what it connotes can be calculated by the formula proposed here. It must be concluded then that this index is a true expression of productive capacity and not a mere comparative scale of the theoretical value of soils. But productivity varies also with the type of crop grown; some plants being able to withstand soil drainage or fertility conditions which others cannot and to give economically satisfactory yields where other plants cannot grow at all. Since it is impossible to review all cultivated plants (whose requirements differ widely) one must consider a level of productivity for the majority of farm crops or for specific crop sequences: grains/fodder legumes, or tree crops/forest. We have taken three cases: shallow-rooting plants (pasture), medium-depth rooting plants (field crops) and deep-rooting plants (trees).

This difficulty of introducing considerations as to the type of crop into the notion of soil productivity is lessened, for instance, when a salt-tolerant plant like cotton will nevertheless give better yields in non-salty, good quality soils. By taking a large range of crops, therefore, it is possible to rate soils for productivity in full cognizance of the fact that productivity is a relative term. Each plant has its own soil-productivity scale, which does not coincide with that of the next plant. Accordingly, "productivity" (i.e., productivity here and now) is employed in the sense of initial soil *capability to produce a certain amount of crop per hectare per annum*; and is expressed as *a percentage of the optimum yield per hectare of that same crop grown on the best soil*. It is the natural fertility of virgin land in its first year of cultivation by simple farming practices (soil preparation, sowing, aftercare, harvesting). For soils already under cultivation it is the productivity of the year in which the soil was mapped, described and analysed–hence prior to its degradation, or improvement, as the case may be.

Assuming scientific development of virgin land or land brought under cultivation after surveying there should be no degradation. Thus, the slope factor (which governs erosion hazard and a soil suitability for machine cultivation) will not be taken into account in determining productivity except insofar as it renders erosion control measures necessary. If a sloping piece of land has already been cultivated, then erosion will have occurred and an equilibrium will have been attained, as may be seen in the soil conditions: low organic matter content, shallowness, more marked dryness, etc. Such characteristics that must be taken into consideration to obtain the actual productivity index.

In special cases where, for political or economic reasons, no conservation measures are taken, slope will be considered (see Annexes).

In distinction to "productivity", the second term to be defined is *potentiality*. This is *that productivity of a soil, when all possible improvements have been made, even then is most difficult and costly*. It is thus the future productivity of that soil taking into account physical and chemical characteristics as modified by conservation practices or improvements, and also those characteristics which are not modifiable by present-day technology.

The theory has been propounded in certain quarters that a soil is of no value in itself because it can be completely changed by modern techniques. We are not of this opinion because there will always be land, particularly in underdeveloped countries which, for material or economic reasons, or even for simply natural reasons (lack of irrigation water for instance) cannot have the benefit of all that modern technology offers. What is more, there will always be certain fertility factors (i.e., texture) that are extremely difficult to modify by modern techniques even in wealthy countries. No matter what improvement measures are taken, there will always be limiting factors of one kind or another. Beyond soil inherent properties influences, the response to management: fertilizers, irrigation, and so on, cannot be neglected.

Principles Underlying the Method

Determination of the Productivity Index

Productivity is a function of the intrinsic properties of a soil, first as determined in the process of describing the soil profile *in situ*, and secondly by laboratory analysis. Soil moisture and temperature are included among such characteristics even though they are directly related to climate. Environmental factors–slope, vegetation and climate–will only be used to determine what set of management practices are necessary.

A soil map and its accompanying report should supply the necessary data to establish the productivity of various mapping units.

From among the countless characteristics that influence soil productivity, the following have been selected :

(a) The most commonly accepted factors of productivity, since a great deal of study is still required to understand these factors, particularly their relative importance;

(b) Those readily found in the literature on the subject or which figure in the definition of soil types;

(c) The most easily measurable;

(d) Those with the fewest possible secondary characteristics in common, so that no minor characteristics will recur several times in the formula thus be exaggerated in significance.

We accordingly consider nine factors as determining soil productivity, viz: moisture (H), drainage (D), effective depth (P), texture/structure (T), base saturation (N), soluble salt concentration (S), organic matter content (O), mineral exchange capacity/nature of clay (A), and mineral reserves (M). Therefore :

$$\text{Productivity} = H \times D \times P \times T \times \begin{matrix} N \\ \text{or} \\ S \end{matrix} \times O \times A \times M$$

Attempt has thus been made to evolve a mathematical formula expressing productivity as a resultant of the various factors at play, following Storie's method of calculation. Each factor is rated on a scale from 0 to 100, the actual percentages being multiplied by each other. The resultant index of productivity, also lying between 0 and 100, is set against a scale placing the soil in one or other of five productivity classes (Table 10.3).

The productivity index thus defined answers well enough to the definition of Storie's index as a "numerical expression of the degree to which a particular soil presents conditions favourable for plant growth and crop production under good environmental conditions", and is "based on soil characteristics which govern its potential utilization and productive capacity". Storie adds that his index is "independent of physical or economic factors, which might determine the desirability of growing certain plants in certain locations".

The main difference between this index and Storie's is in the actual choice of productivity factors. Here only intrinsic soil characteristics are used, all extrinsic, physiographic factors such as erosion, microrelief or slope being disregarded, and the factors attributed by Storie by which soil types (only the soil types of California) are explicited.

The formula clearly is not perfect because the relationship between productivity and soil characteristics is more complex–possibly exponential or asymptotic in form. However, the mathematical approach advocated by Storie has four advantages :

1. The least favourable factor dominates, just as in nature the greatest limitation is often decisive in assessing the ultimate value of a soil;
2. Interplay of the different factors is considered. For instance, a shallow but chemically rich soil may be just as productive as a deeper but less rich one;
3. By manipulating coefficients, it is possible :
   (a) To avoid a linear impact of one factor on the final index (example: the first 30 cm of soil profile are much more important for plant growth than are the 30 cm between 90 and 120 cm depth);
   (b) To attribute to certain secondary or simply corrective factors less weight than the main factors (for example: the nature of the clay is rated between 90 and 100, while soil depth has a wider range from five to 100.
4. It is permissible to disregard one of the factors assumed to be constant, for example soil moisture within a climatic region, and the soil classification according to productivity remains valid.

The coefficients are entirely empirical, but we have been at pains to incorporate in some way factors used by Storie, the Canadian Irrigation Service and Clarke, which have been tested in the field. The remaining coefficients are determined by successive approximations. The index proposed here has been used to forecast yields of peanuts in Madagascar maize, cotton in Swaziland, maize in Argentina (see Table 10.9), with accurate enough results even though other influences, namely pests, type of seed, weeds, etc., were not eliminated from the experiment.

Our formula, then, constitutes a first approximation. It is more scientific than preceding systems, yet is not wholly quantitative. It allows a simpler, numerical classification, and can be applied almost automatically by agriculturists not specialized in soil science (the collaboration of all concerned in order to perfect the system would be welcomed). In the Annexes, equivalences are suggested for characteristics that may be lacking (Table 10.1). Variants will be proposed in future with factors more readily measurable if this becomes possible, for example, available water content (to replace moisture); Henin's structural stability index (to replace "structure") conductivity of soil solutions (to replace "base saturation") and so on.

Factors used in Calculating the Productivity Index

Factors to be used in calculating the productivity index have been selected with the above criteria in mind. An attempt has been made to group them in some sort of logical order, though it is recognised that there is a certain arbitrariness in including such dissimilar elements in the same formula. The reasoning behind the choice of factors is as follows :

A soil is the more fertile when more volume of it is at the disposal of plants (depth: P), the richer it is in bases (base saturation: N) and the more water and the more nutrients it contains and the more readily penetrable it is to roots (texture and structure: T). Hence productivity P × T × N. Certain corrective terms or additional factors are brought in, namely organic matter content (O), nature of the clay (A) and mineral reserves (M), since the more organic matter there is, the more the nutrients are available and the more stable is the structure. The greater the cation exchange capacity the more the nutrients are retained by the soil, with less leaching of fertilizing elements. The greater the mineral reserves, the more nutrients will be replaced as they are used up by the plants. Consequently, A and M correct N and T and give a final productivity value equal to P × N × T × (O × A × M). Finally, the soil moisture factor (H) or excess water factor (D) also affect productivity.

The definition of productivity has been worked out by comparing various soils with the same climate; but the productivity of otherwise identical soils changes from one climate to another. If we use a productivity index to compare soils of one continent or fairly large region (small scale map) to those of another then the climate factor, which may be ignored on a large scale map, must be introduced. Climate may, however, be disregarded on a small scale map in certain situations, say when considering irrigated soils in parts of Africa where temperature is not limiting. Again, climate may be overlooked if the index is considered not as an index of productivity but of soil quality or value. Without encroaching upon the domain of the ecologist, one readily notes that productivity increases as soil temperature and moisture content increases. These factors, therefore, cannot be considered as entirely extraneous to the soil, since they are features of the soil itself–which is precisely why they are introduced. However, in order to determine them, climatic data have to be taken into account because direct measurements of soil temperature and moisture content are very rarely available. We accordingly propose to take the number of dry months per year and the number of months during which the temperature falls below 10°. When the rooting zone is too dry, growth comes practically to a standstill, and the annual soil productivity per hectare diminishes. In arid zones, only one crop may be produced. If the soil is too cold the growing period is also shortened.

Hence the need for superimposing on a soil classification based on fertility under a given climate a second classification according to climate or micro-climatic zones. The water factor is disregarded where irrigation is practiced–i.e., it does not appear on the soil potentiality map–and the temperature factor may be eliminated when for instance one is considering the case of the greenhouses of northern Europe.

Method of Calculation

Calculation tables are given in the Annexes. Here one soil type will be used for illustrative purposes, a vertisol in a region with five dry months a year; depth below the surface of the parent rock (basalt), 110 cm; high clay content; prismatic structure; 70 per cent base saturation; no soluble salts in the rooting zone; 1.2 per cent organic matter and a mineral exchange capacity of 42 mEq/100g of clay; average reserves of minerals alterable by weathering and other processes, hence a fairly mature soil. Therefore, the formula for such a vertisol would be (using symbols explained in Table 10.1) :

$$H_{4a} \times P_5 T_{5a} \times N_4 \times O_2 \times A_3 \times M_{20}$$

Referring to Table 10.2, we read H_{4a} carries a rating of 80 per cent.

P_5 = 100 per cent, continuing to read of the values for each of the remaining symbols, we have therefore :

$$\text{Productivity index} = \frac{80}{100}\ \frac{100}{100}\ \frac{50}{100}\ \frac{80}{100}\ \frac{100}{100} = 25.6$$

This figure is now referred to Table 10.3, where the particular vertisol under consideration is found to belong in Class III, i.e. of average productivity.

Determination of the Index of Potentiality

The index of potentiality is required to express potential productivity after soil management. It is first necessary to determine which management practices are necessary, then what their repercussions are on potentiality. Two groups of management are to be considered :

(1) Each limiting factor requires a soil management :
H (dryness)–requires irrigation (A and B)
D (poor drainage)–requires drainage (C)
P (shallowness)–requires deepening (D)
T (poor texture or structure)–requires stone removal (E_1) or mechanical working (E_2)
N (low nutrient content)–requires application of fertilizers (F)
C (salinity)–requires desalting (G_1 or G_2 if Na_2CO_3 is present)
O (low organic matter content)–requires application of organic matter (H).

Table 10.4 has a list of appropriate management measures and Table 10.5 the characteristics that can be improved and what happens to them following such treatments.

(2) Other types of improvement are imposed by physiographic conditions and environment (situation, climate, vegetation, etc.) the control of wind erosion (J) and water erosion (K and L) and land clearance (M). The soil scientist must obtain information (in addition to that supplied by the soil map) regarding slope, climatic agressivity (distribution of rainfall, wind speed), etc. in order to decide what management measures are necessary. These data are essential in calculating the potential productivity of a soil and they have to be noted down in the field during soil surveys or must be taken from other maps (topographic map for slope, climate maps, vegetation maps, etc.) or from reports.

When the necessary management measures have been determined (those that are feasible under local circumstances and those that are impossible due to certain soil characteristics–see Table 10.6) the next subject to be considered is which improvements will in fact be attempted. For example, by application of fertilizers in suitable quantities and proportions, the base saturation can be raised from N_3 to N_5.

That done, one is in a position to calculate the *potential* productivity index with the same formula as that for actual productivity but according to improved soil characteristics as shown in Table 10.7.

For the management measures necessitated by conditions extraneous to the soil (which often affects several characteristics simultaneously) we have used a flat 10 per cent or 20 per cent rise in value of the index. For instance, erosion control may also increase soil moisture, organic matter content and depth.

The potentiality index is calculated from the improved characteristics and percentages of increased productivity resulting from management and is useful for classifying soils against a potentiality scale (the indices of which are identical with those of the productivity scale, see Table 10.3).

The fact that a soil has been improved is shown by a change of class or, better, by the ratio of the two indices, i.e., the coefficient of improvement.

For instance, the vertisol taken as an illustration of the calculation for productivity (P = 25.6) is improvable:

- by supplementary irrigation (B) and H_4 becomes H_5
- by mechanical working of soil (E_2) in order to improve structure, and T_{5a} becomes T_{5b}
- by amending the organic matter content (H) and the final index will gain 10 per cent.

Then, the formula for potentiality becomes:

$$\begin{aligned} P_1 &= H_5 \times P_5 \times T_{5a} \times N_4 \times O_2 \times A_3 \times M_{20} + 10 \text{ per cent} \\ &= 100 \times 100 \times 80 \times 80 \times 80 \times 100 \times 100 + 10 \text{ per cent} \\ &= 51{,}2 \times 5{,}12 \doteq 56{,}3 \end{aligned}$$

This index reported in Table 10.3 gives us the potentiality class II (good).

The coefficient of improvement of this soil is expressed by

$$\frac{P_1}{P} = \frac{56{,}3}{25{,}6} = 2{,}2$$

It means that the productivity can be multiplied by more than 2 by the application of all suitable management techniques.

Productivity Map and Potentiality Map

Several systems of representation can be used.

1. The productivity and potentiality maps for Nigeria can be taken as a first example. Each mapping unit on the productivity map is coloured according to soil productivity class, letters being used to express the soil characteristics considered in determining the productivity index and also specific crop suitabilities (Table 10.8). The potentiality map likewise has coloured portions showing potentiality classes and letters indicating the improvements necessary in order to attain the level of potentiality it is proposed to work for, i.e., the type of management recommended and used in calculating the potentiality index. (a) If the new management practice is difficult because of environmental conditions (for example, irrigation in desert regions) or for economic reasons, the letter is underlined, though this type of management is still considered in calculating potentiality; (b) should the user of the map seem the particular type of management to be absolutely impractical due to external circumstances, he may re-calculate the index without this item in order to obtain the true potentiality; (c) if, on the other hand, it is the intrinsic properties of the soil that make the improvement impossible, for example drainage of a sodium montmorillonite clay soil (see Table 10.6 which shows incompatibilities) the letter is circled. The presence of a circled letter almost automatically places the soil in Class V.

Maps are drawn up in accordance with the procedure schematized in the diagram 10.1 and 10.2

Diagram 10.1: Productivity Map

Soil type from soil map ____	Soil characteristics ____ (in letters)	formula ____	Productivity index ____	Productivity class (in colour)

Diagram 10.2: Potentiality Map

Data from climate, vegetation & erosion maps etc.	—	Management measures	—	Charac-teristics modified	—	Formula	—	Potentiality index	—	Potentiality class (in colour)

2. Another example is to be had in maps for Togo. The area occupied by a soil series is coloured according to its productivity class on the productivity map and its potentiality class on the potentiality map. A table is appended to these maps indicating for each soil series its characteristics, the appropriate management and the two indices, together with the coefficient of improvement. This system is to be preferred to others when the areas occupied by certain soil series are so small that it is not possible to show characteristics and management measures on the map itself. It also allows the symbols referring to the soil map legend to be retained, making for greater ease of comparison of soil characteristics before and after management.
3. Both types of map can be combined into a single map, in which case it is to be recommended that actual productivity be indicated by a colour and potentiality, i.e., improved capability following upon management, by overprinting. An Arabic numeral might be used for the productivity class and a Roman numeral for the potentiality class.

Soil Resources Appraisal: Coefficient of Improvement

Appraisal of Value of Soil Units

In the equation P = f (a, b, c .....), P represents the productivity of a given soil unit and a, b, c, are the soil characteristics. Some of these factors cannot be modified (for instance, texture, reserves of alterable materials) whereas others can be improved by agricultural practices (irrigation, drainage, amendments). Hence the potentiality P′ of the same unit can be appraised by applying an identical formula P′ = f (a′, b′, c′.....) in which a′, b′, c′.... represent characteristics as corrected by the proposed management.

Some purpose will then be served if one can deduce from this what may be called latent improvement of the soil under study. For this coefficient of improvement we have used the expression C = P′/P in which C is the number by which the soil productivity index must be multiplied in order to obtain the potentiality index.

Theoretically this figure may be anywhere between unity and infinity but in practice it lies between 1 and 100 (the highest value calculated to date being 33). Generally value ranges between one and five.

A low coefficient indicates little possibility of improvement either because actual productivity is already very high and it is, therefore, impossible to expect much better [example: Agni (An) series of Table 10.9] or because whatever the actual productivity, it is subject to limiting factors which cannot be corrected even by modern technology [Atchasi (At) series, in which the limiting factor is the presence of a lateritic hardpan near the surface, or the Vokouteme (Vo) series, whose productivity is limited by the excessively light texture].

A high coefficient of improvement indicates a state of inadequate development or immaturity. It refers to soils whose productivity is low at the moment but which could be raised by a programme of land improvement [examples: Kezou (Kz) series after drainage, improvement of structure and application of organic matter]. Obviously for management to be economically worthwhile it should be introduced on soils having a high coefficient of improvement and a fair potentiality.

Such a coefficient is a non-dimensional number which can be applied to any expression of soil productivity, e.g., crop yield in tons per hectare; forest yields in m^3 of wood per hectare; or yield in kg of liveweight per hectare for livestock grazing on a given type of land. It goes without saying that soil productivity and the yield of a crop are parallel where soil factors alone are considered in making the comparison. It is more appropriate to see present crop yields as dependent upon soil productivity, and *increase in yield* as a function of the coefficient of improvement. This can be expressed by the equation R′ = R.v (c), where R′ is improved yield and R is yield before management.

Example

To apply the coefficient of improvement to productivity for peanuts, x represents the index of productivity P, and y = yields R in tons/ha with the equation R′ = R f (c), or Y′ f(c).

We have in this particular example: y′ = c.y + (c–1) 0.55

Let x = 25 and x′ = 50, c = P8/P or x′/x = 2 and for the equation of

the straight line Y = 0.08, x = 0.55
$Y = (0.08 \times 25) - 0.55 = 1.45$ T/ha
$Y' = (0.08 \times 50) - 0.55 = 3.45$ T/ha
One can also find y′ as a function of y and c applying formula (1):
$y' = 2 \times 1.45 + (2-1) \times 0.55 = 3.45$ T/ha.

Evaluation of a Heterogeneous Area

The concepts "productivity," "potentiality" and "coefficient of improvement" can be extended to regions (subscript r) with soils of different values. A region with an area S_r having n soil series with respective productivities of P_1, P_2...P_n on areas S_1, S_2... S_n will have an average productivity shown by the formula

$$P_r = \frac{(P_1 \times S_1) + P_2 \times S_2) + ... + (P_n \times S_n)}{S_r}$$

Simplifying: $$P_r = \frac{(P_n \times S_n)}{S_r}$$

Likewise: $$P'_r = \frac{(P'_n \times S_n)}{S_r}$$

And $$C_r = \frac{P'_r}{P_r}$$

The average coefficient to improvement thus calculated has the same meaning, on a regional scale, as the exact coefficient for the soil category. High potentiality combined with high coefficients is indicative of regions yet to be developed and where the execution of a management plan has the best chances of producing satisfactory results.

Summary and the Future of this Method

It is the authors' view that the agricultural value of a soil depends primarily on its characteristics and properties which can be determined by soil surveys or by the interpretation of an existing soil map. A mathematical formula summing up its properties will provide an index of the value of a soil, expressed in terms of productivity. Limiting factors such as unfavourable physiographic conditions call for management, conservation and development work which, in turn, will modify the soil. Hence the need for an additional index which expresses the capability following upon management, i.e., "soil potentiality".

Three Types of Data

Value of soil in the natural state, value of that soil when improved and the magnitude of the management work needed to produce that improvement are indispensable for any one considering land utilization. Up to now, soil classification efforts have been directed solely to determining what set of management practices is necessary, but here the emphasis is on the soil itself–the basis for any such work. Soil maps are all the more valuable to the extent that they can serve as the point of departures for the entire methodology.

A practical means of condensing a great quantity of data that can be useful for agronomists, engineers, economists and planners seems to be to present the findings on two separate maps, one showing productivity classes and the other potentiality classes, i.e., fertility factors and work to be carried out. Some persons, however, may prefer a single map with a table appended.

Much still has to be done by way of evolving a method of estimating yields from a piece of land as a function of its characteristics. Variants are allowable depending on the goal set–for example, adaptation of the formula for determining productivity for particular plant species to use for a large scale map, or employing a fuller and more comprehensive climatic coefficient–for comparing soils of one climate with those of another and so on. However, the main purposes of this new methodology are :

(1) To make the chief line of approach that of identifying and combining productivity factors, without neglecting their interaction;
(2) To draw up a balance sheet and synthesize findings of research;
(3) To use the concept of productivity to compare soils;
(4) To evolve a quantitative approach to the assessment of soil value –the only basis for mutual understanding between soil scientists, engineers and economists; and finally
(5) To arrive at a coefficient of improvement for appraising the development possibilities of a region.

By this method, a soil resources map can readily be compiled simply from interpretation of existing soil maps and the use of supplementary data such as climate, relief and vegetation. It will show the value of various soils, the conditions governing their utilization and their future potentialities.

ANNEXES

Table 10.1: Soil Characteristics used to Determine Productivity

H *Soil moisture content*

H_1 Rooting zone below wilting point all the year round
H_2 Rooting zone below wilting point for 9 to 11 months of the year
- H_{2a} 11 months
- H_{2b} 10 months
- H_{2c} 9 months

H_3 Rooting zone below wilting point for 6 to 8 months of the year
- H_{3a} 8 months
- H_{3b} 7 months
- H_{3c} 6 months

H_4 Rooting zone below wilting point for 3 to 5 months and wet below field capacity for over 6 months of the year
- H_{4a} 5 months
- H_{4b} 4 months
- H_{4c} 3 months

H_5 Rooting zone wet above wilting point and below field capacity for most of the year

Note: 1. If data on actual soil moisture is not available, it is possible to use instead the number of dry months per year calculated from weather intelligence (Gaussen's ombrothermic diagram for instance) at least for small scale maps.
2. For cold countries, the months during which frost occurs as also the months of average temperature 10°C (threshold of productivity) are considered as dry months.

D *Drainage*

D_{1a} Marked waterlogging, watertable almost reached the surface all year round (Hydromorphic horizon at a depth from 0 to 30 cm)
D_{1b} Soil flooded for 2 to 4 months of the year
D_{2a} Moderate waterlogging, the watertable being sufficiently close to the surface to harm deep rooting plants (hydromorphic horizon at a depth from 30 to 60 cm)
D_{2b} Total waterlogging of profile from 8 days to 2 months
D_{3a} Good drainage, watertable sufficiently low not to impede crop growing (hydromorphic horizon at a depth of 60 cm below the surface)
D_{3b} Waterlogging for brief periods (flooding), less than 8 days each time
D_4 Well drained soil, deep watertable (hydromorphic horizon at over 120 cm depth); no waterlogging of soil profile.
In this case see H

Note 1. If the hydromorphic horizon is not recognizable from morphological characteristics, the height of the watertable is the only point to be considered. If, on the other hand, it is fossilized, it should be ignored altogether.

Table 10.1: (bis)

Table of Equivalents to Table 10.1.

This table is to be used only where certain characteristics are missing and which can be replaced by close, though not entirely inter-changeable, equivalents. These are listed below by way of guidance and have no rigid value :

T

T_{1a}	Stones and pebbles: 30 per cent by volume
T_{1b}	Stones and pebbles: 20 to 30 per cent
T_{1c}	Stones and pebbles: 10 to 20 per cent
T_{2a}	HE = equivalent moisture < 10 per cent
T_{2b}	HE = equivalent moisture < 10 per cent
T_3	A + L > 40 per cent and pH 8.5 or Na/T > 15 per cent (A = clay; L = silt)
T_4	HE from 10 to 15 per cent
T_5	HE > 30 per cent
T_6	HE from 25 to 35 per cent
T_7	HE from 15 to 25 per cent

N

N_1	pH (in water 1/1) from 3.5 to 4.5
N_2	from 4.5 to 5.0
N_3	from 5.0 to 6.0
N_4	from 6.0 to 7.0
N_5	from 7.0 to 8.5

Note: The use of pH instead of base saturation is advisable in cases of very sandy soils with a low cation exchange capacity. In such cases base saturation given by analysis is often unreliable.

S	Content of salts in percentage of soil	Conductivity in milli-mho of saturation extract	Conductivity in micro-mho of saline extract 1/5	Conductivity in micro-mho of saline extract 1/10
S_1	0	0	0	0
S_2	0.2	2	1000	500
S_3	0.4	6	1750	875
S_4	0.6	8	2500	1250
S_5	0.8	12	3000	1625
S_6	1.0	16	3500	2000

Note: These figures cannot be taken for an exact correspondence between the different conductivities, as they may vary according to the water capacity in the soil, and the degree of solubility of salts, thus, according to their nature. However, these figures give an order of extent available in the proposed formula. In column 2 the American classification limits of Riverside have been chosen.

O *Organic Matter Content O Carbon × 1.7 Nitrogen × 20*
O_1 Thickness of the humus-forming horizon < 10 cm
O_2 Thickness of the humus-forming horizon from 10 to 20
O_3 Thickness of the humus-forming horizon from 20 to 30
O_4 Thickness of the humus-forming horizon > 30
A *Exchange capacity of clay*

TmEq/100 g of soil — K × per cent organic matter × 100 per cent clay
and K = 2,50 for very humid soils peaty soils or soils of cold or high regions
K = 2,00 for soils of temperate regions
K = 1,50 for tropical soils with little humus

M_1 Sum of total bases determined by treating with hot nitric acid: Total bases < 10 mEq
M_2 Sum of total bases determined by treating with hot nitric acid: Total bases 10—50 mEq
M_3 Sum of total bases determined by treating with hot nitric acid: Total bases 50—300 mEq.

Table 10.2: Tentative ratings of different characteristics

	For crop growing			For pasture			For forest and non-forest tree crops		
H									
H_1		5			5			5	
H_2	H_{2a}10	H_{2b}20	H_{2c}40	20	20	30		10	
H_3	H_{3a}50	H_{3b}60	H_{3c}70	30	40	60	10	20	40
H_4	H_{4a}80	H_{4b}90	H_{4c}100	70	80	90	70	90	100
H_5		100			100			100	
D	H_4	H_5	H_2	H_3					
D_1		10—40			60			5	
D_2		40—80			100			10	
D_3		80—90			90			40	
P									
P_1		5			20			5	
P_2		20			60			5	
P_3		50			80			20	
P_4		80			90			60	
P_5		100			100			80	
P_6		100			100			100	
T									
T_{1a}		10			30			50	
T_{1b}		30			50			80	
T_{1c}		60			90			100	

(Contd.)

Table 10.2 Contd.

	For crop growing			For pasture	For forest and non-forest tree crops
	$H_4H_5H_6AB$	H_3	H_1H_2		
T_{2a}	10	10	10	(Same ratings as for crop growing)	(Same ratings as for crop growing)
T_{2b}	30	20	10		
T_{2c}	30	30	30		
T_3	30	20	10		
T_{4a}	40	30	30		
T_{4b}	50	50	60		
T_{5a}	50	60	20		
T_{5b}	80	80	60		
T_{6a}	80	80	60		
T_{6b}	90	90	90		
T_7	100	100	100		
N					
N_1		40		60	80
N_2		50		70	80
N_3		60		80	90
N_4		80		90	100
N_5		100		100	100
N_6		80		90	100
S				$T_1T_2T_4$	$T_5T_6T_7$
S_1				100	100
S_2				70	90
S_3				50	80
S_4				25	40
S_5				15	25
S_6				5	15
S_7				60	90
S_8				15	60
S_9				5	15
O				$H_1H_2H_3D_3D_4$	$H_4H_5D_1D_2AB$
O_1				85	70
O_2				90	80
O_3				100	90
O_4				100	100
O_5				70	70

(Contd.)

Table 10.2 Contd.

	For crop growing	For pasture	For forest and non-forest tree crops
A			
A_0		85	
A_1		90	
A_2		95	
A_3		100	
M		H_1 H_2 H_3	H_4 H_5 AB
M_1		85	85
M_{2a}		85	90
M_{2b}		90	95
M_{2c}		95	100
M_{3a}		90	95
M_{3b}		95	100
M_{3c}		100	100

Table 10.3 : Classes of Productivity (P) and Potentiality (P′)

P	Classes	Rating	P′
1	Excellent	65-100	I
2	Good	35-64	II
3	Average	24-34	III
4	Poor	8-19	IV
5	Extremely poor to nil	0-7	V

Table 10.4: List of land improvements necessary for development (over and above prevailing agricultural practices)

A. Irrigation (essential) and drainage (usually required)

B. Supplementary irrigation : B_1 by sprinkling
B_2 by flood or furrow irrigation

C. Excess water removal: by reclamation, ridging, drainage or protection against floods.

D. Deepening of top soil: by ridging, deep plowing or breaking up of soil crust

E. Improvement of texture and structure:
   - E_1 by stone or rock removal
   - E_2 by mechanical working of soil (difficult and costly — requiring heavy machinery)
   - E_3 by improvement of organic soils

F. Fertilizers, amendments, liming in large quantities (application of fertilizers—particularly those containing nitrogen—is considered indispensable for all soils)

G. Desalting:
   - G_1 by irrigation and drainage
   - G_2 by irrigation and drainage + application of gypsum ($CaSO_4$) to eliminate sodium salts (Na_2CO_3)

H. Enriching and maintenance of organic matter content, application of manure, green manure, mulching, crop rotation, forest fallow, etc.; also improvement of humid condition of peat and semi-peat soils.

J. Measure to control wind erosion: windbreaks, mulching

K. Measures to control severe water erosion: of banquettes, terraces, etc.

L. measures to control mild water erosion: digging of ditches, planting of bedgerows, etc.

M. Large scale land clearance

Table 10.5: Improvement of Soil Characteristics or Properties by Management

Management practices	A	B_1B_2	C	D	E_1	E_2	E_3	F + H (with A_0)	F (with A_1 or A_2)	F (with A_3)
Initial soil properties	H_1H_2	H_3H_4	D_1D_2	$P_1P_2P_3$	T_{1b}	$T_{5a}T_{6a}$	T_{2c}	N_1N_2	$N_1N_2N_3$	$N_1N_2N_3N_4$
Improved soil properties	H_5	H_5	D_3	$P_2P_3P_4$	T of fine soil materials	$T_{5b}T_{6b}$	T of sub-soil	N_3	N_4	N_5

*Note: $A_0A_1A_2A_3$ refer to GEC data.

G_1	G_2	H	J	KL	M
S_3S_4	S_9	$O_1O_2O_5$	H_1H_2 + $T_1T_2T_4$		
S_1S_2 For T_6 and T_7 For T_2 improvement of 4 soil classes rated according to salinity For T_5 improvement of a single soil class rated according to salinity	S_7	O_4 Add 10 per cent to final index O_4 (T_{20}T of sub-soil)	Add 10 per cent to final index	Add 20 per cent to final index (10 per cent) if improvement of organic matter (H) has already been taken in consideration	0 per cent

Table 10.6: Incompatible Management Practices and Characteristics

1.	A and B_2 with P_{12}, $P_3 + T_{1247}$, $P_4 + T_{1a}\ T_2\ T_3$	E_2 with T_3
2.	B_1 with P_1 and T_3	F with A_0; However F + H is compatible A_0
3.	C with T_3 (C and T_3 are compatible if G_2 is used)	L with P_{12}, T_3, T_{5a}
4.	S with T_1	K with P_{123}, T_3, T_{5a}
5.	E_1 with $T_{1a}\ T_{1b}$	

Table 10.7: Illustration of Soil Suitability for Different Uses Depending on its Characteristics

Envisaged land-use	Rice growing			
Soil characteristics permitting the proposed use	H_4 to H_5 or H_1 to H_3 and A or B	H_5 or H_1 to H_4 and A or B	N_4 to N_5 H_1 to H_3 and A or B	N_4 to N_5 H_1 to H_3 and A or B
Other characteristics preclude or considerably hamper the (proposed use)	D_1 to D_2 D_3 to D_4 and/or B P_4 to P_6 $T_5T_6T_7$ N_1 to N_5 S_1 to S_5 and G O_1 to O_5 A_1 to A_3 M_1 to M_3	D_3 to D_4 or D_1 to D_2 and C P_5 to P_6 $T_{10}T_4T_6T_7$ N_3 to N_5 S_1 O_3 to O_4 A_1 to A_3 M_1 to M_3	D_3 to D_4 P_4 to P_6 $T_{2ab}T_4T_7$ N_1 to N_5 S_1 to S_5 & G O_2 to O_4 A_1 to A_3 M_1 to M_3	D_2 to D_3 P_2 to P_6 T_{10} 5 6 7 N_1 to N_5 S_1 O_2 to O_4 A_1 to A_3 M_1 to M_3

Soils with Several Horizons of Different Textures

These are soils of heterogeneous textures (e.g., certain alluvial soils with alternate sandy and clay horizons) or simply highly developed soils with a horizon where there has been accumulation of different materials (soils leached into clay).

We arbitrarily divide the soil into two horizons :

(a) The horizon from 0 to 50 cm in depth, which is the most significant as regards the supplying of plants with water and nutrients;

(b) the horizon from 50 to 120 cm, supplementary to the first either because it is impermeable and holds water or because, on the contrary, it is too sandy and drains the profile; or because it hampers deeper rooting, or else allows a tree to survive when the uppermost horizon is too sandy. Only the dominant texture is considered in each of these two horizons.

Table 10.8: Special Cases

Horizons from 0 to 50	Horizons from 50 to 120	Crops and pasture	Forest and non-forest tree crops
Clay dominant	Clay dominant	T_{5a} or $_{b}$	T_{5a} or $_{b}$
	Loam dominant	T_{5a} or $_{b}$	T_{6a} or $_{b}$
	Sand dominant	T_{5a} or $_{b}$	T_{4a} or $_{b}$
Loam dominant	Clay dominant	T_{6a} or $_{b}$	T_{5a} or $_{b}$
	Loam dominant	T_7	T_7
	Sand dominant	T_7	T_{4a} or $_{b}$
Sand dominant	Clay dominant	T_{6a} or $_{b}$	T_{6a} or $_{b}$
	Loam dominant	T_{4a} or $_{b}$	T_{6a} or $_{b}$
	Sand dominant	T_{4a} or $_{b}$ or T_2 if there are 30 cm of coarse sand in the top horizon (0 to 50 cm in depth)	T_{4a} or $_{b}$ or T_2 if there is over 30 cm of coarse sand in the top horizon (from 0 to 50 cm in depth)

Generally speaking (1) a coarse-sand horizon of over 20 cm in the top horizon (from 0 to 50 cm in depth) places the soil in class T_2

(2) a compact clay horizon of over 10 cm in the top horizon (from 0 to 50 cm in depth) places the soil in class T_{5a}

Note: The following are excluded from this table: fragipan, hardpan, gypsum horizon, because where these exist the effective depth of the soil is that of the upper surface of these horizons.

Sloping Soils

These soils are cultivated without special precautions, particularly without conservation practices. It is assumed that degradation occurs until a state of equilibrium proportional to the slope has been reached. In this case the usual productivity index is multiplied by a slope factor. The latter factor is to be applied whenever agricultural productivity after forest clearance, for instance, shifting cultivation in tropical countries, is being calculated.

Slope Percentage	*Factor*
0 – 2	100
3 – 8	95 – 100
9 – 15	80 – 95
16 – 30	70 – 80
30 – 45	30 – 50
45	5 – 30

Depending on the "aggressivity" of the rainfall and soil erodibility, the upper, middle or lower figure is taken.

Toxicity or Deficiency Cases

Special cases of toxicity (excess of soluble and exchangeable aluminium, excess of manganese, presence of acid sulphate–catclays– etc.) or of deficiency in micro-elements (copper, zinc, boron, etc.), or deficiency in phosphorus have not been treated in the general formula. The excess or the deficiency being relative, and the curative treatments being very easy or very difficult, according to the cultivated plant and the type of soil, the consideration of these several special cases would singularly complicate the formula. Besides, the diversity of analytical methods and the still inadequately determined critical concentrations mean that the damages caused are not calculable as a function of the intensity of the toxicity or of the deficiency. The output of the culture may vary from 0 at the natural state to 100 per cent after improvement of these soils.

The toxicity or the deficiency will be indicated by a particular sign on the map of productivity and the productivity index will be modified by a factor X that the interpreter of the map will fix himself according to his knowledge. On the potentiality map another particular indication will be noted for the legend, where the proposed improvement will be indicated (ex. liming to reduce an excess of aluminium). The potentiality index will be modified in the same way.

Table 10.9 : Specimen Presentation of Data
(Taken from Etudes pedohydrologiques au Togo FAO/SE: 13/TO — Calculations made for crop growing)

Soil series & improve	Productivity (P) Potentiality (P')	Coeff. of imp. P'/P	H	D	P	T	N	S	O	A	M	X*
Agble (Ab)	P 4 (11)		H5:100	D2b:60	P6:100	T4a:40	N4:80	—	02:80	A1:90	M1:85	
C.H	P:IV(19)	1.72	H5:100	D3:90	P6:100	T4a:40	N4:80	—	02:80	A1:90	M1:85	+10 per cent
Agni (An)	P 2(58)		H5:100	—	P6:100	T6b:90	N4:80	—	03:90	A2:95	M2b:95	
	P' II(58)	1	H5:100	—	P6:100	T6b:90	N4:80	—	03:90	A2:95	M2b:95	
Agove(Ag)	P 4(10)		H5:100	D3a:80	P6:100	T4a:40	N4:80	—	02:80	A1:90	M2a:90	
H	P'IV(19)	1.90	H5:100	D3a:80	P6:100	T4a:40	N4:80	—	02:80	A1:90	M2a:90	+10 per cent
Atchasi (At)	P 4(9)		H3:60	—	P3:30	T7:100	N4:80	—	01:85	A1:90	M2a:85	
B	P'IV(9)	1	H3:60	—	P3:30	T7:100	N4:80	—	01:85	A1:90	M2a:85	
Awito (Aw)	P 5(6)		—	D2a:40	P6:100	T4a:30	N4:80	—	01:85	A1:90	M2c:95	
C.H	P'IV(17)	2.83	—	D3:90	P6:100	T4a:30	N4:80	—	01:85	A1:90	M2c:95	+10 per cent
Canne (Cn)	P 4(18)		H5:100	D2b:60	P6:100	T5b:80	N3:60	—	02:80	A2:95	M2a:90	
C.F.H	P'II(55)	3.05	H5:100	D3:90	P6:100	T5b:80	N4:80	—	02:80	A2:95	M2a:90	+10 per cent
Dasikpe (Dp)	P 5(3)		H3:60	—	P4:80	T2b:20	N3:60	—	01:85	A1:90	M1:85	
B.F.H.	P'IV(14)	4.66	H5:100	—	P4:80	T2b:30	N4:80	—	01:85	A1:90	M1:85	+10 per cent
Doukpo (Dk)	P 4(12)		—	D2a:40	P6:100	T5a:50	N4:80	—	03:100	A2:95	M2a:85	
C.E2	P'II(47)	3.91	—	D3:90	P6:100	T5a:80	N4:80	—	03:100	A2:95	M2a:85	

(contd.)

Table 10.9 (contd.)

Soil series & improve	Productivity (P) Potentiality (P')	Coeff. of imp. P'/P	H	D	P	T	N	S	O	A	M	X*
Eko (Ek)	P 5(6)		H3:60	—	P6:100	T4a:30	N3:60	—	01:70	A1:90	M1:85	
B.H.	P'4(19)	3.16	H5:100	—	P6:100	T4a:40	N4:80	—	01:70	A1:90	M1:85	+10 per cent
Ese (Es)	P1 5(3)		H5:100	D3a:90	P5:100	T2a:10	N3:60	—	01:70	A1:90	M2a:90	
F.H.	V(4)	1.33	H5:100	D3a:90	P5:100	T2a:10	N4:80	—	01:70	A1:90	M2a:90	+10 per cent
Ganove (Ga)	P1 4(18)		H5:100	D2b:80	P6:100	T4a:50	N4:80	—	01:70	A1:90	M2a:90	
C.H.	III(22)	1.22	H5:100	D3:90	P6:100	T4a:50	N4:80	—	01:70	A1:90	M2a:90	+10 per cent
Hompou (Hp)	P1 4(15)		H3:60	—	P4:50	T7:100	N4:80	—	01:85	A1:90	M2a:85	
B.H.	III(29)	1.93	H5:100	—	P4:50	T7:100	N4:80	—	01:85	A1:90	M2a:85	+10 per cent
Keklome (Kk)	P 4(8)		H3:70	—	P6:100	T4a:30	N3:60	—	01:85	A1:90	M2a:85	
B.F.H.	P'III(22)	2.75	H5:100	—	P6:100	T4a:40	N4:80	—	01:85	A1:90	M2a:85	+10 per cent
Kezon (Kz)	P 4(12)		—	D2a:40	P6:100	T5a:50	N6:80	—	01:85	A2:95	M2c:95	
C.F.2.H.	P' II(49)	4.08	—	D3:90	P6:100	T5b:80	N6:80	—	01:85	A2:95	M2c:95	+10 per cent
Kodjin (Kj)	P 2(40)		H4:90	—	P6:100	T7:100	N4:80	—	01:70	A1:90	M2a:90	
A.H.	P' II(50)	1.25	H5:100	—	P6:100	T7:100	N4:80	—	01:70	A1:90	M2a:90	+10 per cent
Kodo (Ko)	P 5(7)		H5:100	D2b:50	P6:100	T4a:40	N3:60	—	02:80	A1:90	M2a:90	
C.F.H.	P' III(20)	2.85	H5:100	D3:90	P6:100	T4a:40	N4:80	—	02:80	A1:90	M2a:90	+10 per cent
Kouble (Kb)	P 4(15)		—	D2b:70	P6:100	T4a:30	N5:100	S1:100	01:85	A1:90	M2c:95	
C.H.	P' III(29)	1.93	—	D3:90	P6:100	T4a:40	N5:100	S1:100	01:85	A1:90	M2c:95	+10 per cent

(contd.)

Table 10.9 (contd.)

Soil series & improve	Productivity (P) Potentiality (P')	Coeff. of imp. P'/P	H	D	P	T	N	S	O	A	M	X*
Kponou (Kn)	P 2(58)		H5:100	D3a:90	P6:100	T7:100	N5:100	—	02:80	A1:90	M2a:90	
H	P' II(62)	1.06	H5:100	D3a:90	P6:100	T7:100	N5:100	—	02:80	A1:90	M2a:90	+10 per cent
Legbako (Lg)	P 3(24)		H4:90	—	P6:100	T4b:50	N4:80	—	01:85	A1:90	M2a:90	
B.H.	P' III(30)	1.25	H5:100	—	P6:100	T4b:50	N4:80	—	01:85	A1:90	M2a:90	+10 per cent
Seme (Sm)	P 5(4)		—	D2a:40	P6:100	T4a:30	N3:60	—	02:90	A1:90	M2a:85	
C.F.H.	P' IV(16)	4	—	D3:90	P6:100	T4a:30	N4:80	—	02:90	A1:90	M2a:85	+10 per cent
Sio (Si)	P 4(12)		—	D2a:40	P6:100	T5a:50	N4:80	—	03:100	A2:95	M2a:85	
C.E2.	P' II(47)	3.91	—	D3:90	P6:100	T5b:80	N4:80	—	04:100	A2:95	M2a:85	
Tankouti (Tk)	P 3(20)		H4:90	—	P6:100	T4b:50	N4:80	—	01:70	A1:90	M2a:90	
B.H.	P' III(25)	1.25	H5:100	—	P6:100	T4b:50	N4:80	—	01:70	A1:90	M2a:90	+10 per cent
Togble (Tb)	P 4(13)		H5:100	D3a:90	P6:100	T4a:40	N3:60	—	02:80	A1:90	M2a:90	
F.H.	P' IV(19)	1.46	H5:100	D3a:90	P6:100	T4a:40	N3:80	—	02:80	A1:90	M2a:90	+10 per cent
Togome (Tg)	P 4(18)		H4:80	—	P6:100	T4b:50	N4:80	—	01:70	A1:90	M2a:90	
B.H.	P' III(25)	1.38	H5:100	—	P6:100	T4b:50	N4:80	—	01:70	A1:90	M2a:85	+10 per cent
Vokoutime (Vo)	P 3(22)		H4:100	—	P6:100	T4b:50	N4:80	—	01:70	A1:90	M2a:90	
H	P' III(24)	1.09	H4:100	—	P6:100	T4b:50	N4:80	—	01:70	A1:90	M2a:90	+10 per cent
Voodau (Vd)	P 4(08)		H5:100	D2b:60	P6:100	T4a:40	N3:60	—	01:70	A1:90	M2a:90	
C.F.H.	P' IV(18)	2.25	H5:100	D3:90	P6:100	T4a:40	N4:80	—	01:70	A1:90	M2a:90	+10 per cent

Table 10.10 Soil Profile in the Region covered by UNDP Project (Togo)*

Terminal Continental Soils		
Legbako	(lg)	
Vokoutime	(Vo)	
Kponou	(Kn)	
Kodjin	(Kj)	
Klekome	(Kk)	". . . . little leached soils (Kodjin) eroded, with cuirass (Atchasi) and colluvium (Keklome). There are also leached soils without colluvium or serious erosion (Legbako, Vokoutime, Kponou) and the entire gamut of sandy colluvium with various moisture regimes (Eke, Agove, Agble, Yonor)."
Ganave	(Ga)	
Togome	(Tg)	
Eko	(Ek)	
Agove	(Ag)	
Agble	(Ab)	
Desikpe	(Dp)	
Atchasi	(At)	
Tankouti	(Tk)	
Hompou	(Hp)	
Soils of the Pre--Cambrian Peneplain		
Kodo	(Ko)	". . . . sandy or loamy--sand soils, pebbly, probably formed from underlying rock (gneiss or migmatite). They have been subjected to surface upheavals, leaching, transportation (indicated by the presence of quartz and concretions). The Pre--Cambrian peneplain has the only tropical, leached, ferruginous profiles that were mapped in the southern part of Togo in the course of these surveys."
Ese	(Es)	
Alluvial Plain Soils		
Agni	(An)	". . . . highly variable from the standpoint of texture, acidity, salinity and moisture regime, their only common character being their alluvial origin and the fact that they are subject to periodic flooding."
Canne	(Cn)	
Sio	(Si)	
Doukpo	(Dk)	
Togble	(Tb)	
Voodou	(Vd)	
Seme	(Sm)	
Kouble	(Kb)	
Awito	(Aw)	
Keson	(Kz)	

*Etudes Pedohydrologiques au Togo FAO/SF: 13/TO.

11

Ground Water Resource Analysis for Drought Prone Areas

Introduction

DUE to successive delay or failure of the monsoon, our country experiences droughts in many districts. Hence, Governmental bodies have set up cells for studying and improving this situation and to combat droughts. As evaporational losses on open surface waters are more, it is better to estimate the reserves of ground-water. As a country in which 70 per cent of the total area is covered by hard rocks we have to turn to hard rock areas not because they are extensive and capable of giving large yields, but because they are extensive and can yield water which is at least sufficient for domestic and irrigational needs of small size farms.

Concurrence and Circulation of Water on Earth

The hydrologic cycle is defined as the circulation of water evaporated from the sea through the atmosphere to the land and then via surface and sub-surface routes back to the sea. (Table 11.1).

Of all water on earth (about 1400×16^6 m^3) 97 per cent is contained in the oceans and seas as saline water. The fresh water (3 per cent of the total water) is distributed as follows: around 75 per cent in polar ice caps and glaciers, around 24 per cent in the sub-soil, around 0.3 per cent in lakes, 0.06 per cent in soil moisture, 0.035 per cent in the atmosphere and 0.03 per cent in rivers.

Table 11.1: Correlation and Regression Equations between Crop Yields and productivity Index

X productivity index		
Y crop in t/ha		
Maize's crop on 16 Swaziland soil series*		
Y = 0,058 x + 0,73	F = 10,687	
	Highly significant (p = 0,01)	F = 8,86
Maize's crop on 26 Swaziland soil series		
Y = 0,042 x + 0,99	F = 17,932	
	Highly significant (p = 0,01)	F = 7,82
Maize's crop on 9 Argentina soil series**		
Y = 0,047 x – 0,43	F = 10,98	
	Significant (p = 0,05)	F = 5,59
Cotton's crop on 17 Swaziland soil series (mean yields of 1957/66).		
Y = 0,030 x + 0,25	F = 5,50	
	Significant (p = 0,05)	F = 4,54

* Agricultural results and index calculation of G. Murdooh.

** Agricultural results of experimental stations of Pergamino and Runcinam (INTA) and index calculation of J P. Cornet.

The general pattern of exchange of water between land and sea areas is as shown in Table 11.2.

Table 11.2: Water Pattern

	Area in 10^6 Km^2	Precipitation (mm Per Year)	Evaporation (mm Per Year)	Run off (mm Per Year)
Land	136	750	545	205
Sea	374	870	940	70

It can be seen that evaporation from land is less than that of the sea (because of the areal extent of the seas and the salinity of the water). Further, most of the rain on land areas originates from the oceans and only a small part comes from evaporation of water from water bodies on the earth.

Surface Water Resources

For our country this has been estimated at about 1,356 million acre feet, almost the entire quantity being derived from precipitation. The available surface water resources of the different parts of the country vary considerably.

It has been estimated that only one-third of the surface water (450 million acre feet) can be used for beneficial purposes owing to various physiographic, climatic and geographical factors.

The quantity utilised has been estimated at about 120 million acre feet representing 27 per cent of the usable flow or 8.9 per cent of total flow. About 70 million acres have been in irrigation. It is considered that the overall ultimate potentialities of all the major and minor irrigation projects are expected to be 100 million acres involving about 170 million acre feet. Thus, even after bringing about 100 million acres under irrigation, a large quantity of water out of usable flow would remain unused.

While a large quantity of water is likely to be lost by evaporation and other processes, there is still considerable scope for increasing the utilizable quantity of water out of the total flow.

When it is realised that in our country large areas are backward on account of non-availability of adequate water supply in time, such an enormous quantity of unused water could be beneficially used in these backward areas.

Ground Water Resources

Ground Water can be developed in sufficient quantities for irrigation or other large scale uses from the alluvial and sedimentary terrains by means of wells. In hard rock areas which form 70 per cent of the total area of the country, water is present in limited quantities and is developed for rural, municipal and industrial purposes by dug-cum-bore and bore wells. Ground water is present in varying quantities in Himalayan terrain where in different types of rocks are met with.

The presence of ground water and its development in sedimentary and alluvial terrain is governed by the nature and extent of the porous and permeable media in them. In other terrains it is largely dependent on the depths of weathering of the rocks and the structural features in them. As the ultimate source of all ground water is chiefly rainfall, its resources in any particular terrain are dependent on the variation in the rainfall over the area and the nature of the terrain (thickness of soil, mantle or weathered rocks, topography, etc.). Depending on the geologic and climatic factors the quantity of water that can be obtained from different types of terrains is variable.

Hydro-meteorological Aspects of Ground Water Potential

The importance of ground-water for the economic development of the country, specially for the development of agriculture in dry farming areas, is being more and more realised. Large scale ground-water development is thought of for many areas but before such developments take place, and for making a success of such developments, it is essential to investigate and make a fairly reliable estimate of the ground-water potential and its safe yield.

Ground-water has some advantages over surface water, the most important of which is that is does not suffer the heavy evaporation losses which surface water in open reservoirs, lakes, etc., with a large surface area, suffers, specially in arid and semi-arid areas. Evaporation from open water surfaces can be as much as 300-350 cm per annum in arid and semi-arid areas and 200-250 cm per annum for most other parts of the hard rock areas of India.

An evaporation of 300 cm per annum is equivalent to a loss of 1,740 million gallons per annum or 2.0 million gallons per day per sq. km. of water spread.

Ground-water Recharge by Rainfall, . Infiltration, Percolation, Evaporation and Evapotranspiration

Rainfall being the source of all ground-water, a study of its incidence, distribution both in space and time, intensity, variability, frequency, etc., is of utmost importance for the study of recharge of ground-water by rainfall.

It is only a small part of the rainfall that goes to recharge and the problem is to determine how much this part is. The recharge occurs in three stages, first by infiltration of water into the soil zone, then downward percolation of water through the zone of aeration and finally it reaches the zone of saturation or the watertable.

If i = rainfall intensity, f_p= infiltration capacity, f.m.d. = field moisture deficiency, P = rainfall depth and F = infiltration depth, then recharge of ground-water takes place only when:

(1) i f_p and P f.m.d. and (2) i f_p and F f.m.d.

In the first case there is no surface runoff, but ground-water recharge is there and in the second case even when surface runoff is there, there is recharge of the ground-water body.

When rainfall occurs after a dry spell on the soil surface which is dry and cracked it infiltrates faster in the beginning but decreases ex-pentially with time. This can be expressed (infiltration rate) at any given time by the formula:

$$f = f_c + (f_o - f_c) - kt$$

Where f_c = the final infiltration rate

f_o = the initial infiltration rate, and

k = a constant

The values of f_o can be as high as 75 mm/hour and f_c can vary from 0.1 – 0.75 mm/hour depending on the nature of the soil.

Water that is not held in the soil water zone by capillary forces percolates down by gravity through the zone of aeration to the zone of saturation. This amount depends on the permeability of the soil and rock material in the zone of aeration including the soil water zone. The maximum water that is held in the soil water zone by capillary forces against gravity is called the field capacity of the soil. It is different for different types of soils and can vary from 50 to 300 mm depending on the nature and thickness of the soil.

The water in the soil water zone, also called the root-zone of plants, is drawn up by plants for their sustenance and growth. Part of the water lost by evaporation from the soil water zone, soil surface and vegetation is called evapotranspiration. As the water is depleted by evapotranspiration, it has to be made up by further rainfall. The soil water zone is, thus, a reservoir which is refilled and brought up to field capacity if possible by precipitation.

If the soil water zone consists of clay material with high moisture holding capacity and very low permeability it will allow very little water to percolate, however high the amount of rainfall it may be. Thus the soil water zone, its moisture holding capacity and the permeability of its material play a decisive role in ground-water recharge.

Apart from permeability and evapotranspiration, the ground-water recharge depends on the amount and the distribution of rainfall in time and space as well as on the intensity and duration of each rain shower.

A specified amount of rain will produce maximum recharge of ground-water if it occurs for a continuous period or persistent rain with an intensity just as fast as it can infiltrate. If the same rainfall amount occurs as occasional rains spread over a long period with intervening long period of no rain, very little water will reach the watertable. If rainfall occurs in heavy downpours of short duration, as it happens in arid and semi-arid areas, most of the rainfall will be lost as direct runoff, and only small amounts will percolate to ground-water recharge.

Water Balance Equation

Ground-water being an important component of the hydrologic cycle, it is better to investigate the water balance for ground-water recharge in the form G = P – (E+R) for an aquifer, basin, sub-basin or a river assuming that there is no inflow or outflow of ground-water and surface water into or out of the area under consideration. G is the recharge of ground-water, P is the precipitation, R is the runoff and E is the evapotranspiration.

P can be considered as the average rainfall over the intake multiplied by the area of the basin. The average rainfall is determined by taking the arithmetic mean of the rainfall recorded by a number of raingauge stations in the area, by Thiessen polygon or isohyetal methods. Of these three, the isohyetal method is the most satisfactory as it considers the topographic situation and the non-uniform distribution of raingauges in the total net-work Radhakrishna (1974) is of the opinion that the existing network of raingauges is inadequate and it should be still closer to get a correct approximation of the quantum of rainfall and its distribution over a basin.

Evaporation (E) is a physical process occurring at a temperature below the boiling point of water by which water vapour escapes from the evaporating medium into the overlying air layers. The process requires a supply of latent heat energy, a *Sink* to accommodate the escaping vapour and an efficient mechanism to transport the evaporated moisture up and away from the evaporating surface.

Evaporative loss from any medium is principally governed by environmental factors such as (1) solar and sky radiations, (2) albedo and temperature of the evaporating surface, (3) gradient of vapour pressure between the medium and the overlying air layers, (4) wind speed at or near the surface, and (5) general state of stability of the lower layers of the atmosphere.

In addition to above-mentioned factors, some more factors like (1) size, depth, configuration, purity and state of surroundings in the case of water bodies, (2) depth of watertable and pattern of rainfall moistening of the top layers of the soil in case of bare soil surfaces and (3) foliar ground coverage, depth of active root zone and watertable, physical properties, chemical composition and moisture characteristics of soils in the case of vegetative surfaces affect this process.

The best way is to use the average evapotranspiration worked out from lysimeter observations obtained from different stations spread over the area. However, lysimeters are extremely few in India and actual evapotranspiration values are not generally available.

In the absence of lysimeter data empirical formulae proposed by Thornthwaite, *et al.*, (1955) is used to calculate the actual evapotranspiration (AET). Potential evapotranspiration (PRT) is the maximum amount of water that would be lost by evapotranspiration by a soil, water or vegetal cover if there is sufficient water at all times in the root zone of the soil. After PET is calculated the AET is calculated on the assumption that AET/PET is equal to the ratio of actual soil moisture storage to the water holding capacity of the soil, which is assumed to be 30 cm. This method has been extensively used in India by Subrahmanyam, *et al.*, (1964), Krishnan (1969) and others. It should be noted that ET calculated this way is still an empirical factor only as the assumption of a uniform soil moisture capacity of 30 cm in all cases is not justified.

The remaining component in water balance is R the surface runoff. This should be available from actual stream gauge measurements over a number of years for each sub-basin. Reliable runoff data from stream gauging are not available in India for many river basins and sub-basins. When these are not available, the runoff can be estimated from rainfall-runoff relationships established for the same or similar river basins and areas having the same characteristics.

If, P, E and R values are available, G can be calculated using the water balance equation. It is necessary to emphasize that as G is a small fraction of P, its value obtained from the water balance equation can be quite unreliable if the probable errors of the estimates of E and R are as high as G itself. Hence, E and R should be known as accurately as possible to obtain reliable values of G from water balance studies.

Subrahmanyam (1964) tabulated (Table 11.3) the PET, AET and annual rainfall for a few stations in Mysore State using the Thornthwaite's empirical method.

It is seen that in many cases AET is equal to rainfall which means that there is no runoff and no ground-water recharge. This does not appear to be quite correct but these values have been obtained because calculations according to Thornthwaite's method take a value of 30 cm for AET/PET for all soils and all areas. Further, it is indicated that the loss due to AET is proportionately less for heavy rainfall stations than for low rainfall stations. Therefore, the loss due to surface runoff would, however, be proportionately more for heavy rainfall areas which are mountainous with steep slopes.

Table 11.3: Annual Rainfall

Station	Annual rainfall (cm)	PET (cm)	AET (cm)
Mangalore	329.1	171.0	125.2
Belgaum	139.9	121.6	96.7
Bangalore	86.5	117.5	86.6
Mysore	79.2	130.5	79.2
Bellary	50.7	170.2	50.7
Bijapur	51.2	153.9	51.2
Raichur	64.8	170.9	64.8
Chitradurga	64.3	142.6	64.3
Balehonnur	263.3	107.6	94.0
Mercare	323.7	94.5	83.4

Estimation of Ground Water Recharge

A good example of a detailed estimation of ground-water potential using water balance method after taking into account all items of input and output, including ground-water inflow and outflow, is by Kumaraswamy (1960) on the Coleroon aquifer. He estimated that the annual ground-water potential of the Coleroon aquifer is 3×10^9 m^3, about half of which can be taken to be the safe yield for pumping and utilisation.

A method of estimating recharge to ground-water is to study the seasonal or annual variation of watertable level in special observation wells provided with automatic water level recorders and knowing the specific yield of the saturation zone to calculate the quantity of recharge. When the annual rise in ground-water level is plotted against the annual rainfall, a more or less straight line relationship can be established which when extrapolated will yield a limiting annual rainfall below which there is no annual change in ground-water level and hence no annual recharge. This limiting annual rainfall is lost completely in ET and runoff. In arid and semi-arid regions where rainfall is small and there is soil moisture deficiency throughout the year, there is such a limiting annual rainfall which does not yield any ground-water recharge. It cannot be assumed that any rainfall higher than this limiting rainfall completely goes to recharge, as this is also subject to ET and runoff.

Relationship of Ground Water to Rainfall

It is obvious from what has been stated earlier that there can be no simple theoretical relationship between ground-water recharge and rainfall because of the complicated nature of the factors involved. Attempts have, however, been made by some workers to work out broad empirical relationships for specific areas based on statistical analysis of observed rainfall and recharge data. The ratio of ground-water recharge to rainfall called the "recharge coefficient" is very small during a period of drought and decreases as the drought period gets prolonged. It starts having higher values only when the soil water zone gets saturated to field capacity.

Uppal and Sehgal (1962) found the relation $Y = 1.35\ (X - 14.23)$ between rise Y in ground-water table in inches for June to October and X the rainfall in inches from June to September. This indicates that with rainfall and irrigation upto 14.23" there was no rise in watertable and that amount of water is lost by ET and runoff.

Sehgal (1970) has found as a result of detailed statistical regression analysis that the average ground-water recharge for various doabs in Punjab State when correlated with rainfall gave a relation.

$$G = 2.5\ (P - 16)^{1/2}$$

Where G = the ground-water recharge and P = the annual rainfall in inches.

Krishna Rao (1971), however, is of the opinion that the general relationship may be of the form

$$G = K\ (P - X)$$

where K is a constant and X is the annual rainfall which yields no ground-water recharge. K and X would vary with different rainfall zones, K dependent on the average permeability of the zone of aeration and X increasing with P, ET and runoff characteristics. Further, he has calculated the values of K and X for Mysore State which can be summarised as follows:

(i) For areas with annual rainfall P between 400-600 mm

$$G = 0.20 (P - 400)$$

(ii) for areas with annual rainfall P between 600-1000 mm

$$G = 0.25 (P - 400)$$

(iii) for areas with annual rainfall P between 1000-2000 mm

$$G = 0.30 (P - 500)$$

(iv) for areas with annual rainfall P greater than 2000 mm

$$G = 0.35 (P - 600)$$

where G and P are expressed in mm.

Diurnal Variation of Ground Water Recharge

ET has a marked diurnal variation specially in arid and semi-arid regions. About 75-90 per cent of the total ET takes place in the daylight hours between sunrise and sunset. It is very small in the night time specially between midnight and 4 a.m. and is maximum in the afternoon hours upto 3 or 4 p.m.

As ET is small during night time, it is reasonable to conclude that there is more ground-water recharge from rain which occurs in the night hours as compared to the same amount and intensity of rainfall occurring in the daylight hours.

In the arid and semi-arid regions the few heavy rain showers are concentrated mostly between 3 and 7 p.m. when ET is maximum. An examination of mean hourly rainfall based on 10 years' data shows that at Bangalore 73 per cent of rainfall is during night while at Mangalore 57 per cent of rainfall is during night time (Krishna Rao, 1971).

Intensity and Duration of Rainfall

It is interesting to note that the whole rainfall in a year occurs in a comparatively short duration of time:

For example at Bellary 522 mm in 125 hours.
At Raichur 764 mm in 143 hours.

Thus, the intensity and duration of rainfall is very important for estimating the ground-water recharge. In arid and semi-arid areas the duration and intensity of rain is such that water which goes into the soil remains in the soil and lost by ET without any recharge.

The interval between rainy days is also of importance because if a rainy day occurs after a long dry spell, the soil may dry up to the wilting point for plants or even below and the rainfall infiltration will have to first meet the need of soil moisture storage upto field capacity before any percolation can take place to recharge ground-water. It is, therefore, essential to have for each station statistics of the frequency of spells of rainy days and non-rainy days of different durations. Most of the rainfall in a region with many long spells of rainless days in the monsoon season will not contribute appreciably to ground-water recharge if the period of rain spells are shorter after the long non-rainy days.

Particular Case Study of Karnataka State as an Example

Radhakrishna (1974) summarised the ground-water development in Karnataka as follows:

1. Karnataka State forms a part of the Deccan Plateau at an elevation of 700 mm and is mostly or wholly composed of hard rocks.
2. Recharge to ground-water occurs mainly by infiltration of rain water and to a lesser extent through seepage from streams, etc., and water applied for irrigation.
3. The fluctuation in watertable between the dry and wet seasons indicates that the weathered mantle and jointed bed rocks have good recharge potential.
4. Areas which receive an average annual rainfall of 700 mm and less have little surplus water to recharge the ground-water body. The districts which fall within this category are Bellary, Bijapur, Eastern parts of Belgaum and Dharwar, Chitradurga and Tumkur.
5. On the basis of the surplus, the probable percentage of rainfall contributing annually to ground-water recharge based on climatic data for 13 districts ranges from 3 per cent in Bijapur and 10 per cent in Bidar districts.
6. Out of the total number of wells existing in the State nearly 72 per cent are confined to Bangalore, Belgaum, Bijapur, Kolar, South Kanara and Tumkur districts. Even though the geohydrological conditions are similar, the unequal distribution of

wells has to be attributed to lack of initiative, non-availability of electric power, want of financial resources, etc.

7. Districts like Kolar and Bijapur have exploited all their available surplus and there is need for a cautious approach in planning further development. They may not be sowing heavy duty crops like paddy and sugar cane and sprinkler or drip irrigation will have to be practised.

Planning of Ground Water Development Schemes

Once the recharge to the ground-water body is known, it is the duty of the concerned to inform the following:

1. The amount of water that can be safely drawn out of the aquifer.
2. The number of wells which can be drilled/dug.
3. The costs and benefits from the project envisaged.

Required data for an integrated large scale ground-water development scheme according to Achutha Rao (1963) are as per form 11.1.

FORM 11.1

---

(1) **Equations used to calculate perennial yield:**

(a) *Based on hydrological equation*
Annual Recharge = Precipitation--Runoff--Evapotranspiration.
Safe Yield = Annual Recharge × recoverable factor in percentage

(b) *Darcy's law*
Perennial flow = transmissibility × cross sectional area of the aquifer × width of the aquifer perpendicular to flow.
safe yield = total flow—minimum flow required to avoid deleterious effects.

(c) *Equations* based on specific yield and rise and fall in watertables*
safe yield = coefficient of storage × area of the aquifer × rise or fall of watertable.

(2) **Water use pattern:** (Present requirement/Potential demand)
(a) Irrigation
(b) Domestic

(c) Industries

(3) **Log of Pump Operation Data collected from existing Wells:**
(a) Installed H.P.
(b) Power consumption for one year
(c) Load factor

---

* These equations are very general and each one has its own limitations and hence to be used cautiously.

This will be a check over the pumpage of water and efficiency of operation (Form 11.2).

FORM 11.2

(a) Total water available for pumping in a basin:
(b) Number of wells planned:
(c) Area proved feasible (sq. km):
(d) Well details:

(i) number of wells drilled
(ii) diameter of the bore holes
(iii) diameter of the casing
(iv) depth of production well recommended
(v) estimated yield
(vi) drawdown
(vii) estimated annual production
(viii) types of pumps and motors recommended.

(e) Cost Estimation.

(i) Well drilling and completion with pump.
(ii) Power available.
(iii) Surface distribution of channels.
(iv) Compensation paid to the existing wells, if any.
(v) Maintenance and their charges.

(f) Irrigation Improving Plans:

- (i) existing cropping patterns and likely improvement (single, double cropping pattern, etc.)
- (ii) Productivity value and the extra income developed

(g) Economic Analysis:

- (i) Total investments
- (ii) Annual cost
  1. Fixed
  2. Recurring
- (iii) Benefit cost ratio: Net annual increase in productivity in per cent total annual costs.
- (iv) Effect on per capita agricultural income:
  - (1) Existing per capita income
  - (2) Total number of persons benefited from this scheme
  - (3) Additional income generated by the use of water

12

Strategies for Popular Participation

THE foregoing chapters describe that popular participation can be an effective means of promoting policies for economic and social development. From available experience, it is possible to identify some of the basic elements of a strategy that will encourage citizens to pursue an active role in development. Essential to such a strategy is a sincere commitment by national political leaders to promote popular participation. This means not merely a verbal commitment but rather a willingness to create the necessary institutional structure and other political conditions that make popular participation possible. These leaders, have to be prepared to accept the consequences of popular participation. This latter condition is crucial, since genuine popular participation often produces differences between the government and various groups in society over development priorities. In economic matters, governments tend to view participation as a means of contributing to development in the form of more taxes and work, whereas people tend to regard it as a means of increasing their consumption of the fruits of development. Where differences become acute, governments at times are not loath to stifle or manipulate popular participation rather than seek an accommodation with it. Attempting to mute the voice of a once aroused citizenry by force may create consequences and lead to a serious confrontation between the people and the government.

Chief among the institutional requirements for successful popular participation is decentralization of the governmental institutions so as to bring public decision-making processes as close as possible to the people. To ensure that the public is informed about major issues and that the government is responsive to their preferences, it is necessary to create an effective rapport between the government and the people. There is also need to establish representative institutions at the village and intermediate levels around which citizens participation can be organized. Whatever form this institutional structure may take, its effectiveness will ultimately depend on the public's perception of how efficiently and effectively it can resolve their problems.

A strategy of popular participation should pay careful attention to the way people are initially motivated for active participation in development. Not uncommonly, governments attempt to mobilize people through promises of immediate benefits. When these are slow in forthcoming, there is danger of a psychological let-down which could give way to public apathy or violence. There is a need to offer the people realistic incentives for participation; emphasis should be placed on the benefits to be derived from the realization of medium and long-term goals rather than on immediate gains that are unobtainable. To encourage the population at large to accept deferment of the present benefits for greater future gains, the governments should reveal their goals and the methods they expect to use in achieving them and also indicate the burdens that the various groups in society can be expected to shoulder. This can be facilitated through educational programmes that attempt to foster among the people a sense of social responsibility. Great care should be given to projecting "authentic and realistic images of the future societies that would justify the striving for development and permit the ordering of objectives and instruments within coherent societal policies. The practicability of popular participation depends largely on progress in this direction but at the same time is a condition of such progress."[1]

Since the roles of government officials, local leaders and the masses of the people for continuing decision-making are highly uneven, training should be an integral part of a popular participation strategy. Such training, on the one hand, should involve orientation about the nature of popular participation in decision-making and, on the other, impart those necessary skills, such as management methods and local development planning techniques, that may be required by the particular institutional arrangements in a given country. The effectiveness of such training has been shown by experience to depend in large measure on the particular techniques used for conveying the desired information, skills and attitudes as well as on subsequent monitoring of activities. For example, experience in successful community development programmes indicates that training techniques, combining theory with practice appear to be the most effective.

Monitoring and evaluation of popular participation constitute a final component of a strategy. Since the effectiveness of popular participation depends on institutional arrangements, it is essential to assess their performance, so that corrections can be made, should they begin to fail. Such evaluation should be approached systematically and for this a number of techniques have come into use.

By taking these components into account, it is possible to outline a popular participation strategy. Such a strategy must focus attention primarily on the local level, where direct participation by the people is most possible, but must also be concerned with linking local institutions to intermediate or national institutions, or both. The existence or establishment of local institutions, around which participation can be mobilized, is an essential condition for achieving citizen involvement. While the nature of these institutions will vary, depending on the social and economic system of a country, they must perform two functions. First they should serve to organize discussion and transmit local opinions to higher level decision-makers, (this could be termed the advocacy function). Next, they should serve as a vehicle for making and implementing decisions of local concern, as in the case of community improvements. Both of these functions have been a part of normal community development practice, but it should be emphasized that they should be performed simultaneously.

There is a little evidence to indicate that popular participation on a sustained basis emerges spontaneously. Rather it must be initially mobilized and then maintained over time. The types of institutions in which the people are to participate can vary from those in which participation is episodic and ritualistic to those which involve people on a continuing basis. Evidence points to the need for institutions which centre on people's most salient concerns and, therefore, can maintain popular interest and involvement. These are most frequently economic institutions, such as factory or farm. Co-operatives and other forms of community economic association are institutions which can give a tangible pay-off and thus stimulate participation. However, much depends on the degree to which the local institution is invested with real authority to take and implement decisions within its area of competence and the extent to which the activities and programmes of one institution are supported by other institutions with different functions.

While the creation of effective local institutions for popular participation is frequently a difficult process, the rewards in terms of development are correspondingly greater. Not only can the institutions serve as focal points for detecting and influencing public opinion about development issues but they can also facilitate increased use of local resource, especially labour, for local development. Moreover, such institutions can help structure economic production and services in a more efficient and socially equitable manner.

An adequate infrastructure of local institutions, the mobilization of the people around them and the training of leaders, local government officials and the people themselves are necessary but not sufficient. There is also a need for procedures to link the diverse local institutions with the national planning and administrative machinery to achieve a balanced development effort. While the exact nature of such procedures will vary from country to country, a type of arrangement which is gaining favour is the creation of intermediate-level institutions at the regional or micro-regional (area) levels. The primary functions of such institutions is to act as a bridge between the local and the national levels. This takes two forms. On the one hand, the regional or micro-regional institutions consolidate the opinions and demands of the local institutions in their areas and present a regional view of development problems, like consolidating cooperative activities, through a regional co-operative union. On the other hand, regional institutions can facilitate disaggregation of national plans. Moreover, they may determine the spatial allocation of development projects based not only on the resources made available from central authorities but also on those that can be generated locally. It is this function which makes popular participation can be most effective, since increases in popular contributions can be obtained and activities performed in an organized sequence. Thus a regional co-operative union can assist in obtaining and administering the necessary large-scale inputs, e.g. credit, and assets marketing of products.

There are a number of conditions for the successful functioning of intermediate-level institutions. These must have direct links with local institutions without which their activities would be largely meaningless. They must have the authority to take decisions on the allocation of available resources within the region. Since the making of a regional plan and the supervision of its implementation are complex technical tasks, there is a need for trained regional development officials. It is also desirable to train local officials and leaders in the essentials of regional development. Moreover, to maintain the links between intermediate-level and the local institutions and ensure that the technical requirements of projects do not give rise to social problems, there is a need for a steady flow of information about programme performance, monitoring and evaluation. Such a flow has proved most useful in promoting the success of popular participation.

In short, a comprehensive strategy for promoting popular participation within an overall framework of the national development strategy can prove most effective if undertaken at all levels of decision-making within a society. At the national level, leaders must give the guidance and symbolic content to mass citizen involvement in decision-making. This requires institutions and procedures that facilitate transmission of popular opinions and preferences. At the local level, individual participation must be aggregated, oriented and given purpose through decentralization of decision-making authority as appropriate to the particular national context. Between the two levels, it has often been found useful to encourage intermediate-level institutions capable of aggregating local preferences opinions and activities and disaggregating national plans, programmes and policies. In this sense, popular participation can become an integral strategy for promoting development at the national, local and regional levels by making available to planners the voluntary efforts and experience of the people.

REFERENCE

1. *Social Change and Social Development Policy in Latin America* (United Nations Publication, Sales No. E. 70 II. G. 3), p. 300.

13

Inter-sectoral Integration of Area Plans

IT is now a well accepted concept that there exists close inter-relations among different sectors of human activities. Development of a particular activity is possible only if these activities which impinge on its development are favourable to it. In other words, other things remaining favourable, a particular change would occur. While for analytical purpose one may dispose of this whole problem by saying 'other things being equal or same', it is of no great help to a practical planning exercise.

Integrated rural area development requires that all sectors of the rural economy are so planned and developed that one supports the other. To this, we must know the relationships among various activities. While, one has to find out these relationships in each area of planning, a practical exercise in this respect worked by J.G. Krishnayya and S.K. Sharma of Indian Institute of Management, Bangalore, is reproduced below as an example of how to attempt inter-sectoral integration of plans.

Agriculture Sector Linkages

'Agriculture' encompasses a whole spectrum of activities like farming vegetables and fruit growing, animal husbandry, poultry and fisheries. Inputs to and or the factors that affect the Agriculture Sector are as follows (grouped in the order of importance):

Farming

Land: Land affects the agricultural sector through the following parameters:

(i) *Soil composition*: determines the type of crops that can be grown, the number of crops that can be grown, the yield per hectare and the mix of fertilizers to be used.

Taking some examples–black loam soil with its moisture retaining property is essential for growing cotton–the nutrients content of the soil is an important variable in determining whether you can grow 2 or 3 crops on the same field and also determines the yield–soil deficient in phosphates will have to be given a strong dose of P-fertilizers.

(ii) *Location*: in conjunction with fertility (soil composition) determines the price of the land which in turn affects the gross area under cultivation. Land nearer to a town or village, an irrigation scheme, the market, a processing industry, which uses the produces, is likely to be costlier.

The climate and topography–dependent on location–influence the technology to be employed and the crops to be grown. For example, if the terrain is hilly, one needs to do terracing–paddy requires heavy rainfall or flooding, etc.

(iii) *Size of land-holdings*: may determine the efficiency with which some inputs like fertilizers, pesticides, mechanical implements (tractors, harvestors) can be used, or the speed at which innovations take place.

Labour: Both skilled and unskilled labour are needed on the field: skilled for ploughing, sowing, irrigation, use of fertilizers and pesticides, and unskilled for purely mechanical operations like harvesting, thrashing. Labour can be the family members of the farmer (which is most often the case) or hired hands.

Water: The pattern of rainfall is most crucial. The whole agro-economy of India hinges around how the monsoon turns out.

Then we have the artificial means of irrigation–canals and wells. Wells again can be of two types (a) dug wells, (b) Tube wells.

Canals and wells provide water when needed removing the uncertainty of monsoons. Adequate water supply can lead to a change in the type of crops grown and also the crop pattern.

Seeds: On seeds depend the yield per hectare and other minor properties like disease resistance, protein content, etc. Seeds can be classified as: (i) Local, (ii) Improved and (iii) HYV.

HYV is a hybrid variety of seeds and by definition of a hybrid, the crops grown from them do give us HYV seeds, so HYV have to be produced through a chain of special seed farms (manned by agro-scientists) and for every crop sufficient quantity of HYV seeds has to be produced. Because of this, HYV seeds become a 'conventional' production = distribution system.

The HYV should reach the farmer in time for sowing and in requisite quantity. Also encountered is the problem of purchasing power. It should be possible for the farmer to purchase the HYV with available funds (which are function of credit facilities). There have been occasional complaints in the press about the inequitable distribution of HYV seeds, largely a responsibility of the government.

In short, efficient production and distribution of HYV seeds are the pre-requisite for sustaining the green revolution.

Fertilizers and Pesticides

Fertilizers supplement the nutrients in the soil to help increase the crop yield. Different fertilizers may be needed at different points in the growth cycle of the crop. They can also be used to make cultivable land with sub-standard soil. Other fertilizers along with rotation of crops are used to replenish the soil nutrients after a crop has been grown. Proper mix of fertilizers can be. used for making the soil more suitable for particular type of crop.

Fertilizers are either: (i) Indigenous or (ii) Manufactured.

Indigenous fertilizers include green manure and compost organic material which can be produced at the village level.

Manufactured fertilizers are the chemical fertilizers: N.P.K. types (Nitrogen, Phosphates, Potash). They again can be viewed as a production distribution system.

In addition to a supply system, fertilizers need educational support in terms of teaching the farmers the 'how and when' and 'what' of fertilizer usage. Also needed are mechanical implements for efficient application of fertilizers.

Pesticides are protective measures. Farmers need to be educated in the safe and effective use of pesticides. There can be different pests infesting a region or field and accordingly rodenticides, herbicides, insecticides or fungicides have to be used. Occasionally *rapid dissemination* know-how and pesticides is required to fight crop disease or pest. Because of the breeding pesticides HYVs are particularly susceptible. Also needed management to effectively apply these pesticides.

Tractive Power

There are two sources of power for use on the field:

(i) *Animal power*: The animals used on the farm differ from region to region–horses, camels, buffaloes, bullocks. Human labour is not insignificant.
(ii) *Mechanical power*: Tractors and power tillers are increasingly being used in the Indian fields.

Tractors and power tillers are an obvious choice (in spite of oil crisis) if the sole criterion is productivity. But they require high initial investment. Tractors are here to use hence inefficient and often uneconomical on the average size of land holding in India, assuming that the farmer could raise enough credit to buy one. Leasing services change the picture as do the secondary uses of the power source, especially for the highly time-critical activities characteristic of modern agriculture.

Mechanical Implements and Servicing

As has been mentioned previously mechanical implements are needed to disperse fertilizers and pesticides on the field, to do the seeding, for irrigation, for harvesting and threshing etc. Attachments to tractors can provide many of these services.

All these implements improve productivity but again, they need high initial investment.

Once these implements are in use it is essential that facilities are provided for prompt servicing and repairing of these. Which means that sufficient technical know-how has to be generated locally or has to be brought in from outside.

Power

'Power' is being spoken here in the sense of static motors or devices which are used in different operations on and around the field: Operations like harvesting, threshing, irrigation.

There can be three types of motive power:

(i) Animal or Manual
(ii) Diesel
(iii) Electricity

In category (ii) it could be a diesel engine or it could be a tractor itself with its power take-off attachment which is acting as a prime-movers.

Electricity taken from a power supply grid requires a complex chain of supporting systems including installation, maintenance and protection of feeder transmission lines and transformers, as well as a metering, billing and collection system.

Now we move over to software inputs.

Credit

All the inputs that we have mentioned above have to be bought with money. It is not possible for a vast majority of Indian farmers to purchase all the 'hardware' inputs to improve their productivity without substantial credit support.

A farmer gets credit from the following four sources:

1. Private Money Lenders
2. Co-operative Societies
3. Banks
4. Personal Savings

The most dominant among these at present is the private money lender and this has far reaching impact on the marketed surplus. Private money lenders also charge high rates of interest. It indicates a need for increasing the reach and effectiveness of bank and co-operative society activities, and for them to provide a full package of services.

Extension Network

Even after the farmer has got the essential inputs for farming, he needs to be educated in the proper use of those inputs. He should be told about HYV and its advantages, mix of fertilizers suitable for his crops and conditions, advantages and dangers of pesticides, etc.

Farmers need to be kept up-to-date in all these areas. Publicity is needed for all the schemes, government devises to improve farm productivity beyond that the farmers should be aided in making use of them by the way they are integrated and presented.

The extension network for this already exists, and it has been utilised reasonably, successfully and efficiently to introduce HYV, and other practices. Included in extension is the effective use of communications media like drama, films, radio, newspapers, pamphlets, etc.

Post-harvest Operations and Marketing

Crops require some post-harvest operations such as threshing and some, such as rice, require major milling activity immediately.

Storage and Transportation: Systems are the link, filter and barrier between the farmers' economic world and the consumers. Disadvantage of good farm level storage facility could increase (speculative) hoarding. On the other hand, the amount of the crop withheld for the farmer's own consumption includes his estimates of spoilage (which is usually 25%). Better on-farm storage conditions should, therefore, release a larger surplus to market. Better transportation facilities reduce the cost of marketing.

Market Structure: There are regulated markets and there are private dealers working through 'Adhetiyas'. The variables that become relevant here are how much the farmer sells, to whom and when?

If the produce is sold through a regulated market it provides a fair price for both the seller as well as buyer with adequate weight and quality control.

But as mentioned earlier the farmer depends for his credit mainly on the *seth* (since banks do not provide credit for marriages and social functions) and is under some sort of obligation to him. Now this *seth* is usually a trader also and he can get the farmer to sell the produce to him, thus interfering with the play of 'market forces'.

How much and when are determined by the economic conditions of the farmer and the prices. If the past one or two years have been good for the farmer, he has a buffer of savings and can afford to sit on his produce waiting for prices to go to a 'favourable' level. Also since he is not in urgent need of money the quantity he will sell will be less.

Conversely, if his economic condition is bad because of bad crops for the past year or two, the farmer will bring the produce to the market as soon as he can and as much as he can, regardless of the prices.

The quantity and timing of the crop sales (assuming the demand to be inflexible) affect the prices.

Co-operatives

Formation of co-operatives is increasingly gaining ground. Co-operatives are organized bodies for providing support to the farmers in the form of credit, storage and marketing facilities. They also form an efficient channel for distribution of fertilizers, HYV seeds and pesticides.

Co-operatives are also a medium for effective dissemination of information about technological and other developments and provide leadership in adoption of innovations.

Prices and Gross Income

If the farmer can afford to wait, the prices will affect the surplus he brings to the market.

Also, in general, prices determine the type of crops that a farmer would like to grow. Everything else being suitable (if he has enough land already under food crops for his own consumption) his preference would be to go in for a cash crop yielding higher earnings.

The prices and the quantity marketed determine the gross income of a farmer. A farmer's gross income in time 't' determines the inputs he can afford to buy in time 't'+1 which in turn affects the quantity produced.

Government Policies

Government is the largest producer and distributor of fertilizers, producer and distributor of HYV, as well the biggest single purchaser of the agricultural produce. It also influences the agricultural sector through rural electrification programmes, extension and development work, finance for co-operatives, directives to banks on credit policy and the purchase prices of various commodities. Crop levies, movement controls and taxes are other forms of government action.

Industry

Proximity of a processing industry, which uses a particular agricultural produce as input, is likely to increase the inclination towards producing that commodity. For example, if there is a sugar mill nearby, it is possible that the farmers would switch over to sugarcane, because they save on the cost, effort and time of transportation.

Then there are some factors which have a direct but not quite measurable impact on agriculture.

Health

The physical condition of the farmer influences the time and effort he can put in on the fields and thus has a direct impact on the productivity. Health of his family members determines the help he can get on the fields and his mental peace.

Education

Education moulds a farmer's attitude towards learning new techniques and applying them as well as determines his capacity to do so.

It also brings about an increasing awareness and consciousness which enables the farmer to take advantage of various developmental schemes and also to make the most efficient use of the available resources.

Influence of Agriculture: Effect of agriculture on other aspects of rural life is predcminantly through a single transducer–economic condition–an individual's as well as of the community.

Taking demand as inflexible, the quantity of output determines the prices; the prices and the quantity marketed determines the gross income. Gross income of the farmer determines the amount of money to be spent on education of the children, health of the family, etc.

The prosperity of an agricultural community determines the spending on public works programmes like building roads and storage facilities and forming of co-operative societies and regulated markets.

A prosperous economy boosts up the level of political goodwill fund. It also attracts industries which can use the main produce of the region as raw material.

Non-economic impact of agriculture is on the socio-cultural scene which includes variables like food habits, festivals, social customs, etc.

A loop type of relationship can also be identified. The gross income of the farmer determines the inputs he could afford for the coming crop and the amount of inputs will determine the quantity produced.

Vegetables and Fruit Growing

The analysis for this activity is also quite similar to that of farming except that:

(i) Greater play of demand and supply, and cost and price

economics; not so much of government interference;

(ii) Mechanical implements needed do not require as high investment; and

(iii) Since these commodities are perishable, the storage facilities (cold storage) and accessibility of market in a short time are critical factors.

Animal Husbandry and Poultry

The prevalent caste system in rural India determines the persons who can take up a particular type of occupation.

For examples 'higher' caste people will not keep cattle except for milking or breeding purposes. Butchering and dealing in meat is left to a different group of people. Same is the case with poultry.

Apart from that, here also the storage facility (for milk products as well as meat and eggs) and proximity to market are important factors.

A completely new type of facility has to be developed for this activity–veterinary hospitals and artificial insemination centres.

Different types of inputs namely nutritious cattle and poultry feeds are needed. The extension network also has to employ a new type of specialist–one who knows about the fauna being promoted.

This activity is dependent upon farming for fodder.

Fishing

Fishing is a specific type of activity in the sense that proximity to natural or artificial reservoirs of water is essential. Coastal, tidal and river and pond fishing are quite different.

It can give us a substitute food as well as substantial foreign exchange earnings. Input 'industries' (for nets, implements, boats) and 'post harvest' operations–cleaning, packing, freezing, canning, etc. are economically significant as a system.

Figures 13.1 and 13.2 depict diagrammatic representation of the analysis of agricultural sector linkages.

(b)

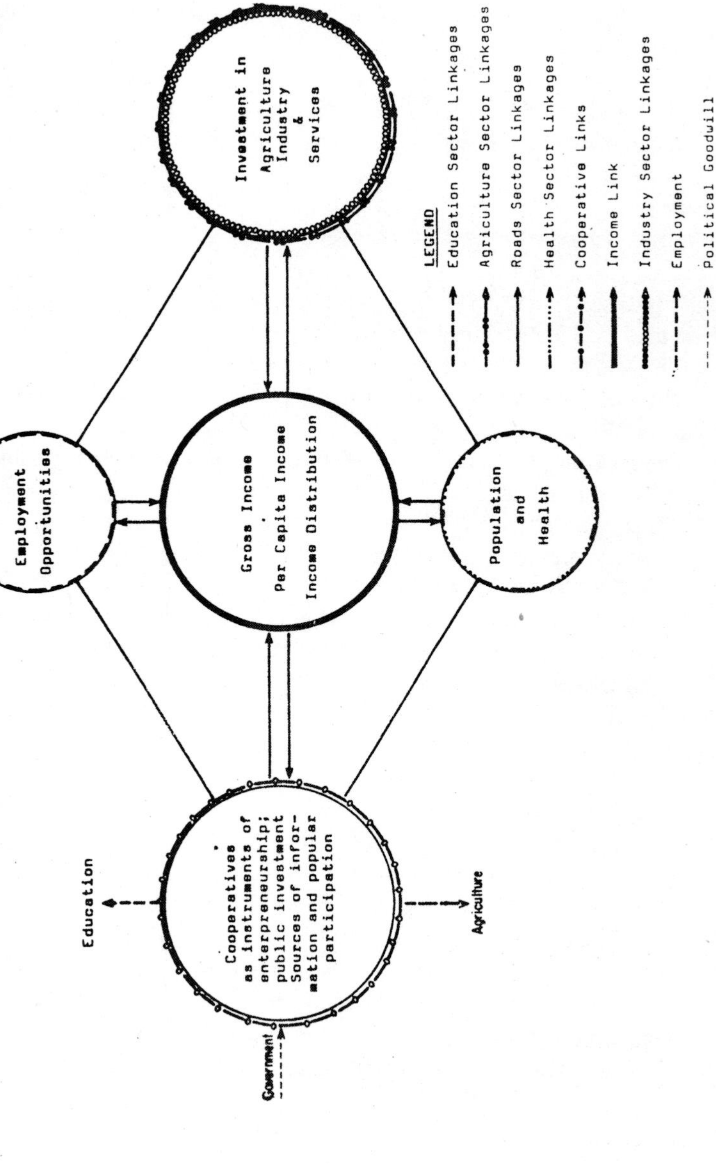
Employment Opportunities
Gross Income
Per Capita Income
Income Distribution
Investment in Agriculture Industry & Services
Population and Health
Cooperatives as instruments of enterpreneurship; public investment Sources of information and popular participation
Education
Agriculture
Government
LEGEND
Education Sector Linkages
Agriculture Sector Linkages
Roads Sector Linkages
Health Sector Linkages
Cooperative Links
Income Link
Industry Sector Linkages
Employment
Political Goodwill

Fig. 13.1

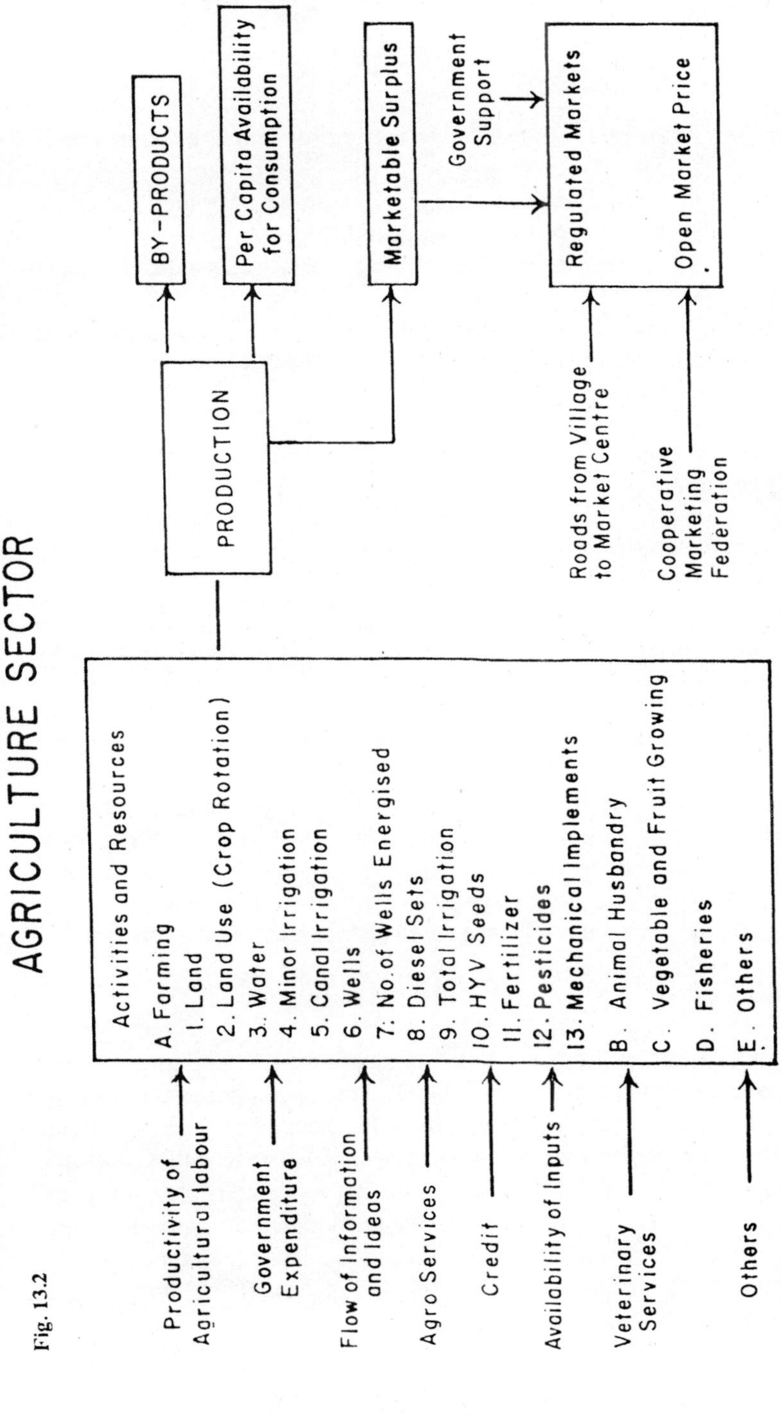
AGRICULTURE SECTOR
Productivity of Agricultural labour
Government Expenditure
Flow of Information and Ideas
Agro Services
Credit
Availability of Inputs
Veterinary Services
Others
Activities and Resources
A. Farming
1. Land
2. Land Use (Crop Rotation)
3. Water
4. Minor Irrigation
5. Canal Irrigation
6. Wells
7. No. of Wells Energised
8. Diesel Sets
9. Total Irrigation
10. HYV Seeds
11. Fertilizer
12. Pesticides
13. Mechanical Implements
B. Animal Husbandry
C. Vegetable and Fruit Growing
D. Fisheries
E. Others
PRODUCTION
BY-PRODUCTS
Per Capita Availability for Consumption
Marketable Surplus
Government Support
Regulated Markets
Open Market Price
Roads from Village to Market Centre
Cooperative Marketing Federation

Fig. 13.2

Industry Sector Linkages

Industry in the rural context, can be categorised into three segments:

1. *Village Artisans*: Like the blacksmith, the carpenter, the ***mochi***, the tailor, the potter, and goldsmith, etc.
2. *Cottage industries*: Like spinning, khandsari, handicrafts, handloom etc.
3. *Conventional industries*: (which generally come to the urban mind when industry is mentioned) like saw mills, printing press, dal and rice mills, workshops, etc.

A particular industry is set up in a region due to any of the following reasons:

1. It uses the main crop of the region as a raw material, or it is involved in supporting the 'inputs' to local agriculture.
2. There is some mineral like iron or copper ore.
3. Preference of the entrepreneur, or as an ancillary to a big industry.
4. Other advantages like tax concessions and land facilities provided by the local government.

These reasons are relevant for the 'conventional' industry only. The first two categories of industry are mostly for satisfying local needs and, therefore, there is no deliberate decision-making process in their location. They flourish in response to the need of the region.

The factors which influence the industrial sector are as follows:

Location

There are different aspects of location which affect not only the decision to locate the industry there but also the operations of the industry. But since these aspects are important by themselves we shall discuss them individually. Here we could just mention that with a particular location, a particular climate and particular topography are tied up and they influence the efficiency of the operations. For some industries, like cotton textiles which requires a certain minimum level of humidity, climate becomes critical. Location also affects the first input to any industry–land prices.

Raw Materials

Availability of raw materials at an appropriate price is critical to the functioning of any industry. Also important is the time factor, i.e., timely and regular inflow of raw materials.

For the village artisan and the cottage industry, raw-materials are easily accessible because they usually utilize locally available resources. It is also quite common that the producer of the raw material and owner of the industry are the same person, e.g., a farmer who grows sugarcane also has a khandsari unit in his backyard. Village artisans, quite often, do not have to worry about raw materials because the customer himself supplies it like in the case of tailors, goldsmiths, etc.

Natural Resources

These include minerals and water. The existence of minerals can lead to mining and/or processing industry. Water is essential for all industries and so a plentiful source of water supply is a major consideration for these industries.

Labour

Unskilled and skilled labour is needed for all the three types of industries. Large skilled labour requirements leads to inflow of labour. Availability of local labour is influenced by education and the skills it has been possible to impart to the local populace through the education system (vocational training institutions). Also to be considered is the opportunity for alternate employment. It has been found that education beyond a certain level leads to expectations of white collar jobs and manual work is shirked by those individuals. Often this results in migration to urban areas.

In industry of first two category skills are passed from father to son and there is no need for formal vocational education.

Health has an important influence on productivity of labour.

Capital

Another most important input to an industry is capital. Sources of capital can be any of the following:

(i) savings (which is a function of per capita income).
(ii) Credit: from
  (a) Banks
  (b) Industrial Development Corporations
  (c) State Financial Corporations
  (d) Private Financiers
  (e) Credit Co-operatives.
(iii) Public subscription.

Technical and Managerial know-how

In industries of first two categories technology involved is very simple and the know-how is transferred from father to son. The management of these enterprises does not require any sophisticated techniques.

But for third category industries, relatively sophisticated technology and management know-how is needed. It is quite obvious that these inputs cannot be available locally and, therefore, there is an inflow of people with appropriate skills.

Some amount of simple technological know-how, more relevant to categories (1) and (2), is provided through extension programmes sponsored by the government.

Co-operatives also assist in providing some managerial support.

Marketing

Before deciding what to produce and how much, one has to look for the demand and needs.

For the village artisan, it is purely the local (either just at the village or at the nearby *mandi*) need, which is meaningful. The cottage industrialist can think of exporting his product but he needs organisational help which is provided by handloom cooperatives or bodies like *Khadi Gramodyog* Commission.

'Conventional' industries export practically 100 per cent of their output and the local needs have no effect on their demand except perhaps indirectly.

Another part of market forces is prices. But they will also be more influential in the 'conventional' industry segment rather than the local market.

Electrification

The amount of electricity consumed is the most appropriate indicator of industrial development.

But again, this won't be fully applicable to category (1) and (2) industries. If the village is electrified, the village artisan will have lighting to work under and some increase in productivity will accrue. The khandsari unit will use an electric motor to run the cane juice extractor. The increase in productivity due to the availability of electricity is an observable phenomenon.

In 'conventional' industry electrification is critical to the setting up of the plant itself.

Major Crops

They might not have such a big impact on category (3) industry unless and until it uses the agricultural produce as its raw material.

The most clearly related to the crops is the cottage industry. Though some activities like handloom and handicrafts might not be dependent very much upon the type of crops in the region but khandsari, spinning, 'ghani', etc., owe their existence to the crops grown in the area. Other 'cottage' industries such as leather are linked to animal husbandry. Canning and food preservation industries also depend upon agricultural output.

The market for the village artisan is essentially dependent upon the prosperity generated by the crops in the region.

Communications

It includes roads and transport. All the items to be exported need efficient connections to the market. Also the raw materials can be imported efficiently through well developed roads and communications network.

Quite evidently category (3) and to some extent category (2) industries are influenced by this aspect of the infrastructure.

Government Policies

'Government' here includes Central, State, and Local governments like *Panchayat* as well as some other bodies like *Khadi Gramodyog* Commission etc.

The following aspects of government policies influence the development of industries in general:

(i) Technical extension services and marketing co-operatives
(ii) Loans and capital grants
(iii) Subsidies and taxes
(iv) Expenditure on developing facilities like industrial estates and other infrastructure

Influence of industry: The output of the industry can be measured in terms of units produced, rupee value of production or values added.

Economy: Apart from satisfying needs through the outputs, the industry also affects the economy of a region through the following two parameters:

(a) Per capita income
(b) Employment level

An increase in per capita income leads to better health and education.

Employment level has an opportunity cost attached to it. For example, a farmer might leave his fields to join as an industrial worker and thus bring down the agricultural production.

Multiplier effect: Once an industry has been established it attracts other supporting industries and services. It also draws an industry which can use its output as an input.

Non-economic influences of the industry are as follows:

Health: There are occupational diseases associated with certain industries.

Education: Setting up of an industry generates a demand for certain types of skills and knowledge. This requires that the education system be geared towards imparting those skills and knowledge.

Population: This is mainly influenced by category (3) industry. As mentioned earlier 'conventional' industry needs lot of manpower with diverse skills and this leads to inflow of people, changing the mix of the population in the region.

Socio-cultural system: Inflow of people of different social and cultural background leads to a sort of cross breeding and emergence of a new configuration of morals, ethics and values. Empirical evidence suggests that there is some degeneration as a result of industrialization.

Political goodwill: Since it improves the economic environment of a region, industrialization is generally welcome. This is supported by the evidence that as the elections draw near, more and more foundation stones are laid for one industry or the other or for some input to the industry.

Diagrammatic representation of the above analysis is given in Fig.13.3.

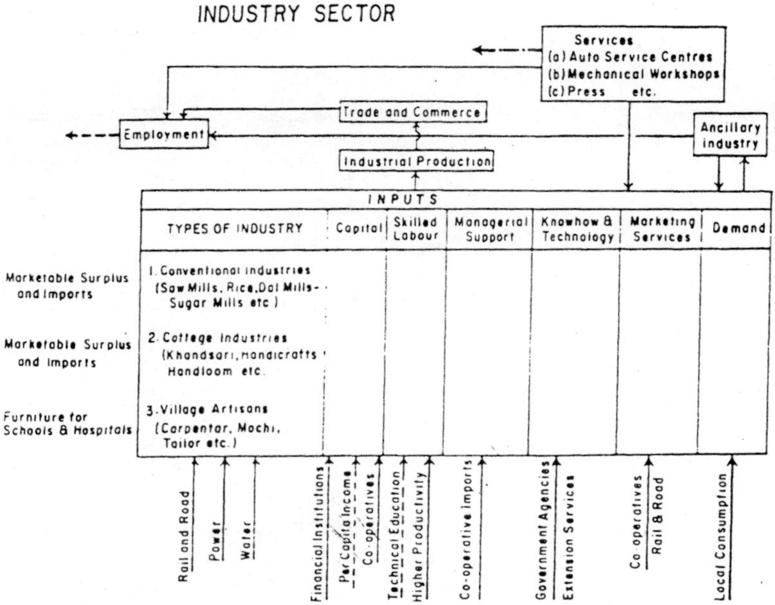

Fig. 13.3

Roads and Linkage Sector

Factors that Influence Road Construction

Roads facilitate the flow of material, men, services and information.

Geographical factors

(i) *Topography*: Influences the cost of construction and maintenance of roads and the type of road by necessitating bridges. But they may also serve as a substitute mode for transport and communication. Cost of roads rises steeply as we move from plains to the hills.

(ii) *Climate*: Most of the rural roads are unsurfaced, and many of them which are covered with clay become very slippery and unusable during the monsoon months. Poor grading, runoff and drainage make the roads unusable for a considerable period of time.

Flow of Materials

Main products which flow out of the village are agriculture, dairy and poultry products, fish, fruits and vegetables.

The demand for roads depends on tons per year of these products (surpluses) moving out of the village.

Production of the above products in turn depends upon the flow of inputs into the village.

Inputs are fertilizers, seeds, pesticides, petrol, oil and lubricants, spare parts, agricultural implements, etc., which can be classified as agricultural inputs. Other inputs into the village system are kerosene oil, cakes and other consumer goods which have to be supplied from the other centres. quantities of these commodities moving inward can be termed as material inflow.

The necessity to have a road, of a particular type would greatly depend on the quantity of inflow and outflow of materials in the village system.

The inflow of materials depends on the number of persons in the system and their purchasing power (i.e., per capita income) as well as the effective crop area and the farm technology in use. The quantity of agricultural surpluses flowing out and inputs into the system depend on the size of the holdings, income level of farmers and level of modernization of agriculture in the village.

Flow of Men

Roads facilitate the movement of:

(a) (i) Persons from home to the field

(ii) People from home to the market centres

(iii) People and livestock from village to hospitals and veterinary centres

(b) (i) Students from home to schools
(ii) Teachers to villages

(c) (i) Village community to their place of worship/entertainment, and
(ii) Village community to their relatives, outside the village.

Flow of Services

Roads facilitate the movement of service personnel, government and private, like extension workers, workers, doctors, craftsmen, mobile dispensary, family planning worker, hawkers, traders, etc.

In sum, *utilization of the road* depends on the number of persons using the road and the amount of material transported over the road. In effect men and material movement create the demand for roads.

The type of road required is interdependent on the mode of transport used/the speed of transport required.

Mode of transport	*Type of road*
(a) on foot	foot path
(b) a + animal drawn carts	cart tracks
(c) a + b + petrol bus, jeep, tractors, etc.	Unsurfaced roads
(d) a + b + c + trucks	Surfaced roads
(e) all types of vehicles	All-weather roads

Number of the above vehicles in the system and the kilometres of the above type of roads per square km. of area of the system give us a set of state variables which influence the demand for roads.

Another set of influential state variables are the distance of the village from major service centres.

(a) Distance from railway station
(b) Distance from market centres
(c) Distance from processing centres like rice mills, cotton gin, oil mills, etc.
(d) Distance from pilgrimage centres
(e) Distance from entertainment centre, hospitals, etc.
(f) Distance from *pucca* road
(g) Distance from all weather road

Road construction depends on the ability to finance and obtain finance for construction and maintenance.

Factors that are Influenced by Roads

The most powerful impact of roads is: (i) creating accessibility and (ii) reducing the time spent on route.

Roads increase the income level of the population in the system through increasing the productivity of agriculture, dairy, poultry and other rural activities and reducing the cost, time and effect involved in marketing.

Improvements in Agriculture

Roads facilitate the inflow of information and knowledge through more visits of extension workers, etc. and over a period of time, are instrumental in changing the attitudes of the villagers towards modern methods. When farmers become more mobile they are likely to be exposed more often to new ideas and methods.

A study has shown that proximity to roads leads (i) improvement in land-use; (ii) more acreage under cash crops, and (iii) specialization in crops.

Seeds, fertilizers, pesticides, etc., and other inputs become more easily available leading to changes in farming methods and increased agricultural production.

Farm mechanization would increase as drilling rig can move to the interior and drill tube wells. Petrol, oil, lubricants, spare-parts, etc., can reach the village and help to maintain pumps, tractors and agriculture implements.

Another very important result of roads is the speedier transportation of the perishable commodities from villages to market centres. Therefore, poultry, dairy, fishery, fruit and vegetable production would go up. These products bring daily cash flow to the villager as against twice a year cash flow if he produces only grains. This leads to flexibility in finance and the farmer would release his surpluses when prices are favourable and thus would realize higher income. Of course, this tendency may lead to storage of foodgrains in poor condition resulting in higher losses in the system.

Education

Teachers would be more willing to go to the villages served by roads. Better attendance may be expected. Female literacy is likely to increase. A broader range of school facilities would be available to the students.

Health

With accessibility to hospitals, dispensaries, etc., and the increased number of visits of health and family planning workers, mobile dispensary visits etc., the health status is likely to improve.

Industries

Rice mills, agro-service centres, ginning mills, oil mills, etc., would be more accessible to the village. Roads may lead to establishment of cycle shops agro-repair shops, etc.

Having sanitation and electricity, easier transport of building materials, would improve the quality of housing sanitation and provision of electric service lines.

Improved connectivity and the resultant increase in economic activity will boost the political goodwill in the populace towards authority.

Decision Variables

In some States 25 per cent of the cost of the road is borne by the local body and 75 per cent is contributed by State PWD. Given the amount of money available with the panchayat, the type of road to be built would be a decision variable.

Relief programmes during famine, floods, etc., lead to availability of labour to build or improve roads.

Octroi levies restriction on inter-district movement of foodgrains, restriction in inter-State movement of trucks, etc., inhibit the growth and use of roads. These should be altered or removed.

Diagrammatic representation of the above analysis, is shown in Fig. 13.4.

Fig. 13.4

ROAD AND LINKAGE SECTOR

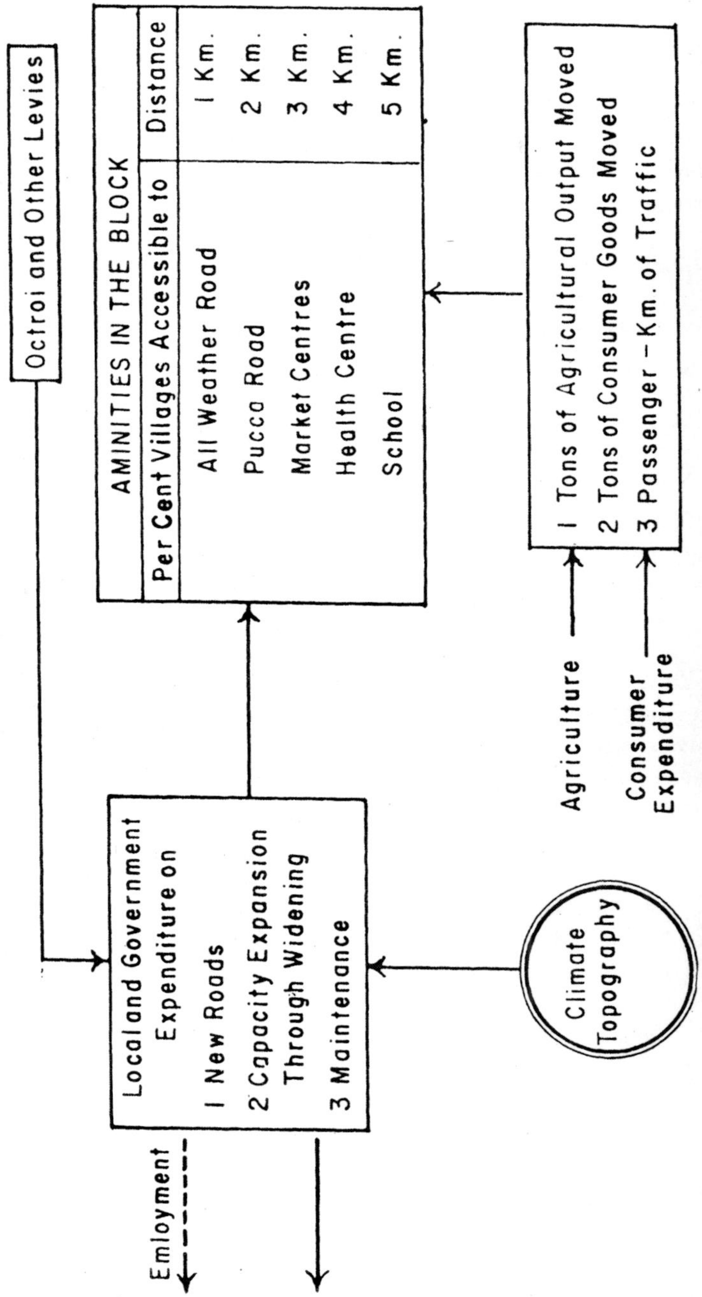

Education Sector Linkages

The level variables in the education sector in our model are:

1. Percentage of primary school age population enrolled in primary schools.
2. Percentage of secondary school age population enrolled in secondary schools.
3. Percentage of population literate (a) male and (b) female.
4. Enrolment in Adult Literacy Centres.

Levels in the education sector are influenced by the following factors:

Physical Facilities

These are considered in relation to the student population and include class-rooms, furnitures, text-books, games, library, etc.

Adequacy or abundance of these facilities as a ratio with student population denotes greater than one multiplier to the developmental effect of education.

Availability of Teachers

This is again denoted in terms of teacher student ratio. A higher ratio is considered to lead to better effectiveness of education.

Distance from School

Great deal of travelling to be done in reaching the school and coming back is a disincentive to enrol. This is true particularly in the case of girls, where the parents do not like to send their daughters to school if it is not within the boundary of the village.

Good roads and convenient transport facility tends to negate the effect of greater distances.

This factor has been quantified in terms of percentage of student population having to travel greater than a specified distance to reach school.

Relevance of Curriculum

Education provides a greater impetus to development if the emphasis is on vocation oriented curriculum. Education is more relevant if it takes into account the predominant occupation of the block and the needs of any nearby industry.

Health

Health has an indirect effect on education. The only quantifiable measure is absentees because of illness.

Cultural Factors

It has been found that in regions with higher proportion of Scheduled Caste population the Enrolment levels are lower.

Income

Per capita income and cost of education, particularly at the higher levels, determine the inclination of the parents to send their children to educational institutions.

Current Literacy Level

We hypothesize that parents with a higher level of education have a greater propensity to send their children to school. This can be generalised to the regional level.

Government Expenditure

Government expenditure on physical facilities, teachers' salaries and training, incentive programmes like free mid-day meals and text books, has a great effect on levels in the education sector.

The impact of education is mostly through second order effects.

Attitude: Education generates a favourable attitude towards family planning, use of health facilities and adoption of new techniques in agriculture. It also brings awareness of public hygiene as well as political awareness.

Availability of labour: Vocation oriented education makes various kinds of skilled labour easily available which encourages setting up of industries in the region.

Migration: Education above a certain level results in expectations of a white collar job. Such individuals look down upon manual labour and the result is migration to urban areas.

Drop-outs: This is an indication of the educational wastage. This is mainly due to economic reasons which include availability of the required level of education in geographical proximity.

The linkage of education with other sectors is shown in Fig. 13.5.

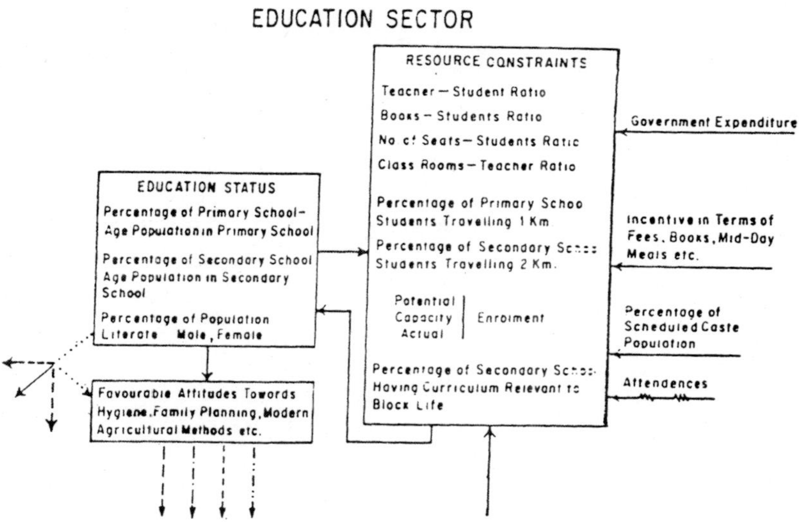

Fig. 13.5

Health Sector Linkages

The health status of a block has been defined, in our model, by means of two parameters:

1. Infant mortality; and
2. Death rate.

The factors that affect health status are as follows:

Supply of Health Services

The health service personnel are doctors (allopathic, homeopathic, ayurvedic and unani, supported by nurses, midwives, compounders, health workers, family planning workers, vaccinators, etc., which can be grouped under para-medical staff. In addition to the personnel, health services include physical facilities like beds, equipment, drugs, etc.

Simply availability of health services is not sufficient to determine the health status of a block. How effectively these services are used by the local population is also an important criterion.

Use of the health services is influenced by the factors, mentioned below:

Education

Literacy in the region determines attitude towards hygiene, awareness of the common rules for maintaining good health and inclination to go to the medical personnel for advice in case of ill-health.

Female literacy in particular has great influence on adoption of family planning ideas.

Expenditure (capacity and preference)

The amount spent by the people on nutrition (measured in terms of per capita calorie and protein intake) has great influence on the health status of the region.

Also to be taken into account is the amount available for spending on drugs and medicine as and when needed.

Both these types of expenditures are dependent on per capita income. Nutrition intake is also dependent upon school feeding programmes sponsored by various agencies.

Public Hygiene

This is one of the most (if not the most) important determinant of the health status. Proper sewerage and garbage disposable system as well as hygienic drinking water facility contribute towards good health.

Houses served by covered drainage system and local government expenditure on sweepers can be indicators of efficiency of public hygiene system.

Connectivity

Easy accessibility of villages by good roads plus the proliferation of health centres to reduce the distance travelled to get to one, contribute towards betterment of health.

Good connectivity also ensures more visits by sectors and health workers as well as mobile dispensary.

Government Expenditure

Government expenditure on drugs, physical facilities, extension work and special programmes like family planning and school feeding directly influence the health status of the block.

Local Leadership

Adoption of health services and programmes by the accepted leaders of the region facilitates acceptance among rest of the population.

Influence of Health

The primary effect of health is on the productivity of labour in agriculture as well as industry, which in turn has a second round effect on per capita income.

Health also affects attendance in educational institutions.

Fig. 13.6 Explains the linkages with other sectors.

Rural Administration

The administrative sector impinges on all other sectors directly and with great importance. It has been asserted that good administration can take care of all other weak linkages in any sector. Below we identify first the general model of rural administration which we have used as our paradigm, and then we specify the abstract parameters to be used in the simulation.

General Model

The apex of the rural administration hierarchy is at the district level—the collector being the highest administrative authority. He has a number of functional specialists supporting him. But here we are confining ourselves to block and lower level administrative machinery.

The block is a unit carved out to facilitate community development work. It is quite possible for a block to coincide with a tehsil in geographical boundaries.

When a block is initially formed it begins a life of eleven years. It receives funds and has complement of personnel depending on its 'stage' of development. There are three stages–a pre-extension stage in the first year, stage I in the following five years and stage II in the final five years.

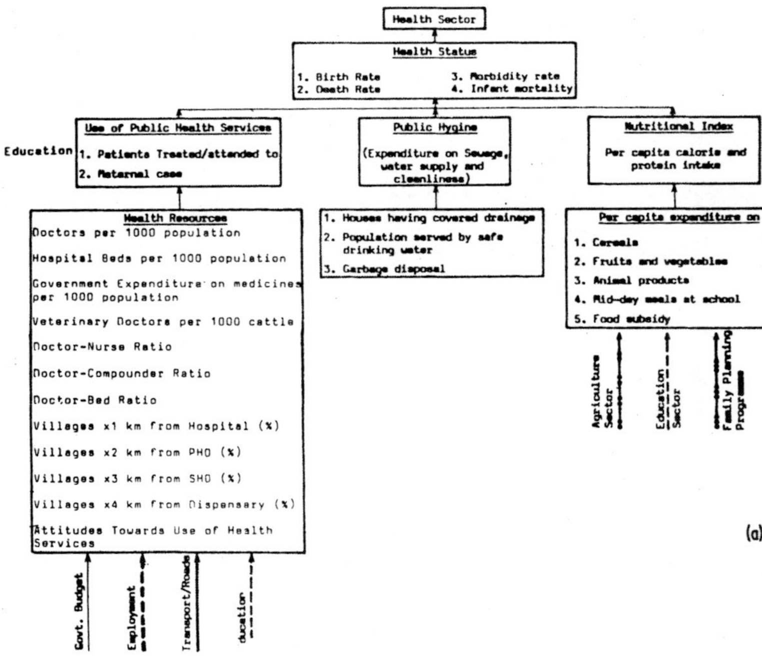

Fig. 13.6

During the pre-extension stage a few of the personnel are deployed to do initial survey work and start agricultural demonstration in the villages. When the block enters Stage I a period of intensive development ensues. The full complement of community development personnel works to ensure that panchayats, village schools, village co-operatives and statutory organizations at the block and district levels are established and begin to function well. During Stage II the responsibility for rural development is gradually handed over to these organizations so that central financial assistance can be withdrawn.

The various functionaries at block level and their involvement with different sectors of the model are as follows:

Block Development Officer is the controlling authority at the block level and reports to the collector or sometimes to the sub-divisional officer. B.D.O. does not have a specific sectoral responsibility but is responsible for the objectives, methods and contents of the various programmes undertaken. He guides the work of the other staff and is responsible for proper utilization of funds at his disposal. He is responsible for building up stocks of necessary equipment, for arranging proper storage and maintaining the supply lines.

Extension officers: There are generally eight–one each for:

Agriculture	
Animal husbandry	Agriculture sector
Rural engineering	Agriculture & Road sectors
Social education	
Programme for women & children	Education & Health sectors
Co-operatives	Agriculture and Industry sector
Rural industries	Industry sector
Panchayats	Administrative liaison

In health sector there is the Medical Officer at the Primary Health Centre.

They assist and advise the B.D.O. in all matters concerning their specialities. They supply knowledge and data to the village people and various organizations. They try to educate the people in the use of new technology and clear their doubts regarding it. They also help the village people in getting external help or supplies or financial aid.

Gram Sevak (Village Level Worker): Gram Sevak is the lowest rung of the administration hierarchy. He is a jack of all trades. His functions include education, information, supply of service and organization in all the sectors. He reports directly to the B.D.O.

Panchayati Raj: There is a parallel administrative machinery in the rural system designated as *Panchayati Raj*. The objective is to bring democratic government down to the village level.

It is a 3-tier (Zilla Parishad, Panchayat Samiti, Gram Panchayat) organically linked system. In terms of importance *Panchayat Samiti* is the linchpin and Zilla Parishad is an advisory and co-ordinating body without executive powers (except in Maharashtra—where *Zilla Parishad* is the executive body).

Zilla Parishad operates at the district level.

Panchayat Samiti: It is a statutory body at the block level having a term of three to five years. It consists of:

(i) All the sarpanches of the Panchayats under it,
(ii) Local MLAs,
(iii) Co-opted members (women, Scheduled Castes, Scheduled Tribes).

There might be some other members nominated by the State government or the collector. These members elect a pradhan from among themselves.

B.D.O. is the chief executive officer for Panchayat Samiti and his staff functions under the jurisdiction of the Samiti.

The Panchayat Samiti's activities, viz., community development, agriculture and animal husbandry, Health and sanitation, education, communications, co-operatives, cottage industries, etc., cut across all sectoral boundaries.

Samitis approve Panchayats' budgets and provide them supervision and assistance. The concept "fund of political goodwill" operates as a brake or accelerator at the stage when programmes require *Panchayat Samiti* support and popular participation.

Gram Panchayats: They are elective statutory bodies at village level. Average number of members in each panchayat is 15 to 20. There is one sarpanch, eight to ten panches, and 3 to 4 co-opted members (women, Scheduled Castes). Panchayats have functions similar to the samitis. In fact, panchayats are field units of Panchayat Samitis.

Critique

This description has been of things as they should be. But often it has been observed that the administration has failed to deliver the goods.

Representation of Administration in the Simulation

Discussed upon various studies, we have identified two critical variables on which efficient implementation of policies depends.

(a) *Efficient working team*: Putting together an effective team involves appropriate selection, rigorous training and motivating factors like good pay and career plans. In the model two parameters have been defined to represent the team performance.

   (i) *Composition of the team*: It is defined in terms of numerical strength of the team and its completeness, which denotes whether the team has all the skills needed for implementation.
   (ii) *Efficiency of the team*: It depends on the money spent and on the duration of training imparted. It also involves a subjective measure of motivation which can be taken as proportionate to economic rewards.

The interaction of the composition and efficiency gives us a multiplier which acts on the inputs (money, materials) and affects the resultant benefits.

(b) *Dissemination of Information*: The rural masses have to be informed and educated for optimum utilisation of facilities already existing and new development schemes.

This process of education is considered to be a draft on the manpower resources or conversely an increase in the quantity of inputs because it requires use of money, manpower (extension workers) and materials. The medium of education can be any combination of mass communication media, extension workers, specialized demonstrations and training programmes.

14

Spatial Integration of Area Development Plans*

What is Spatial Planning?

A REALISTIC planning exercise should have three essential dimensions, i.e., economic, social and spatial. It is not enough to say which sectors should develop and to what extent; what is equally important is to tell who should benefit from the development and to what extent. In other words, planning development should lead not only to an improvement in income measured in average or absolute terms but also to progressive reduction in the disparities in per capita and areal incomes. Wide differences in the earning capacities of urban and rural areas and populations, industrial and agricultural areas and populations, and socially privileged and under-privileged populations must be progressively reduced.

The equity and distributive aspects of planning did not receive the attention, they ought to have, in the earlier stages of planning largely because of the desire of the underdeveloped countries to catch up with the developed ones in economic growth, as fast as possible, and the important assumption that economic growth automatically benefits the people in the long run. Experience of these countries, however, indicates that this need not always be so. In most countries, notwithstanding the high rate of economic growth disparities in income and production capacities increased because modern technology and production processes tend to favour those who had the intellectual, organizational, and financial capacity to utilise them best. Those who were most illiterate, had poor economic base and were slow in adopting themselves

* This chapter is largely based on a report of Service Planning brought out by Ford Foundation, New Delhi.

to the changing circumstances and modern methods of production benefited least.

Had such under-privileged people been few, the developing countries could ignore them. They could have rationalised this by saying: "the society must pay for economic growth". It, however, so happens that such people form a large group; in some countries they form a majority. If this group is ignored, national development would have no meaning to them. A small minority would reap the fruits of development; economic differences would widen; social tensions would increase; and the orderly development of the national economy would be jeopardized. It is, therefore important that planning should aim at not only rapid economic growth but also better distribution of the fruits of economic growth inter-personally as well as inter-regionally and areally.

Disparities in socio-economic development manifest themselves in two ways: inter-personal and inter-regional (or inter-areal). Often the two go together. Inhabitants of backward areas are relatively poorer than those of forward areas. Spatial planning attempts to create conditions for the poorer areas and regions to catch up with the richer areas and regions. Where inter-personal disparities in economic and social development are significant, spatial planning is oriented to the poorer sections of the society within the framework of overall areal or regional development goals.

Spatial Organization

To understand spatial planning, one should first understand the spatial organization of national economy and human activities. Spatial organization means the functional organisation of a given set of activities in space. We can appreciate this better when we fly at an altitude of, say, 30,000 feet. From that elevation, we see a number of nodes: cities, towns, villages, etc. We see them linked with each other by a network of communication lines radiating from each of the nodes. The networks consist of railways, highways, etc. If we fly at a still lower level, we see more details of the nodes and networks. The larger nodes specialise in activities which are not space consuming such as factories, commercial establishments, etc. The smaller nodes specialize in space-consuming activities such as agriculture, mining, etc. The intermediate nodes such as small towns have a mixed activity pattern. We also notice that network linkages weaken as the size of nodes decreases so that some of the tiny nodes inhabited by a few people and located in resourceless, poor areas have no or extremely poor linkages.

What binds the various nodes with each other is the network of flow of people, goods and services. Larger nodes attract consumer goods and industrial raw materials. In return, they send out finished products and render a variety of other services to the smaller nodes.

The amount of interaction among various nodes depends on their relative productive capacities and the surplus of goods and income they generate. The nodes which have no surplus have limited interaction. Those having surplus have a relatively more interaction. The area of interaction of a node is often referred to as hinterland or the zone of influence. Urban geographers call it urban field.

The networks, the nodal activities and the flows together constitute spatial organization. The spatial organization as seen at a particular time cannot be seen in the same state again. It is always changing. Each birth of a baby, each investment in the factory or farm, each improvement in communication, and each new input in transportation changes the organization. Many of these changes are not perceptible to us because, taken individually, they are minute. Cumulatively, they, however, force the spatial system to re-adjust itself to a new situation. New cities come into being; villages are transformed into towns; many communities disappear, small farms become large, crop patterns change and new communication lines give a new pattern of linkages. All this happens in response to the decision of the people to locate themselves and their activities at some, but not other, places.

Spatial Structure

The arrangement of nodes networks and associated activities in space in relation to each other is called spatial structure. Each country or region has its own unique spatial structure. It has resulted from the past decisions of individuals and governments. Economically developed countries have one type of spatial structure; the under-developed countries have another type; and those in between have a third type. The typology is, however, not as simple as given above. In fact, one can think of a continuum of spatial structures from highly polarized to highly dispersed. Each country or region can be identified on this continuum.

A closer study of the continuum reveals that the highly developed countries have evolved spatial structures which are different from those evolved by the less developed countries. It happens because of the inter-dependence between socio-economic development and spatial structures.

The above analysis leads us to conclude that:

(a) Planning should be sectoral-cum-spatial.
(b) Each country or region has to evolve its own organization and structure of space to meet the specific goals and objectives of planning.
(c) Developing countries with a highly polarized spatial economy have to evolve a spatial structure which difuses the benefits of planned development to those who are poor and under-privileged.

Spatial Planning

Spatial planning is the sum total of the concepts, approaches, methods and techniques of evolving a desired spatial organization and structure. It is often used as coterminus with regional planning. Theoretically speaking, space is a dynamic and open system. Unlike a region, it has no boundaries. Spatial planning is an exercise to determine the allocation of sectoral resources in places and areas in a way that:

(a) Sectoral investments give highest social and economic returns and maximum support to each other.
(b) Productive activities and social facilities are available to all those who need and deserve.
(c) Differences in incomes and welfare among the people and areas are reduced, if not eliminated.
(d) A spatial structure conducive to planned development is evolved.

It may be recalled that spatial organizations and structures of human activities are determined by the nodes, the networks and the flows among the nodes through the networks. The efficiency of a spatial structure depends upon the location, rise and distribution of the nodes, the shape and density of the networks, and the quantity, quality and direction of the flows. The task of spatial planning is to analyse the spatial structures and to generate structural changes in them to facilitate planned development.

How are the structural changes brought about? To answer this question let us take a hypothetical case of a country which has decided to invest Rs. 1,000 million on health services to cover the total population of the country. This country has 10 urban centres and 1,000 small villages spread over in space rather randomly. The economic condition of the rural population is rather poor and is based on subsistence agriculture. The links between the urban and rural places are weak and are maintained by a set of intermediaries who collect the surplus rural products in small bits at a subsistence price and transport the same to the urban centres. They also carry the urban products to the tiny villages and sell them at a pre-determined price.

Now the question is: How and where to invest the funds to carry the benefits of health services to the rural population? It is obvious that the health plan should attempt to develop rural health centres with resident doctor and supporting staff. Where should such health centres be built so that they should be easily accessible to the people? The spatial planner would develop distance norms or standards and prescribe the number of health centres required to serve all or a maximum number of people. Then, he would suggest the vertical linkage between the health centres and better equipped hospitals so that specialized medical service can be secured.

The spatial planner would thus tell: Where to locate these various levels of health services? What norms or standards about distance and population should be adopted? But his problems would not be over with these. If it were only the question of health services, the problem would have been easy. He has to carry out the same exercise for all other sectors such as education, agriculture, commerce, etc. If he decides to locate each facility independent of the other, he would be using the limited resources at so many places and would find it difficult to match the changes in the spatial structure economy with the planned growth of the economy.

Thus one of the important tasks of spatial planning is to integrate the spatially dual economies through successive locational decisions leading to the development of a spatially balanced social and economic structure. Next is to identify the economic activities, which can be located in space to help fill the gaps in the nodal hierarchy and generate greater flow of goods and services among the places. Thirdly, spatial planning attempts to evolve a system of transportation and communication network which facilitates the expected flow. And finally, spatial planning specifies the institutional infrastructure including administrative and planning which can help build a well structured space economy.

Distance Standards for Services

For different services and activities, there should be different distance standards. Establishing distance standards which are realistic in the light of the local and regional conditions is an essential step in spatial planning specially for the rural areas. This must be done for every area or region to be planned with respect to each kind of service or activity mentioned in the plan.

Let us take the example of education. What is the range of distance from each children can be drawn for primary schooling? One may say, that the school should be located where the children live. But, what to do if the rural settlements are small and none of them can singly provide enough children for the school? Or, if enough resources–financial or human–are not available to provide a primary school to every village? One of the several small villages would have to be selected for provision of school. If the school is so located that most of the children would have to walk for, say, 10 km to reach it, it would not be efficient because the objective is to provide primary education to every child within a walking distance.

India has made primary education compulsory. To make this policy a success, primary education must be accessible to each child of school-going age without impairing the effective functioning of the school, i.e., there are enough children within a radius set by the planners. Let us say 2 km radius can be taken as a standard for primary school. If possible, it should be less, but, barring very exceptional situations, it should not exceed 2 km. Now we will call 2 km as the distance standard for primary schools. We would then take up each activity and set distance standard, remembering that within a given activity, say education, we will have to set distance standards for primary, middle, secondary, college, etc., levels separately.

Setting Population Threshold Standards

Along with the distance standard, a population standard has also to be evolved. For each activity, there should be a minimum population in its catchment area carved out by the distance standard. For example, a primary school should have at least 100 children, i.e., 25 children in each class. If we take 15 per cent of the population being in the age group of 6-11, and if we assume that every child in the primary school age-group should or would attend school, there should be at least 800 persons in the catchment area of the school. The required population will increase, as the strength of the school in terms of children enrolled increases. Thus we arrive at a population standard.

Conflict between Distance and Population Standards

After distance and population standards are set for different levels of each activity, the two should be empirically tested to determine their applicability to different situations. Population density in some areas or regions may be so low that sufficient number of people may not live within the distance standard to make the offering of a particular service feasible. Or there may be too many people within the radius of the standard distance. In such circumstances, necessary adjustments would have to be made between the conflicting standards. The nature of this compromise will depend upon considerations such as future development possibilities, possibility of improving transport impediments, possibility of providing mobile service, even on a selective basis, etc.

The conflict between the distance and population standards raises the question of equity *versus* efficiency in spatial planning. If equity expressed as a maximum travel distance, is the governing factor, then the efficiency question is: What is the minimum number of places required to put all places in the area of operation within that distance of a centre and where should the services be located? If the efficiency governs in terms of minimum population base, then the equity question is: where should a given number of service be located so that the maximum level distance from all the places selected to the most remote villages they serve is least but that around each place the minimum number of people necessary to support the facilities are present? Spatial planner has to resolve these conflicts.

Setting the Hierarchy of Services and Activities

Another problem that the planners have in spatial planning is the hierarchy of services and activities. Certain services are needed by the people too frequently to be located at long distance; e.g., primary school, health clinic, extension agent, grocery store, agricultural marketing. Some are not needed so frequently such as specialised hospitals, colleges, wholesale market, etc. We set the distance and population standards for various services and activities, keeping the hierarchy of services and activities in view.

It is, therefore, important that the services and activities to be located to meet the equity and efficiency criteria are classified and standards for each class are worked out.

Each class of the educational services requires a separate set of standards. It should be emphasized that the classification is illustrative. For each country and region, different hierarchies would have to be worked out for each service.

Constructing the Hierarchy of Settlements and Services

An important problem in spatial planning is the determination and construction of a hierarchy of settlements which can provide an efficient framework for location planning. By hierarchy of settlements, we mean the order in which settlements stand with respect to each other in terms of population and activity. An idealized settlement hierarchy tree is illustrated in Figure 14.1. In this Figure, the first level settlement is the most important settlement. In its area of influence, there can be several second level settlements (for want of space, only one is shown here). There are six settlements of third level and each of these has several settlements in the area of its influence.

The hierarchic ordering of settlements pre-supposes that higher the place of a settlement in the hierarchy, the higher the levels of functions or activities located there. It also pre-supposes that the functions, present in a place of lower order, would be present in places of next higher order. For example, if there is a primary school in the lowest order settlement, there would be primary schools in all settlements of third, second and first orders. Starting from the top, if the first order has a hospital, the second order may have a health centre, the third order, a small clinic, and the fourth order, only a health visitor.

The hierarchy is based on the size of population. It can also be based on the number and the levels of functions. The first level would ordinarily have largest population. It would also have the highest levels of various functions. Thus the order of a settlement in the hierarchy is indicative of the level of services and activities it has or should have.

At this point, one may ask the question: Why construct the hierarchy? Why is it important?

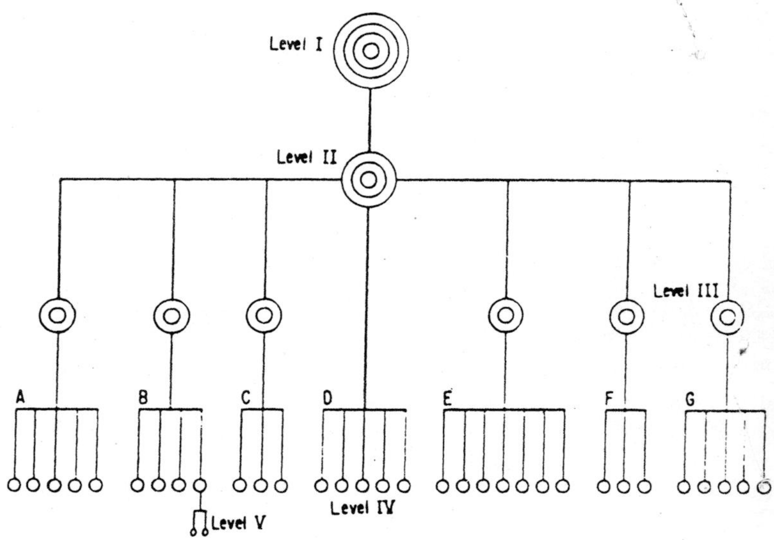

Fig. 14.1: Ideal Hierachical Settlement Organisation Tree Structure

The answer is rather simple. We do not construct hierarchy. Hierarchy of settlements is already there. We only identify what already exists and give a scientific base for it and then use it for planning purposes. Some human activities are space consuming. Agriculture is the most important among them. Such activities are generally dispersed. Most other activities are not space consuming to the extent agriculture is. These activities produce goods in large quantities or they serve a large number of people. Such activities are localized at few places. For example, steel plants have to be located only at a few places, similarly, a large specialized hospital or a wholesale market has to be located only at a few places. But a small clinic or a retail shop can be located at several places. So the hierarchy in human activities already exists. This together, with the population, gives rise to the hierarchy of settlements.

An ideal hierarchy of settlements is given in Fig. 14.1. When we put it horizontally, we get a picture as given in Fig. 14.2. In these figures, the second level centre serves six smaller centres, let us say small towns. And each of the small towns serves so many villages. The people meet their primary needs in the villages, for secondary needs they go to third level centres; for tertiary needs, to the second level centres, and for the most infrequent quaternary needs to the first level centres.

Now, let us consider a situation in which the third level centres do not exist. People would either go to the second level centre or they would remain deprived of the secondary needs. An inefficient hierarcy of settlements has missing gaps like this. Spatial planning attempts to fill the gaps.

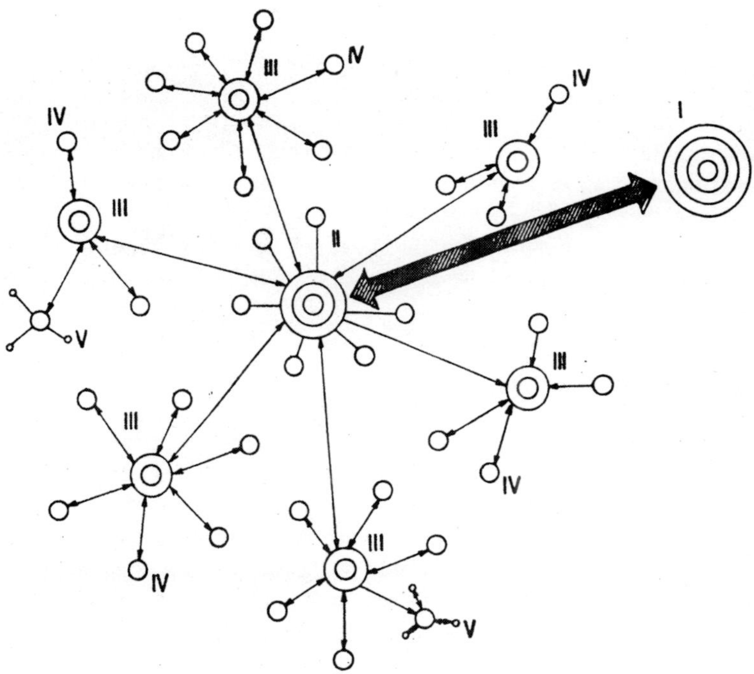

I. GROWTH CENTRE
II. GROWTH POINT
III SFRVICE CENTRE
IV. SUBSIDIARY SERVICE CENTRE (Central Village)
V. VILLAGES

Fig. 14.2

Population as a Centrality Index

The role, a particular place plays in relation to other places, as a centre of services, facilities, goods and social interaction, is referred to as centrality. The indicator of the centrality is called centrality index. Centrality and thus the hierarchical rank of a given settlement in a region is a function of its development. The simplest method is to take population as an index assuming that its magnitude correlates well with its development.

After noting down the population of each settlement of the area under study, the settlements may be grouped together for typological purposes using one or the other criterion of grouping. The census classification of towns is based on this principle. We, however, find certain problems with this type of classification. We do not take into account the functions the settlement, falling in each category, perform. Two places with same or approximately same population may not be equally important. One may have several service functions to serve a large population living in surrounding villages. The other may be just a subsistence farming community with none or much lower level of functions.

In spatial planning we, therefore, rarely take population alone as the criterion for constructing settlement hierarchy.

Institutional Scalogram

Another method of arriving at a centrality score is derived from Guttman Scalogram technique. This method uses the presence or absence of institutions providing services, economic activities, etc., as the criterion for classification. This method is superior to the first one, specially when the objective of the exercise is to select places which can provide various services to the rural population within a given range of distance. But in a situation where institutional information is not readily available, the first index method (population) can be used as a basis for constructing hierarchy of settlements.

The methodology for constructing a scalogram is as follows:

Step 1: Using a large sheet of paper, list all the settlements in order of their population on the left hand side and list all the institutional facilities of significance in a row at the top. Significant institutions are those which are found in various settlements and are permanently located. The format is given in Fig. 14.3, which refers to a scalogram prepared for Kazerun Shahrestan of Iran.

Step 2: Write down for each settlement the number of institutions present in the appropriate column.

Step 3: After step 2 is completed, sum the types of institutions and number of different institutions regardless the type for each settlement. In our example (Fig. 14.3) total number of types of institutions in Zhesht is 20 and the total number of units of all institutions is 78.

Step 4: At the bottom of the table give the number of places having each type of institution in the appropriate column. And below this row give the total number of units of each institution in each column. For illustration see Fig. 14.3.

Step 5: In the extreme right hand side of the table rank all settlements in order of the total number of units of various institutions given in the preceding column. The place with the highest number gets first rank. At the bottom of the table rank all the institutions in ascending order. The institution with largest number of units in all the settlements gets first rank. When all five steps have been completed, first stage in the construction of the scalogram is over. One can treat this as final or go to the next step. It is optional. Before we go to the next stage, let us return to step 5. What happens when two places get the same rank on the basis of the number of units that the institutions present? In such case we look at the population column. The settlement with larger population gets the superior rank. This is one way to break the tie.

Step 6: After completing the ranking of settlements and institutions, as stated above, the institutional scalogram for the area will show circles around the number and types of institutions. A pattern of hierarchy can be visually seen from this. Now reorder the settlements in column one of the table, so that least number of holes (zeros) appear in row of the first settlement. The number of holes (zeros) will increase as one moves to the second, third and so on settlements. This shows the hierarchy of settlements much better.

Step 7: Repeat step 6 for institutions also. Add the number of settlements having each type of institution. Write this at the bottom of the column. Next add the units of each institution present in each of the settlements and write below in another row. In the last row, rank the institutions. The first rank goes to the institution having largest number of units in all the settlements. This institution is needed most.

Fig. 14.3

	Services → / Places ↓ Name	Pop.	*	•EDUCATION Nursery	Primary	High School	Secondary	Technical	University	HEALTH	ADMINISTRATION	COMMERCE	TOTAL	RANK
	1	2	3	4	5	6	7	8	9					
1.				1										
2.														
3.														
4.				1										
5.														
6.														
7.				1										
8.														
9.				1										
10.														
11.														
12.														
13.				1										
14.														
15.														
Total				5										

3. No. of types of ins tion
4. No. of units of institutions

KK/90

When all these steps are completed, the institutional scalogram is ready. It gives the hierarchy of the settlements, as well as the hierarchy of institutions. We interpret the scalogram in following way:

(a) The higher level settlements have lower demand for institutions which get higher score in the ranking;
(b) The lower level settlements such as villages have higher demand for institutions which get higher score in the ranking;
(c) The institutions getting higher ranks are those which people need closer to their place of residence; and
(d) The institutions getting lower ranks are those which are less frequently needed and hence can be located at longer distances.

If we decide to evolve a three tier hierarchy of places for rural development, we should be able to select the places which can qualify for each of these levels using the rank of settlements. The rank gives candidate settlements for rural choice. The actual choice will be made after taking the distance standard for each service and activity incorporated in the scalogram and the population of the area to be served.

Uses of Hierarchical Organization

To this point, the concern has been to find spatial patterns of centres that can satisfy a given distance or other standards. In addition to the compromises often required to reconcile conflicting standards for a particular activity, a second kind of compromise is often required when different activities with different standards are to be located in the same area with the proviso that the location for one activity should be chosen from the centres in which the other activity is to be located. This "hierarchical" organisation of activities has the following advantages:

(a) It is convenient and efficient for the consumer because it enables the satisfaction of several different needs on the same trip out of a village;
(b) It reduces the amount of public transportation required to connect villages to facilities because, from among the many possible transport links between places, those few links connecting villages to their local service centre and connecting the service centres to more important places will be recognized by all to be

the priority links where public transportation facilities should be provided;

(c) It reduces the length of roads that require improvement before every village is connected to places having facilities to which they need access;

(d) It economizes on the cost of providing services to the facilities themselves because these costs can often be shared among several facilities located in the same place. The cost, for example, of providing banking service facilities is obviously reduced if they are grouped together in few places rather than scattered among many;

(e) It enables a more economical and effective monitoring of the regulated activities;

(f) It facilitates the exchange of information and qualified personnel between related activities; and

(g) It focuses development efforts for a region on a few places with superior locations and resources and this increases the likelihood that some of the places will spontaneously generate additional activities catering to the needs of their hinterland region.

The disadvantages of such a hierarchical organization of activities is that the distance standards and other requirements of individual activities must be adjusted and shaped at discrete levels. Frequently, individual standards must either be stretched to fit into the level of place or shortened to fit into a lower level set of places. In the first case, the maximum distance of villages from their closest centres with the required activity may be unacceptably long and, in the second case, the number of facilities that would be required might be more than investment funds permit or that can economically exist.

Graphical Methods of Service Centre Planning

Circle Method

In this section we propose to demonstrate one of the two graphical methods of selecting various levels of service centres from amongst the several settlements which qualify for selection. We get the qualified settlements from a scalogram.

Step 1: Prepare at least ten copies of a working map of the area of planning extended in all directions beyond its boundaries to include settlements of 500 or more population located within a distance approximately equal to its dimension in that direction. Unless the area is extremely long in one or more directions the map should be prepared on a scale of 1:200,000. All maps scale show the transportation system, settlements and major features such as rivers, slopes, forests, lakes, swamp canals, etc. The exact locations of settlements having latest populations of more than 500 are crucial; those with smaller populations may be approximate. It is preferable to show all settlements located in the planning area, big and small, irrespective of population size. But outside the planning area, only settlements with 500 + population are to be marked.

Step 2: Prepare a list of all settlements shown on the map ranked in the order of their latest populations. In three adjoining columns note the actual population of each settlement, the number of types of institutions found in each settlement, and the number of units of these institutions in each settlement. Column four need only be completed for settlements having more than 500 population.

15

Project Formulation and Evaluation— I: Cost-benefit Analysis*

COST benefit analysis is a very useful tool of analysis with wide-ranging application. The basic notion in this analysis is very simple. If a certain project is to be undertaken we need to use resources which are scarce. In other words, we cannot do everything that we would like to because the resources that we require are scarce whereas the things we would like to do are practically innumerable. Secondly, resources are not only scarce, they have alternative uses. Every resource can be used for more than one purpose. Therefore, how do we decide whether a certain project should be undertaken?

Next, we cannot undertake a project unless it is feasible in the sense that it will yield an appropriate return. That is, no project is worth undertaking unless its benefits exceed its costs. Further, if we decide to undertake one particular project (call it A) it means that we have to give up another project (call it B). If we do A, we lose the benefits of B. These benefits which we lose really are the cost of doing A.

At this point it is convenient to become familiar with a term often used in economics, namely, opportunity cost. Opportunity cost is the cost of not doing a particular thing. Suppose we have a choice among doing A, B, C and D with limited resources. The choice finally lies between A and B. We decide on A. B is the nearest alternative but we forego it. B is the opportunity cost of A.

If this principle behind cost-benefit analysis is so simple, one may wonder why it is to be treated at great length. The fact is that there are plenty of problems connected with the measurement of costs and benefits. Precisely what should be included under costs and benefits is

---

* By V.K. Natraj, Institute of Development Studies, University of Mysore, Manasa Gangotri, Mysore-6.

a highly controversial matter. Secondly, how they should be quantified and measured is another tricky issue. Unless we have some common denominator, it would be impossible for us to compare two alternative projects. What we shall do is to consider the main principles behind what items are germane to a particular technique known as the discounted measure of estimating the return from a project.

Basic Issues

Definition of a Project

Generally, the nature of the project being analysed is clear. But sometimes complications arise. Let us assume, we are analysing project A. The goods produced by this project may be related to some other goods, say those produced by project B. Take another example: there is a river valley authority responsible for a long stretch of river. If a dam is constructed at a point upstream, this will affect the operations of existing or potential dams downstream. In all such cases, in calculating the costs and benefits of a particular project, allowances must be made for these side-effects. In Jargon we say that where there are strong relationships on either the supply side or the demand side, allowances must be made for them in cost-benefit calculations.

Externalities

In the case of most projects, there are costs and benefits which accrue not to the persons/authority responsible for the project but to a third party. Let us take a hypothetical illustration. A State government builds a reservoir upstream along an inter-State river. As a result the lower riparian State has to go in for more dredging. This has to be taken into account while calculating cost and benefit. The reason is that in this case the action of the upper riparian State has led to an alteration in the physical production possibilities of the lower riparian State from the river. Wherever this happens, the external effects of a particular project are taken into account.

In some cases, the external effects operate not directly but through the prices of products or of factors of production. Assume that a highway is improved. One result of this is that garages and restaurants along the highway become more profitable. They begin to employ more workers. They pay higher rents to the landlords of their premises.

These benefits are not taken into account. They are not credited to the investment on the highway. The increase in profitability is a result of the fact that more journeys are now performed on the improved highway. It would be double counting if the extra trips plus their efforts are taken into consideration. It needs hardly be stressed that it is never easy to make this distinction and there will always be borderline cases.

Secondary Benefits

What has been said above would indicate that pecuniary (monetary) spillovers (side-effects) are generally not taken into account. But there are some cases where it is held, they should be included in the estimation of benefits. As usual we shall use an illustration to grasp this point. There is an irrigation project. On completion, this leads to an increase in grain production. The increased output leads to greater activity by merchants, transport companies, etc. It leads to an increase in their profits. Should these secondary benefits be taken into account? One view is that these should be but not certain other secondary benefits (known as induced secondary benefits) which arise from extra profits made out of activities. Some authors are critical of this view. The most acceptable compromise is this: if the output of a project has a market value (irrigation leads to increase in foodgrain production and this has a market value) then the problem is somewhat simplified. In our example, the worth of irrigation water to farmers is worked out as follows: The water helps increase grain production. The worth of the water to the farmers is the excess of the value of the increased output (made possible by the water) over the cost of the increase in the other inputs of the farmers. This is because when water is made available, the farmers will also have to incur extra cost over other inputs.

Project Life

Estimating the life of a project is another complex issue. This problem is discussed again below with reference to the discount rate. It should be noted that estimating the length of life is a subjective process and depends upon changes in technology, emergence of competitive products, changes in demand for the output of the projects, etc.

We shall now turn to an examination of the selection of values in cost-benefit analysis.

Selection of Values

If costs and benefits are to be compared, they must be valued. The common denominator for valuing our commodities is money. The price of commodity is its value expressed in terms of money. Therefore, if costs and benefits are to be valued, it means that we must find the proper prices at which they should be compared.

Prices Reflect Values

As mentioned above, the price of a commodity reflects (or should reflect) its value. The problem is that due to a number of reasons the market price of a commodity may not reflect its value. One of the reasons is that prices accurately reflect values only when the market is perfect or near perfect. There is a whole body of literature in economics dealing with perfect markets. A perfect market is highly competitive, it has many buyers and sellers. In such a market, every commodity is priced at its marginal value product. All that this means is that the price of every commodity will reflect the value which the last unit of that commodity contributes to production. For example, the price of labour (wages) will be exactly equal to the contribution made by the last worker employed to the output. If a factor of production can earn more in some other activity, its price will rise and it will be attracted to that activity. Prices not only reflect values but allocate scarce resources among competing uses. The price mechanism (also referred to as the market mechanism) is supposed to perform this function. In a situation where the country is in "equilibrium", the marginal value product, the price of the commodity and its opportunity cost–what can be earned by the commodity in the next best alternative use–all these will be equal. In such a situation, resources are optimally allocated. Nothing would be gained by transferring any resource from one use to another

In actual fact, such perfect markets rarely exist. Therefore, prices do not accurately reflect value. For example, in an under-developed country, the price of capital (the rate of interest) may not truly reflect its scarcity. Hence entrepreneurs may use more capital than is actually warranted. Although we know that often prices do not accurately reflect values, we cannot abandon prices, that is, market prices altogether. There is an alternative to market prices known as shadow prices or accounting prices. That again is a highly controversial matter and economists are sharply divided on their use. In most cases, it is better to find the appropriate market price rather than an alternative (shadow) price. Perhaps what is required is an attempt to find the correct market price rather than replace it with some other notionally mere accurate value. This is recommended although we realise that prices are often proved to be inaccurate.

The next problem to tackle is this; if you decide to use market price, you are still confronted with a choice among several alternatives such as point of first sale, farm, gate price, etc. Let us consider each of these briefly.

Point of First Sale

The point of first sale is, under normal conditions, the best price to use. If the market for the commodity in question is relatively competitive and if the market price can be accepted as a reasonably accurate reflection of value, then the price at the point of first sale can be taken as a good measure of this value of output.

Intermediate Goods

In many productive activities there are intermediate goods. These are used as inputs and are not freely sold such as irrigation water. This means its price is not determined by market forces but by administrative decision. In this case, the irrigation system cannot be separated from the production which it helps. If the separation is tried it would become essential to determine the value of irrigation water–not an easy job. Therefore, what is generally done is that the value of the agricultural production at the point of first sale is taken as the basis for calculating the benefit from irrigation.

Farm Gate Price

This is the price which the farmer gets when he sells his output at the boundary of his farm. In an agricultural project which is exclusively production-oriented, the farm gate price is the correct price to be considered. The product will no doubt acquire additional value when it is processed and marketed. But this is to be attributed to the marketing and processing service and not to the project itself. However, if the project includes marketing, we will then be concerned with the farm gate price, as well as the market price.

There is one difficulty that must be considered. It is not always possible to determine the farm gate price. In many cases, the only prices available may be those which include marketing and/or other services which are not to be included in the project proper.

Another complication is introduced by taxes and subsidies. A subsidy may be given in order to encourage local production and reduce imports. In some cases, a tax may be levied on exports. In all such cases, the price will not accurately reflect the true value of the product.

Seasonal Fluctuation

Most agricultural commodities are subject to seasonal fluctuation. This raises a question. At which point, in the seasonal fluctuation, should the price be decided? The answer is to choose the farm gate harvest price at the peak of the harvest season. This will most likely be the lowest price during the cycle. The justification for this choice is as follows. During the cycle, prices will rise but at least a part of the increase in prices will be due to factors other than the farmers' productive activity. However, this ignores another important problem. Farmers are often forced to sell their output immediately after harvest in order to meet debts. In such a case, it is justifiable to select a higher price than the farm gate harvest price at the peak of the season.

Grades

Agricultural commodities are often graded. Prices vary with grades. In picking the correct price for project analysis, decisions regarding grades are to be taken. Two solutions are possible here: one is to assume that even after a certain project is undertaken, farmers will produce almost the same quantity as before. But, in many cases, the very purpose of a project is to improve the quality of the product. In this case, the proper procedure is to select the average price expected for the improved quality to be produced.

Future Prices

During the lifetime of a project, commodity prices may change. The question is how to predict future prices. It is best to assume that past prices can be taken as a guide to future prices. This is reasonable since the likelihood of a change in relative prices is not very great.

Inflation

This is a severe problem specially at present when most countries are experiencing quite severe inflationary trends. It is most realistic to as sume that inflation will continue. Further, it is assumed that all prices, both on the cost side and the benefit side, will rise uniformly by the same proportion. This means that their relative values are not altered. Therefore, as the future money prices will rise, we can value all future prices at present levels. A difficulty will arise only when some prices will rise more than others. In such a case, the relative structure of prices will be altered. For instance, inflation might effect costs more than benefits. In this situation, it is advisable to assume constant prices for all items except for those which will be differentially affected by inflation.

Accounting (shadow) Prices

It has been mentioned above that markets are often imperfect. This is especially true of under-developed countries. Markets may be imperfect due to interference by middlemen (institutional factors), administrative controls, monopoly control, lack of communication regarding prices between producers and sellers, and many other reasons. As a result, market prices may not reflect accurately the values of commodities. To overcome this, the use of accounting or shadow prices is recommended.

What are accounting prices? They are prices which would prevail if the market were in equilibrium. In other words, an accounting price is that price which would bring the supply of and the demand for a commodity into equality. As mentioned above the subject of accounting prices bristles with much controversy. But it is enough to note that it is difficult to estimate the accounting price of any commodity. This is specially so because the price of a commodity, say, rice, is influenced not only by the supply and demand conditions in that market but also by conditions in other related markets, say, substitutes–like wheat. It is extremely difficult to possess full knowledge of the whole matrix of prices; economists generally ignore institutional and social factors but these are important in under-developed countries.

There is a view that accounting prices rather than market prices are useful with regard to agricultural products in three areas–foreign exchange, commodities important in world market and unskilled agricultural labour.

Foreign Exchange

In the case of foreign exchange it is advisable to use the rate of exchange which the central planning authority is using. This is necessary because an accounting price for foreign exchange is used only so that inputs are valued properly. If different projects use different accounting prices, the whole purpose would be defeated.

World Market Prices

Generally world markets are more perfect than domestic markets, particularly where the latter are protected. Hence for commodities which enter the world market in a big way, world market prices would be a better guide than domestic market prices.

Labour

In a perfectly competitive market, the price of labour (wages) would be equal to its marginal value product. The Table 15.1 illustrates this.

Table 15.1: Labour Wages and Product Marginal Value

Number of workers	Total number of units produced	Wage per day	Price of product
10	50	Rs. 4	Rs. 2
11	54	do	do
12	57	do	do
13	59	do	do
14	60	do	do

It is seen from the Table 15.1 that as the number of workers increases so does the total production. But each extra worker adds less and less to the total output. The 13th worker adds 2 units to the production. These 2 units fetch a price of Rs. 4 which is exactly equal to the wage of the worker. If the 14th worker is employed he adds only 1 unit to the production. The value is Rs. 2, but he has to be paid a wage of Rs. 4.

Therefore, it does not pay the entrepreneur to hire him. Hence, he will stop at the 13th worker.

This neat little piece of theory does not always work in countries like India, there is a surplus of agricultural labour. The addition of one extra labourer adds nothing to the output. In technical language, the marginal productivity of labour is zero. In such a situation, if the extra labour is removed from agriculture, the output will not fall. These workers could be put to work somewhere else where they make a positive contribution to production. There is no cost involved in this transfer of labour from agriculture to some other occupation. Therefore, in project analysis, in economic terms, the proper price to charge would be zero.

It is extremely difficult to determine the true marginal product of agricultural labour. All that can be said is that in labour-surplus economies it tends to be near zero. There is another problem, however, when surplus workers are taken away from a farm, the output may fall because those left behind do not put in extra work. The point is that when there are extra workers, the required work is being performed by too many people. It does not mean that too much labour is being used. It is that too many workers are putting in the required labour and no one is fully employed. Therefore, those left behind on the farm have to compensate by working harder. Keeping this limitation in mind, agricultural labour may be shadow priced at zero.

Yet another problem here is that agricultural employment is seasonal. Hence, almost everyone can find work during the peak seasons. At such times, the marginal product is certainly not zero. The proper procedure here is to value agricultural labour on an annual basis. This can be determined by multiplying the wage when labour is scarce by the number of days in a year when labour can be considered to be reasonably fully employed. Assume that labour is scarce for 70 days a year and earns Rs. 5 per day. Then the annual wage can be shadow priced at 5 × 70 = Rs. 350. This would be reasonable even when we expect that labour is actually employed for 200 days a year.

In other cases–where there is no disguised unemployment (namely a situation where some people appear to be employed although they do not contribute anything to the output) agricultural labour can be priced at the wage it commands.

Finally, agricultural labour which is currently unemployed or underemployed may improve its position during and after a project has been completed. In such a case, initially shadow price agricultural labour at zero; later shadow price it at half the annual wage. Finally, use the actual wage rate. This system of shadow price is generally applicable to unskilled labour. Skilled labour is normally scarce and, therefore, it is not reasonable to shadow price it at or near zero. It may even be necessary to shadow price it above the prevalent wage to reflect its true scarcity.

Capital

There is a general feeling that capital should be shadow priced because, in underdeveloped countries, its price (rate of interest) does not reflect its true scarcity. Frequently, instead of the actual borrowing rate, the opportunity cost of capital is used as a measure of its value and proposed projects are compared to the opportunity cost of capital.

Measurement of Cost and Benefits

To find out how costs and benefits are to be measured, it would be useful to see the distinction between two major aspects of project analysis–the financial and the economic.

The financial aspect deals primarily with the revenue earning consideration of a project. In financial analysis, we are concerned with whether a project can be financially viable. In this analysis, we always use market prices, never accounting prices.

In economic analysis, we attempt to determine whether a given project is likely to contribute to the development of the economy as a whole. Our attention is focused on finding out if the contribution of the project justifies the use of the required scarce resources.

The basic aim of all cost-benefits analysis is to assess whether a certain project is worth undertaking in the sense that benefits exceed costs. We must, however, caution ourselves against a danger. We should not consider only the benefit-cost ratio as a static entity but should also consider whether extra benefits exceed extra costs. For example, between A and B we may find that A has a higher benefit cost ratio. Yet we may prefer B because its extra benefits clearly exceed its extra costs.

We shall first take up undiscounted measure of project worth:

Undiscounted Measure of Project Worth

Let us take four hypothetical pump irrigation investments to illustrate some of the problems associated with using undiscounted measure to choose among projects Table 15.2 (a), (b), (c), (d). All may be thought of as being more or less alternatives for each other.

Ranking by inspection: Project II is better than project I because with same investment they produce same NVP in two years, but one continues to produce for three years. IV is better than III because it has more of flow earlier in the same time sequence. But is project IV better than project II?

Payback period: It is one of the common rough means of choosing specially if there is high degree of risk. We can rank the four projects as per Table 15.2(b).

Table 15.2a: Four Hypothetical Pump Irrigation Schemes

(in '000 rupees)

Project	Year	Project costs			Gross costs	Gross value of production	Net value of production (NVP)
		Capital items	O & M costs	Production costs			
I	1	20	2	3	25	15	10
	2	—	2	3	5	15	10
	3	—	—	—	—	—	—
	Total	20	4	6	30	30	20
II	1	20	2	3	25	15	10
	2	—	2	3	5	15	10
	3	—	2	3	5	5.972	0.972
	Total	20	6	9	35	35.972	20.972
III	1	20	2	3	25	10	5
	2	—	2	3	5	11	6.5
	3	-	2	3	5	17.5	12
	Total	20	6	9	35	38.5	23.5
IV	1	20	2	3	25	10	5
	2	—	2	3	5	17	12
	3	—	2	3	5	11.5	6.5
	Total	20	6	9	35	38.5	23.5

Table 15.2b: Payback Period

Project	Payback period (years)	Ranking
I	2.0	1
II	2.0	1
III	2.8	4
IV	2.7	3

Note: Payback means return of the capital items, in these cases Rs. 20,000.

Here projects I and II are equal but by inspection we know II is better than I.

This method has two weaknesses:

1. It fails to consider earnings of the payback period;
2. It fails to take into consideration differences in the timing of proceeds.

Proceeds per rupee of outlay: Sometimes, investments can be ranked by the total proceeds divided by the total amount of investment. [Table 15.2 (c) and 15.2 (d)].

Table 15.2c: Total Proceeds Per Rupee of Outlay

Project	Project cost Capital items	Net value of production	Proceeds per rupee of outlay	Ranking
I	20,000	20,000	1.00	4
II	20,000	20,972	1.05	3
III	20,000	23,500	1.18	1
IV	20,000	23,500	1.18	1

By this criterion, projects III and IV receive equal ranking, even though we know by simple inspection that IV is better than III. This method also fails to consider timing.

It also fails to take length of time into account as it is biased towards short-lived investments with high cash proceeds. Project I is better than project II although by inspection project II is better than project I.

Table 15.2d: Average Annual Proceeds Per Rupee of Outlay

Project	Capital items	Total NVP	Average NVP	Average annual proceeds per rupee of outlay	Ranking
I	20,000	20,000	10,000	0.50	1
II	20,000	20,972	6,991	0.35	4
III	20,000	23,500	7,833	0.39	2
IV	20,000	23,500	7,833	0.39	2

Average income on book value of the investment: In this measure of investment worth, the ratio of annual benefits to the book value of assets (after subtracting depreciation) is the criterion (Table 15.3).

Time Value of Money

Every project yields a stream of benefits. The benefits are not yielded just at one particular time but are likely to be spread over a number of years in the future. This problem can be illustrated by a simple example. When we lend money, we expect an interest for lending. Why do we expect interest? First, we are depriving ourselves of the use of that money for consumption purposes for a given period and, therefore, expect a reward. Secondly, we are deprived of the opportunity of using that money for some productive purpose. In other words, we are for going an opportunity of earning an income in the present. We expect to be compensated for this by an interest on the money we lend.

Table 15.3: Average Income on Book Value

Project	Average net value of production	Average depreciation	Average income (proceeds less depreciation)	Average book value (of the depreciation)	Income of book value	Rank
1	2	3	4	5	6	7
I	10,000	10,000	0	10,000	0	4
II	6,991	6,667	324	10,000	3	3
III	7,833	6,667	1166	10,000	12	1
IV	7,833	6,667	1166	10,000	12	1

Note : Timing of profit not accounted adequately.
Col. 6 is percentage of Col. 4 over Col. 5.

Suppose that we lend Rs. 650 to someone who promises to return this after five years at an interest rate of nine per cent. At the end of five years we expect to receive Rs. 1,000. The question is how much that promise is worth to us today. In other words, what is the present worth of Rs. 1,000 five years in the future assuming an interest rate of nine per cent. This is easy to estimate. It can be understood clearly if we first remember how we calculate how much money is due to us at a certain interest after a certain period. If we lend Rs. 650 in 1975 at an interest of nine per cent, we expect to receive in 1980 Rs. 1000. We multiply the amount due each year by 1.09. If we reverse this procedure, we get the present worth. This is shown in Table 15.4.

We can see from Table 15.4 that the present worth of a future income of Rs. 1,000 five years hence is Rs. 650. This procedure is known as discounting. The interest rate assumed for discounting is the discount rate. There is no difference between the interest rate and the discount rate. Only the interest rate looks from now to the future whereas the discount rate looks backward from the future to the present.

Table 15.4: Discounting

Year	Amount promised at the end of the year	Interest rate	Worth at the beginning of the year
1980	1000	1.09	917
1979	917	1.09	841
1978	841	1.09	772
1977	772	1.09	708
1976	708	1.09	650
1975	650	—	—

It is time consuming to calculate as per Table 15.4 but is simpler to use Compounding and Discounting tables. These tables give the discount factors (also known as the present worth factors) for various rates for different periods. For example, for a discount rate of 10 per cent, the discount factor for one year is 0.009. Such a table is appended to Gittinger's book.*

* J Price Gittinger: *Economic Analysis of Agricultural Projects*, Johns Hopkins University Press, 1972.

Stream of Income

Often we may expect to receive a stream of income spread over a number of future years rather than a single amount at the end of a particular period. This kind of question is specially important in project analysis since many projects yield the same benefits every year for a number of years. It is essential to know the present worth of a future stream of benefits. Only then can we estimate how much we would be justified in investing today to receive that stream. This is illustrated in the Table 15.5 (a).

Table 15.5a: Future Stream Benefits

Year	Income to be received	Discount factor at 15 per cent		Present worth
1975	6,438	.870	=	5,001
1976	6,438	.756	=	4,867
1977	6,438	.658	=	4,236
1978	6,438	.572	=	3,683
1979	6,438	.497	=	3,200
1980	6,438	.432	=	2,781
1981	6,438	.376	=	2,421
1982	6,438	.327	=	2,105
1983	6,438	.284	=	1,828
Total	57,942	4.772	=	30,722

We see that the present worth of a stream of income of Rs. 6,438 received each year for nine years at a discount rate of 15 per cent is Rs. 30,722. The undiscounted value of the income stream is Rs. 57,942 but this is not the present worth. What this means is that Rs. 6,438 received in 1983 is not worth Rs. 6,438 today. This is, of course, the whole purpose of discounting.

The calculations made in the Table 15.5 (a) can be simplified if we simply take the sum of the discount factors (present worth factors) and multiply it by the annual income to be received. Hence, Rs. 6,438 × 4.722 = Rs. 30,722.

What does this mean for project appraisal? It implies that if the current rate of interest is 15 per cent, then it is worthwhile investing Rs. 30,722 in a project which would yield an annual return of Rs. 6,438 for nine years.

Let us now turn to an interesting problem. There are several projects which do not yield benefits from the first year. Take the example of a project which begins to yield benefits only from the fifth year. Then we would be concerned only with the present worth of a future income stream which begins from the fifth year and continues up to the life span of the project, say, twenty-five years. We shall illustrate this with the example given above but assuming that the income stream starts from the fifth year and continues up to the ninth year. [Table 15.5 (b)].

Table 15.5b: Income Streams

Year	Income to be received		Discount Factor (15%)		Present worth
1979	6438	×	.497	=	3,200
1980	6438	×	.432	=	2,781
1981	6438	×	.376	=	2,421
1982	6438	×	.327	=	2,105
1983	6438	×	.284	=	1,828
Total	32,190	×	1.916	=	12,335

There is a short-cut for getting to this result. This is shown below.

Present worth of an annuity factor for nine years at 15%	=	4.772
Minus, present worth of an annuity factor for four years at 15 per cent	=	–2.856
Present worth of an annuity factor from years five to nine at 15 per cent	=	1.916

Armed with this fundamental notion of discounting, we shall proceed to see how it is applied. The simplest measure is the benefit-cost ratio which is computed as follows:

$$\frac{\text{Present worth of benefits}}{\text{Present worth of costs}} = \text{Benefit - Cost ratio.}$$

How do we decide what discount rate is to be used? There are three solutions. The best is to use the *opportunity cost of capital*–the profitability of the last possible investment in the economy given the total available capital. The difficulty here is to estimate the opportunity cost. It is commonly observed that in underdeveloped countries the opportunity cost of capital is between eight and 15 per cent.

Alternatively one would use the borrowing rate for the project to be financed. The difficulty here is that the benefits of a project will be unduly influenced by the financing terms available rather than by the contribution made by the project to the economy.

The third discount rate is the social rate of return. This is the benefit which reflects what is called the time preference of society as a whole. The rate of time preference indicates the preference for present consumption over future consumption (Table 15.6). This again is difficult to calculate.

The calculation of the benefit-cost ratio is given below:

$$BCR = \frac{\sum n_{t=1} \frac{B_n}{(1+i)^n}}{\sum n_{t=1} \frac{C_n}{(1+i)^n}}$$

Where BCR = Benefit-cost ratio

C_n = cost in each year

i = interest

n = number of years

B_n = benefit in each year

Concept of Multiplier

The marginal propensity to consume helps us to express in a systematic manner the relationship between a given increment in investment and the resulting change in income. Suppose on a given day an investment of Rs. 100 takes place. Now, the first impact of this change will be that income of persons engaged in investment activity will go up by Rs. 100. The process, however, does not end here. The recipients of income will spend a part of the additional income and save the rest–the magnitude of the additional spending will depend on the marginal propensity to consume (mpc).

TAble 15.6 Preference for Present Consumption over Future Consumption

Project	Year	Capital items	O & M cost	Project cost	Gross cost	DF 12 per cent	Present worth 12 per cent	TV of Proj. GB	DF 12 per cent	Present worth 12 per cent
	1	20,000	2,000	3,000	25,000	0.893	22,325	15,000	0.893	13,395
	2	—	2,000	3,000	50,000	0.797	3,985	15,000	0.797	12,955
	3	—	—	—	—	—	—	—	1.690	—
Total							Rs.26,310			Rs.26,350

			Net present worth
I	Benefit-Cost ratio at 12 per cent	$= \dfrac{25350}{26310} = 0.96$	$26350 - 26310 = 40$
II	-do-	$= \dfrac{29602}{29870} = 0.99$	
III	-do-	$= \dfrac{30200}{29000} = 1.01$	
IV	-do-	$= \dfrac{30667}{29870} = 1.03$	

DF = Discount Factor
TV = Total Value
GB = Gross Benefit

Suppose mpc is 3/4. They will spend Rs. 75 and save Rs. 25. When they spend Rs. 75 in buying goods and services, the income of the sellers of these goods and services go up by Rs. 75. They will in turn spend a part of it, depending on their marginal propensity to consume. If their mpc is also 3/4, they will spend Rs. 56.25 and save the rest. Thus one primary round of expenditure creates income much higher than original amount. If the marginal propensity to consume is stable, the series of successive expenditures grows in a geometric progression as shown below.

$$100 + 100 \times 3/4 + 100(3/4)^2 + 100(3/4)^3 + 100(3/4)^4$$

$$\Delta Y = \{100\,[1 + (3/4) + (3/4)^2 + (3/4)^3 + (3/4)^4 + ...]\}$$

$$= 100\ \frac{1}{1 - 3/4}$$

$$= 100 \times 4$$
$$= \text{Rs. } 400$$

Thus we see that an initial primary investment of Rs. 100 gives rise to an increase of Rs. 400 in the national income. The investment measures the relationship between an increase in income caused by a primary increase in investment.

$$\text{Investment multiplier } \frac{Y}{I} = \frac{400}{100} = 4$$

$$= \frac{1}{1\text{-mpc}} = \frac{1}{\text{mps}}$$

If mpc is 4/5, multiplier will be 5; and
if mpc is 9/10 it will be 10,
mps = marginal propensity to save.

Discounted Cash Flow

In this method the worth of a project is estimated by subtracting the costs from the benefits on a year-to-year basis and thus arrive at the incremental net benefit stream (known as the "cash flow") and then discounting that.

Derivation of the Cash Flow

Every project earns a stream of gross benefits. From this we must deduct the capital investment and the costs of other inputs. We are then left with a residual. This residual is available for two purposes:

(a) To recover the investment made in the project—this is the return of capital.
(b) To compensate for the use of capital used in the project—this is the return to or on capital.

This residual is the cash flow. The cash flow includes both the returns *to* and *of* capital. In effect the whole thing can be represented as follows.

Gross return less capital items and inputs less labour and management costs = cash flow.

The above is a derivation of cash flow in economic analysis in which some prices may be shadow prices. In financial analysis all prices are market prices. Also taxes and subsidies are included. Then,

Gross return less capital items, inputs and taxes less labour management costs = cash flow.

Two points should be noted. In the beginning of the project the investment costs and initial operating and maintenance costs may well exceed benefits. Therefore, we may have a negative cash flow. Secondly, the cash flow may contain some non-cash elements.

Net Present Worth

This is referred to as NPW. It is the present worth of the cash flow stream. It can be computed by finding the difference between the present worth of the benefit stream *less* the present worth of the cost stream. Even here we would bc confronted with the problem of choosing the right discount rate. Mostly use of the opportunity cost of capital is recommended.

Internal Rate of Return

In this method we attempt to find that discount rate which just makes the NPW of the cash flow equal to zero. Such a discount rate is known as the internal rate of return. It represents the average earning power of the money used in the project over the life of the project. The internal rate of return drives the NPW of the project to zero. At that discount rate the project breaks even. In other words it will earn back all the capital and operating costs spent on it and also pay the project-sponsors 18 per cent for the use of their money in the meantime. Such a rate of return will make the benefit-cost ratio equal to one.

The problem is that there is no readily applicable formula for finding a discount rate which will make the cash flow equal to zero. It can only be found by trial and error. There is, however, a method of estimating the internal rate of return which will help avoid making too many errors. This is shown in the Table 15.7; but before that consider the example of a project where the internal rate of return makes the cash flow equal to zero.

The Table 15.6 illustrates how a particular rate of discount, in this instance 18 per cent, makes the NPW equal to zero and benefit cost ratio equal to one. You will see that the present worth on both the cost side and the benefit side is derived by multiplying the gross costs and benefits, respectively, by the discount factor. To get at the discount factor for one year for any rate of discount one should consult Discount tables.

It was mentioned earlier that there is no formula for choosing the discount rate. The only way is to begin with a quick guess and choose a rate which commonsense tells is in the right neighbourhood. There is a method of making a first approximation which is given below: The figures in the Table 15.7 (a) are taken from the Table 15.6.

Initial Estimate of the Internal Rate of Return

Find:

1. Average annual benefits/Total initial costs = 4700/13500 = .35
   This .35 = estimated internal rate of return in decimal terms.
2. Next we have to reduce the estimate of step 1 by the approximate amount which is given by the Table 15.7(a) [*Note* that we do not have the derivation of Table 15.7(a) which is like an annuity or discount table].
3. Next we reduce the estimate of step 2 according to the Table 15.7(c).

4. If there is a lapse between end of investment period and beginning of benefit period, adjustments have to be made as per Table 15.7(d).
   In ample there is no lapse and hence no need for adjustment.
5. If benefits are larger in early years than in later years; we increase the step 4 estimate somewhat. If benefits are greater in later years than in early years, we decrease the step and estimate somewhat.
6. Obtain the estimated internal rate of return in percentage terms (Step 5 estimate–in this case steps 4 and 5 do not apply –multiplied by 100)
   So, $.20 \times 100 = 20$ per cent.

The next step is to discount the cash flow by 20 per cent. The cash flow figures are found in column 10 of the Table 15.7(a). If this is discounted by 20 per cent it will be found that the present worth is Rs. 560. This indicates that the present worth of the costs is greater than the present worth of the benefits. The project cannot pay such a high rate of interest and still recover the capital investment. Hence the discount rate is too high.

On the other hand, if we choose 15 per cent and discount the cash flow, we get a value of Rs. 977. This positive flow indicates that the present worth of the benefits is greater than the present worth of the costs. This implies that the project could pay a higher rate of interest and still recover the capital invested. Hence 15 per cent is too low.

Instead of using a trial and error method to find the correct rate we would do it by interpolation. This is done as follows:

Internal rate of return =

$$\text{Lower discount rate plus difference between the two discount rates} \times \frac{\text{Present worth of cash flow at the lower rate}}{\text{Absolute difference between the present worth of the cash flow at the two discount rates.}}$$

Reverting to the example used above we, therefore, get:

$$\underset{\text{(lower rate)}}{15} + \underset{\text{(difference between the two rates)}}{5} \times \frac{977 \text{ (PW at lower rate)}}{1537 \text{(absolute difference)}}$$

$= 15 + 5\,(.64) = 15 + 3.2 = 18$ per cent.

Table 15.7a: Initial Estimate of the Internal Rate of Return

Year	Capital items	Operation and maintenance costs	Production costs	Gross cost	D.F. 18 per cent	Present worth	Total value of production (Gross benefits)	Present worth	Increase benefits (Cash flow)	Present worth 18 per cent
1	7,500	0	0	7,500	847	6,352	0	0	–7,500	–6,352
2	6,000	0	0	6,000	718	4,308	0	0	–6,000	–4,308
3	0	600	700	1,300	609	792	6,000	3,654	+4,700	+2,862
4	0	600	700	1,300	516	671	6,000	3,096	+4,700	+2,425
5	0	600	700	1,300	437	568	6,000	2,622	+4,700	+2,054
6	0	600	700	1,300	370	481	6,000	2,220	+4,700	+1,739
7	0	600	700	1,300	314	408	6,000	1,884	+4,700	+1,476
8	—	—	—	—	314	—	331	104	+331	+104
Total	13,500	3000	3500	20,000	3,811	13,580	30,331	13,580	10,331	0

Note: The figures 314 and 331 in the last row are omitted. The former is omitted from the total to avoid double counting. The latter represents salvage value (described below).

Benefit — cost ratio at 18 per cent = 13,580,000/13,580,000 = 1.0

N.P.W at 18 per cent' 13,580,000 — 13,580,000 = 0

Internal rate of return = 18 per cent

Table 15.7b: Estimated Value of Step 1

Duration of the benefit stream year	Estimated value in Step 1			
	Less than 0.1	0.1-0.2	0.2-0.3	Less than 0.31
5	–	–	0.18	0.13
10	0.08	0.07	0.05	0.02
15	0.05	0.03	0.02	0.0
20	0.02	0.01	0.0	0.0
25	0.02	0.01	0.0	0.0
More than 25	0.0·	0.0	0.0	0.0

Taking the benefit stream as years we get .35 – 0.13 = .22

Table 15.7c: Estimate of Step 2

Investment Period	Subtract from step 2 estimate
1	0
2	1/2 (Step 2 estimate)^2
3	(Step 2 estimate)^2
4	1.5 (Step 2 estimate)^2
5	2 (Step estimate)^2

Taking this period as 2 years we get
.22 × .22/2 = .02, hence .22 – .02 = .20

Table 15.7d: Lapse Year and Subtraction Estimate of Step 3

Lapse (Year)	Subtraction Step 3 estimate
1	(Step 3 estimate)^2
2	2 (Step 3 estimate)^2
3	3 (Step 3 estimate)^2
4	4 (Step 3 stimate)^2
5	5 (Step 3 estimate)^2

Note that absolute difference is merely the sum of the two values ignoring the plus or minus sign attached to them.

Note that I have not reproduced the entire table to show how the present worth of the cash flow is arrived at after discounting. This is with a view to keeping the essay from getting absurdly long. All that is done is to take the cash flow figures from Table and multiply them by the approximate discount factors for 15 and 20 per cent, respectively.

In evaluating projects they are to be ranked in the order of the value of the internal rate of return.

It should also be noted that a project which continues longer with the same investment is always to be preferred. Similarly a project with earlier return is preferred to one with later return.

Another important question is: for how long cost benefit analysis should be carried out? Normally we should choose a period of time roughly comparable to be economic life of a project.

At the end of a project the capital asset will not have been used up completely. There will be a *residual* asset. This is the salvage value and is treated as a benefit from the project in the last year of the analysis. This is how the figure Rs. 331 in column 8 of Table 15.7(a).

One final point on this subject. I have described the steps for deriving the internal rate of return. The derivation on the table is not presented. It is adopted from J. Price Gittinger's book and is itself taken from another source.

Treatment of Uncertainty

In the course of construction of a present costs may increase. Can the project's internal return bear this? In other words how sensitive is it to increased costs or fall in prices of lengthening of the implementation period? To see what happens in such changed circumstances the analysis has to be reworked. This is called sensitivity analysis.

There are four main aspects to sensitivity analysis in relation to agriculture–prices, delays in implementation, cost overrun and yields.

Prices

It is necessary to every agricultural project to find out how its profitability will be affected if the price assumption move wrong. For this purpose, we have to make alternative assumption about future prices and see how these effect the internal rate of return.

Delays in Implementation

Most projects are subject to delays. Therefore, the effect of delay on a project has to be examined.

Cost Overrun

This is specially important in projects where there are significant consumption costs.

Yields

These occupy an important place because there is a tendency to be over optimistic about future yields, particularly with regard to new cropping patterns, etc. It is, therefore, necessary to test how sensitive a project's returns are to lower yields.

16

Project Formulation and Evaluation–II: Critical Path Method (CPM)

V.T.D. BALARAMAN*

Introduction

DURING 1956-57, the Engineering Control Group of EI duPont De Nemours & Co. of USA was seriously exploring the possibilities of using the modern computers in handling the complex problems encountered in managing various engineering projects. Their major aims were:

1. The development of a Master Schedule coverinք ıl projects.
2. The procedures to monitor, update and r. .se the Master Schedule in the most *economical* manner.
3. The built-in provision by which all concerned persons are informed of the progress and consequential revisions, if any.

Their research efforts resulted in the development of the CPM approach.

The use of network techniques of models resulted in providing a systematic procedure for denoting the inter-relationships among various activities. Besides distinctly separating the planning and scheduling functions.

CPM Approach

CPM stands for Critical Path Method. The name itself implies that the procedure identifies the most critical of all paths available through the

* Dr. V.T.D. Balaraman, Indian Institute of Management, Bangalore

network. Analysing the network we can identify those activities which should be expedited and by how much, in order to accelerate the project completion time. As indicated earlier, CPM is oriented towards cost. Cost was selected as the criterion, since labour, materials and equipment can easily be measured in terms of cost. Given the project schedule time, the most economical schedule is that which minimises total project cost.

The cost-time curve for a typical activity is shown in Fig. 16.1

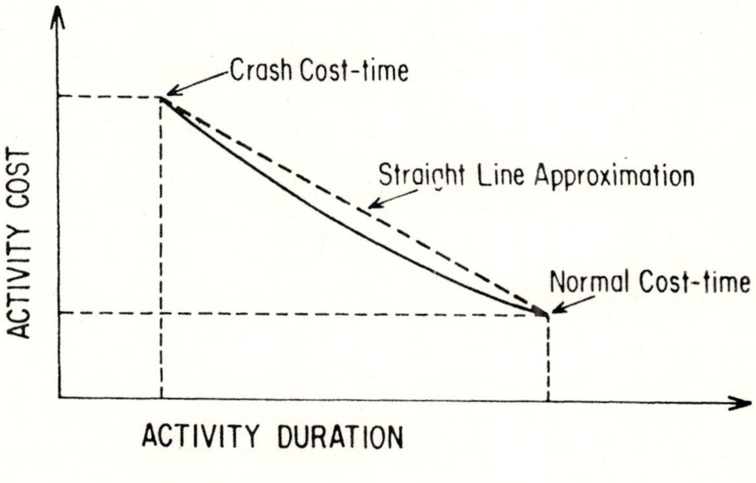

Fig. 16.1

For each activity, there are two cost-time combinations. The first one plans the normal time needed to execute a task and the associated normal cost. The second one considers the minimum time needed to do a job as a crash programme and the maximum cost of this crash programme. This minimum time is known as the crash time and the associated maximum cost is known as the crash cost. Decreasing the time below the crash time is considered not possible. Increasing the time duration beyond the normal time will usually increase the cost because of inefficiencies associated with unnecessary extension of time (See Fig. 16.1).

Since the normal and crash points are derived by estimating procedures which are only approximate, the time-cost curve can be represented by a straight line between the crash and normal points without any loss of significant accuracy. The slope of this line gives the rate at which the cost increases as the activity time is decreased. This slope can be used as the criterion for deciding which activities are to be expedited. Obviously, those activities with the smallest values of slope must be expedited first. This will result in the smallest increase in total project cost.

After the network has been prepared, normal and crash costs and durations are estimated for all activities. Dummy activities are assigned zero cost and zero time for both the crash and normal situations. By analysing the network using only the normal times and costs for each activity, the normal project completion time, the earliest and latest start and completion times for the activities and the normal project cost can be determined. Using the crash times for each activity, a minimum or crash project completion time can be computed. The difference between the normal and crash completion times provides a range of possible project completion times. For each project completion time within this range, a minimum cost schedule can be computed. Each cost schedule gives a duration time for each activity, the earliest and latest start and completion times for each activity, and the total project cost.

Since the project completion time is equal to the sum of the time durations for the activities on the critical path, compressing the critical will reduce the project completion time. The critical path is compressed by expediting the critical activities with the smallest cost rates, first so as to provide the smallest amount of increase in total project cost. The computational procedure expedites each activity to its crash time before expediting an activity with the next larger rate of cost increase. If two activities on the critical path have the same cost rate, the mathematical procedure is indifferent as to which activity is expedited. The activities are expedited only to duration times which are equal to, or greater than, the crash duration times, and which will cause the length of the critical path to equal the pre-assigned project completion time.

When the most critical path is compressed to a length equal to the length of the next most critical path, then both paths must be compressed to achieve any further reduction in project completion time. The process of selecting activities to expedite now becomes more complex. An activity on each path is selected according to the criterion previously stated. Since both paths must be shortened by the same amount of time, the two selected activities must be expedited by the same amount. The increase in total project cost will be equal to the sum of the cost slope for each activity multiplied by the amount of time by which the activities are in common, the cost increase rates for those common activities are examined. Should the cost rate for common activities be the same, then expediting the common activity will decrease both critical paths by the same amount of time, and will increase the total project cost by an amount equal to the cost increase rate for that common activity multiplied by the expedited amount of time. As the project completion time is compressed, the number of critical paths (network paths whose lengths equal to project completion time) generally increases. This makes the computation of a minimum cost schedule complicated, because of the number of comparisons which must be made. For each selected project completion time and a minimum cost schedule can be computed. Figure 16.2 gives a typical plot of minimum total project costs over the range of possible project completion times. In general, the minimum total project cost for the minimum or crash project duration is less than the total project cost based on expediting all activities as shown in Fig. 16.2

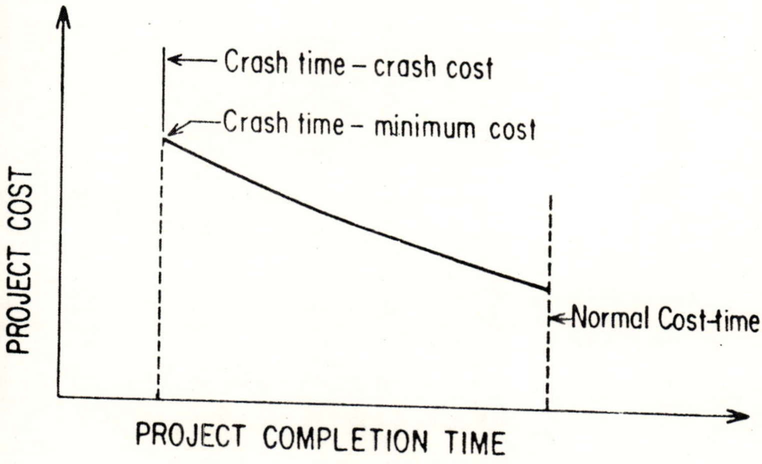

Fig. 16.2

The normal and crash costs described above were direct costs. For most projects, indirect as well as direct costs are usually involved. The indirect costs normally include such things as overhead, general, administrative and other distributive expenses. To arrive at a more representative picture of overall project costs, these indirect costs should be added to the direct costs. In some cases, indirect costs are directly related to the activities and can be estimated when the range of direct activity costs are estimated. More generally, however, indirect costs are related to the total project duration or to the project's direct cost. Incentive fees and penalties, if applicable, should also be included in the total cost structure.

Example

Consider the simple network as shown. It consists of five activities. The activity durations and direct cost for each activity are shown in tabular form. The problem is to develop the alternative cost schedules for this project (Schedules 1 to 6).

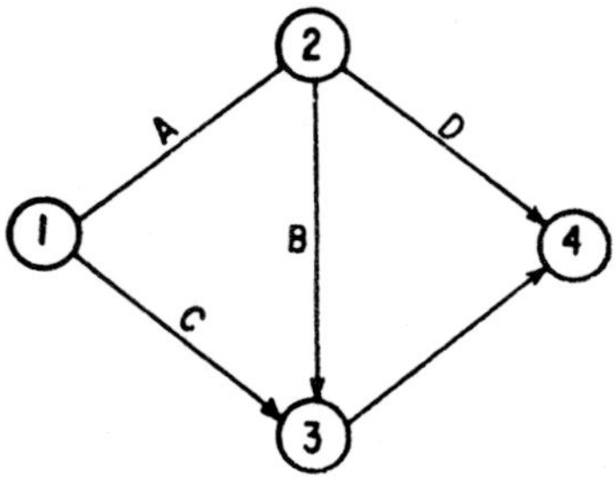

Activity	Duration (week)		Cost (Rs.)		Slope (Rs/week)
	Normal	Crash	Normal	Crash	
A	8	2	3,000	6,600	600
B	6	3	2,000	3,200	400
C	8	6	2,500	4,500	1000
D	9	9	5,000	5,000	—
E	5	2	1,200	3,900	900

Indirect costs: Rs. 500 per project week.

SCHEDULE 1: All Activities at Normal Time

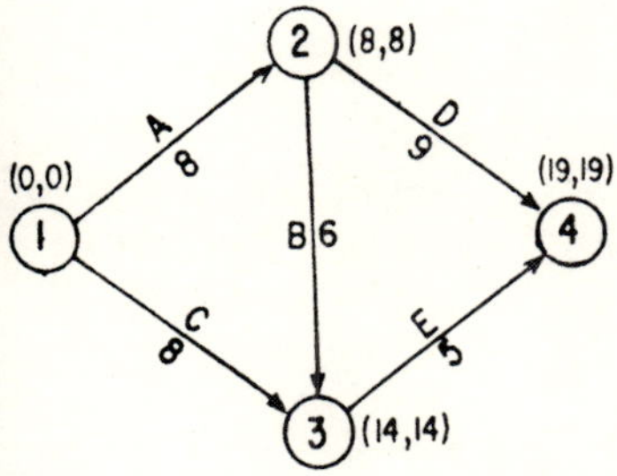

	Present		Plan	
Act	Weeks	Rs.	Crash	Slope
A	8	3,000	2	**600**
B	6	2,000	3	**400**
C	8	2,500	6	1000
D	**9**	5,000	**9**	—
E	5	1,200	2	900
Total		13,700		

Project time: 19
Project cost: 13,700

Decision :
Shorten B by one week

SCHEDULE 2: Shorten B by One Week from Schedule 1

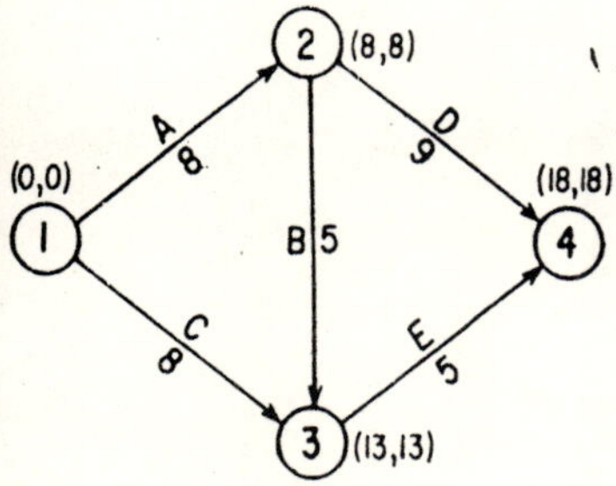

	Present		Plan	
Act	Weeks	Rs.	Crash	Slope
A	8	3,000	2	**600**
B	5	2,400	3	**400**
C	8	2,500	6	1000
D	**9**	5,000	**9**	—
E	5	1,200	2	900
Total		14,100		

Project time: 18
Project cost: 14,100

Decision :
Shorten B by one week

SCHEDULE 3: Shorten B by One Week from Schedule 2

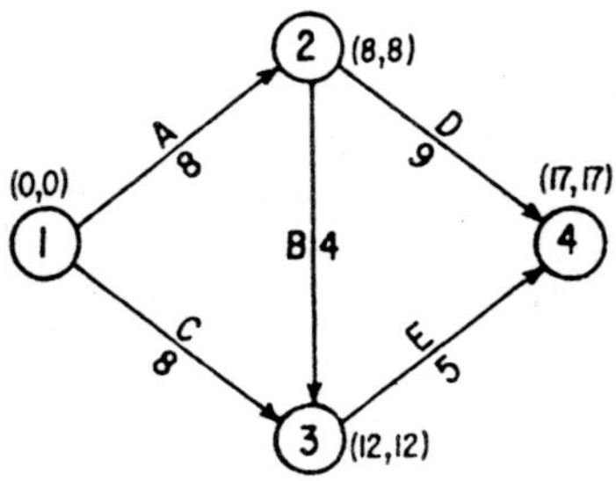

Act	Present Week	Rs.	Plan Crash	Slope
A	8	3,000	2	**600**
B	4	2,800	3	**400**
C	8	2,500	6	1000
D	9	5,000	9	—
E	5	1,200	2	900
Total		14,500		

Project time: 17
Project cost: 14,500

Decision :
Shorten A by four weeks

SCHEDULE 4: Shorten A by Four Weeks from Schedule 3

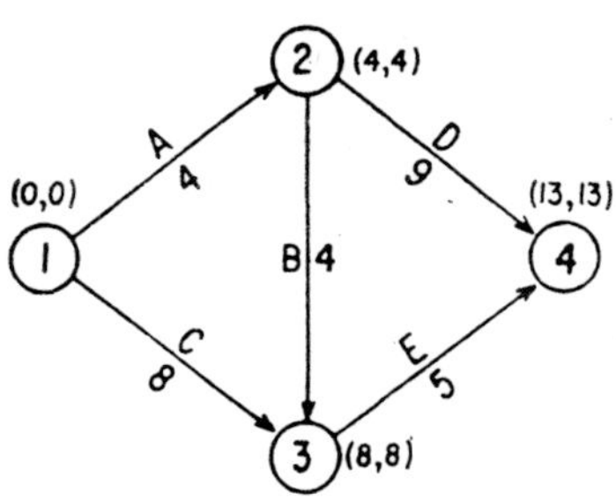

Act	Present Weeks	Rs.	Plan Crash	Slope
A	4	5,400	2	600
B	4	2,800	3	400
C	8	2,500	6	1000
D	9	5,000	9	—
E	5	1,200	2	900
Total		16,900		

Project time: 13
Project cost: 16,900

Decision : Shorten A by two weeks and C by two weeks

SCHEDULE 5: Shorten A and C by Two Weeks from Schedule 4

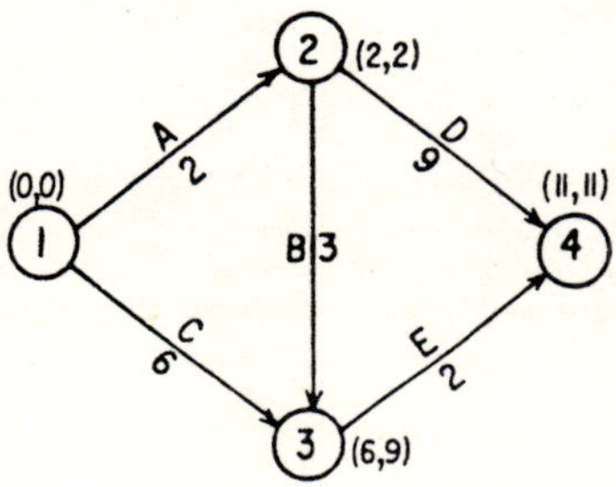

	Present		Plan	
Act	Weeks	Rs.	Crash	Slope
A	2	6,600	2	—
B	4	2,800	3	400
C	6	4,500	6	—
D	9	500	9	—
E	5	1,200	2	900
Total		20,100		

Project time: 11
Project cost: 20,100

Decision :
Crash all activities

SCHEDULE 6: Crash all Activities

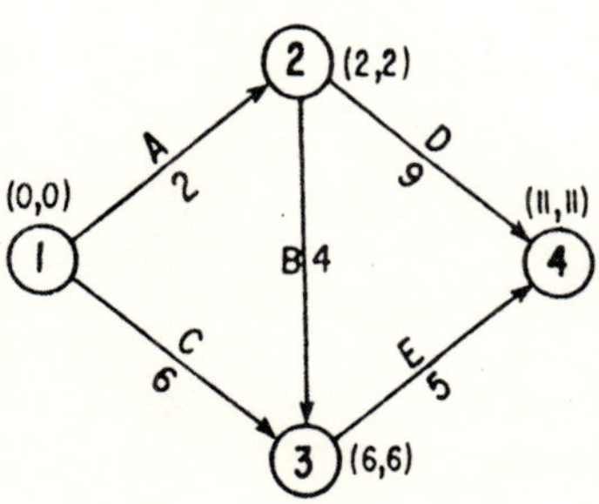

	Present		Plan	
Act	Weeks	Rs.	Crash	Slope
A	2	6,600	2	—
B	3	3,200	3	—
C	6	4,500	6	—
D	9	5,000	9	—
E	2	3,900	2	—
Total		23,200		

Project time: 11
Project cost: 23,200

Summary of Calculations

Schedule	Time	Cost		
		Direct	Indirect	Cost Total
1	19	13,700	9,500	23,200
2	18	14,100	9,000	23,100
3	17	14,500	8,500	23,000
4	13	16,900	6,500	23,400
5	11	20,100	5,500	25,600
6	11	23,200	5,500	28,700

Use of CPM

One of the most difficult problems in using the Critical Path Method of planning and scheduling is the derivation of the normal and crash durations and costs for each activity. The normal durations and costs usually do not present as much of a problem as the crash estimates. In general, the only way to arrive at realistic crash estimates is to critically analyse each activity and cost out of the possible ways of performing it. For example, when overtime and extra shift operations are permitted, several possible alternatives may have to be synthesized and costed.

Even when overtime and extra shift operations are not used, complexities may still arise. For the first project application of CPM by duPont, only a 40–hour week was authorised for the project. Crash times for various activities were obtained by considering only the maximum reasonable increase in manpower for each job and the effect on elapsed time. As the size of crew increased, additional costs were found necessary because of the extra labour congestion. The crash cost was obtained by adding the extra labour costs to the normal cost with an allowance for labour congestion.

The cost-time curve for some types of activities is purely approximated by a straight line between the crash and normal points. For example, consider transportation type activities for which there may be only two rates: a normal rate and a premium or expedited rate. In such cases, the curve consists of only two distinct points, and to connect these points by a straight line is meaningless since there are no possible transportation times between the normal and expedited times. For other types of activities, the cost-duration curve may consist of a succession of discrete points and the use of a value between any two points would correspond to an impractical time cost relationship.

In practical applications, it has been observed that approximately 10 to 20 per cent of the activities in a network are critical, and that the majority of activities are scheduled at their normal time. Only a few activities are scheduled at durations corresponding to their crash cost, and the others are expedited to times between the normal and crash durations. These observations led to the conclusion that much of the time-cost data was not being used in the computational procedure. As a result of this conclusion and the fact that construction of time-cost relationships is often quite burdensome, the technique has been modified to a ".cut-and-dry" or sequential computational method. With the modified CPM technique, the network plan is prepared in the usual manner-durations and costs are estimated for each activity. The project direct cost is computed and the network is analyzed using the normal time durations to determine the critical path and the various slack paths. The indirect costs associated with the computed project duration is also computed and a point on the project cost curve determined. Next, the activities on the critical path are analyzed in detail, and time-cost data collected for expediting these activities by small time increments. The CPM technique is now employed to expedite the activities on the critical path. The resulting project duration direct cost and total cost are again computed. The procedure is repeated with time-cost data collected for activities as they become critical, and for as long as the project total cost decreases. When total project costs begin to increase, the procedure can be stopped because the optimum project duration and cost have been reached.

The step approach offers the following advantages:

1. Less effort is involved since estimates of crash and durations are not required for all activities.
2. The provision for review after each computational cycle offers an opportunity for better understanding of the manner in which activities are expedited to achieve successive comprehensions in project duration time.
3. A smaller computer and a much simple programme can be used. The complete technique with the minimum cost expediting fea-

ture is not easily programmed and requires a large scale computer.

Illustrations of schedule/cost outlook and cost time status have been given in Figure 16.3 and Figure. 16.4 respectively. The specimen proforma for programme status report has been provided in fig. 16.5.

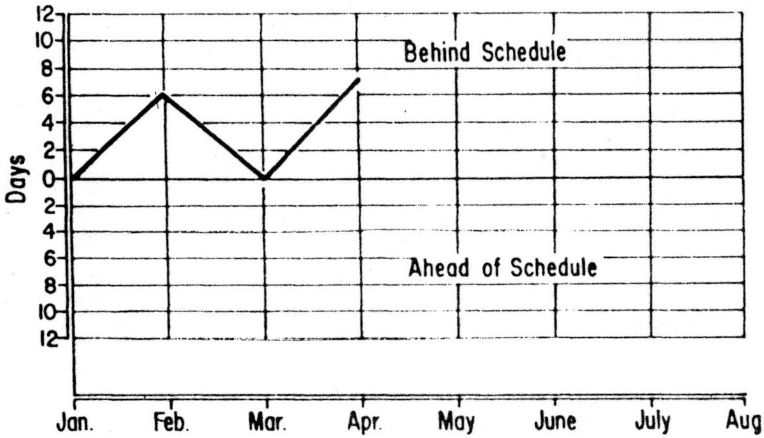

Fig. 16.3 (A)

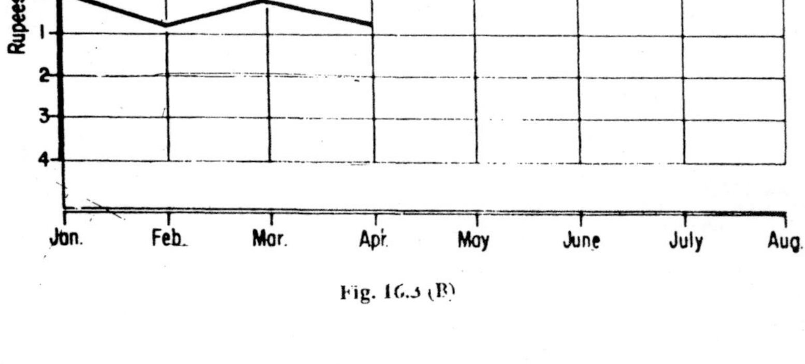

Fig. 16.3 (B)

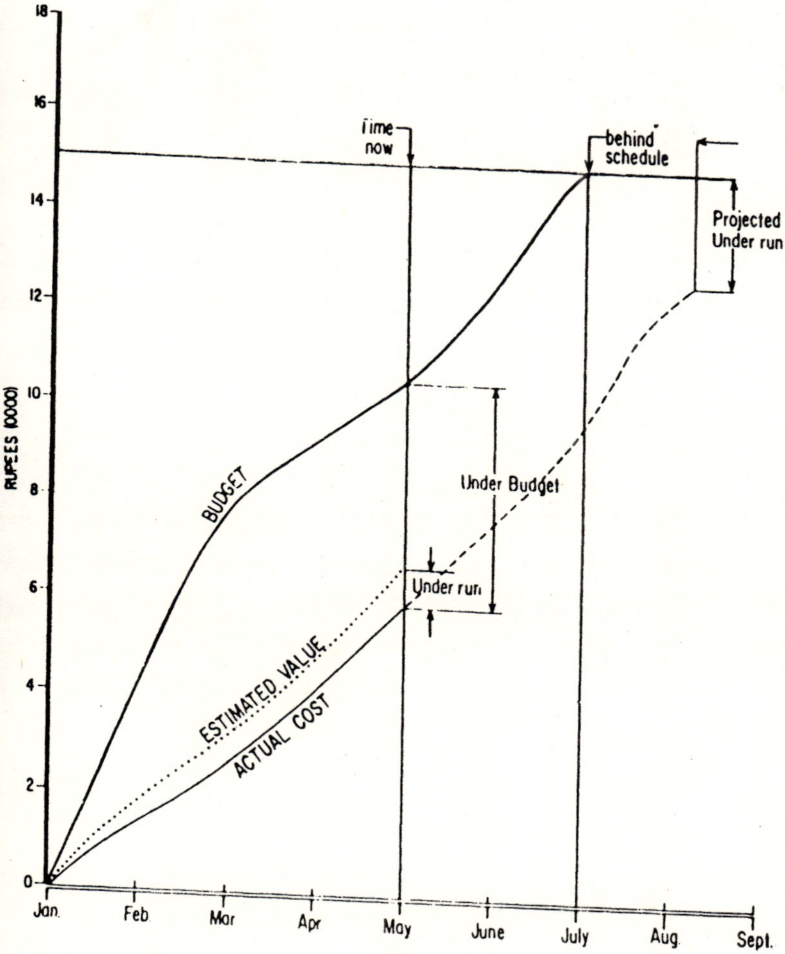
RUPEES (0000)
18
16
14
12
10
8
6
4
2
0
Time now
behind schedule
Projected Under run
BUDGET
Under Budget
Under run
ESTIMATED VALUE
ACTUAL COST
Jan.
Feb
Mar
Apr
May
June
July
Aug.
Sept.

Fig. 16.4

Fig. 16.5: Programme Status Report

ACTIVITY DETAILS		Date Completed	Earliest Finish date	Latest Finish date	Float	Actual Cost so far	Original Estimate	Revised Estimate	Overrun/ Underrun
Name	Code								

17

Project Formulation and Evaluation-III: Programme Evaluation and Review Technique (PERT)

— V.T.D. BALARAMAN

Introduction

DURING 1957, the US Governmental agencies responsible for the development of Polaris Fleet Ballistic Missile were faced with the problem of co-ordinating the activities of several thousand contractors and agencies participating in the development programme. The conventional planning techniques using Gantt Charts did not provide them with a way to identify and achieve the optimum plan.

So the planners searched for new planning techniques. The result of their search is the "Programme Evaluation and Review Technique" (PERT). The entire programme was portrayed as a network of activities. They also found that PERT can be used very effectively to monitor and control the progress. The successful way in which PERT was used for Polaris programme encouraged many other governmental agencies and private industries to adopt it.

The primary objective of PERT is to determine the probability of meeting specified deadlines.

Simultaneously, the private industries participating in complex developmental activities were searching for better planning tools to determine a plan yielding optimum cost. Coincidentally, they too came up with a network technique Critical Path Method (CPM).

The main objective of CPM is to determine a schedule at 'minimum' cost.

During the past decade the term PERT is used to denote the network approach to planning where both time and cost are taken into consideration.

Network

A project or programme is represented as a network of activities in PERT. The network does not merely portray the activities. It presents them in a logical sequence, identifying activities that can be done simultaneously and their chronological sequence.

Definitions

Activities are definite tasks which are necessary to complete a project. They use resources, cost money and consume time. Each activity is represented by an arrow.

Event is a recognisable moment in time when a certain objective is achieved. An event, for example, can be the completion or start of one or more activities. Every activity begins and ends in an event. Each event is represented by a circle.

Network is the graphical portrayal of a project. It is drawn by connecting the various events by appropriate activities, indicating which activities can be done simultaneously and which necessarily must follow in sequence.

A dummy activity is an activity which consumes no time and requires no resources, deliberately introduced by the planner to maintain proper relationships between related activities. A dummy activity is represented by a broken line.

Points to be noted

An event is achieved when all the activities leading to it are completed.

An activity can start *only* after its starting event has been achieved.

Any one path of activities should not include an event more than once. In other words, no looping is allowed. (Fig. 17.1)

Example 1

A petrol bunk operator desires a network to represent all activities to be performed on an incoming car. The services offered are: cleaning wind-shields, check tyres, check oil, check battery and check petrol tank. For the purposes of drawing the network he assumes that all activities are performed. If any one or more activities need not be performed he will assign a zero time value for those. The activities are listed below. Draw the network.

Activities

(A) Raise bonnet
(B) Add petrol
(C) Check tyres
(D) Check radiator
(E) Check battery
(F) Check oil
(G) Lower bonnet
(H) Clean windshield
(I) Compute bill
(J) Collect payment

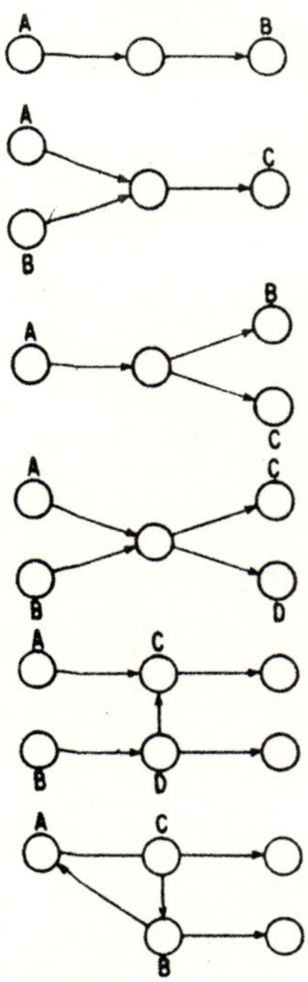

Activity A must be completed before activity B can start.

Activity C cannot start until both activities A and B are completed.

Activities B and C cannot start until activity A is completed.

Activities C and D cannot start until both activities A and B are completed.

Activities A and B must be completed before activity C can start. However only activity B must be completed before activity D can start. (Note use of dummy).

Improper network; since A,C,B form a loop.

Fig. 17.1: Basic Logic of Network Notation

Example 2

A network of the steam pipe maintenance project (Fig. 17.1) has to be drawn. The project begins by moving the required material and equipment to the site (5 hrs). Then we may erect a scaffold and remove the old pipe and valves (3 hrs); while this is being done, we may fabricate the new pipe (2 hrs). After the old pipe and valves are removed and the new pipe is fabricated, we can place the new pipe (4 hrs). However, the new valves can be placed (1 hr) as soon as the old line is removed. Finally, when everything is in place, we can weld and insulate the pipe (5 hrs).

Activity Time Estimates

How long does it take to perform a specific activity? One can answer this with some confidence if he has performed the same activity once or twice before. Even then he cannot be fully sure to give an estimate that will be exact. In other words, there is always a certain amount of uncertainty involved in such estimates. Any effective planning technique must have a way by which the uncertainty can be quantified and evaluated. PERT does this by asking that three time estimates be made for each activity. They are:

the most likely time = m
the pessimistic time = b
the optimistic time = a

These estimates are to be made by persons most familiar with the activity involved.

Interpretation of the Three Time Estimates

Optimistic time is an estimate of the minimum time an activity will take. This can be realised only if unusual good luck is experienced and everything works out right the first time.

Most likely time is an estimate of the normal time an activity will take. If the activity could be repeated a number of times under similar circumstances, this result will occur most often.

Pessimistic time is an estimate of the maximum time an activity will take. This will occur only if unusual bad luck is experienced. This estimate is given by taking into consideration the possibility of initial setbacks, failures and consequent re-starts. However, this must not reflect such factors as strikes, fires, etc., unless such are inherent risks in the activity.

Expected Time Estimate

The manner in which the three time estimates are defined, it is clear that the optimistic and the pessimistic times should occur rarely; and that the most likely time should occur often. Giving more weight to the most likely time and assuming that the time-estimates follow a better distribution, the expected time is defined as

$$t_e = \frac{a + 4m + b}{6}$$

Since a and b are the two extreme values, it is assumed that the range (b–a) is equal to six times the standard duration.

$$\text{Hence} \qquad \sigma = \frac{b - a}{6}$$

Even though these assumptions appear arbitrary, many studies conducted to test the validity of these assumptions have proved they are valid indeed. Also, they have been proved to be valuable in many successful applications.

Preliminary Data

The steps taken so far are summarised below: The data collected can be presented in the tabular form shown in PERT Form 1

(1) Identify all activities.

(2) For each activity identify the immediate predecessors.

(3) Using a logical approach organize the activities into a network.

(4) For each activity, obtain time estimates a, m and b, and calculate expected time and standard duration. Also calculate the variance (= square of the standard deviation for each activity).

PERT FORM 1

Activity		List	Time Estimate				Std.	
Code	Name	Predecessors	a	m	b	Te	Dev	Var
1	2	3	4	5	6	7	8	9

Network Analysis

Definitions: Event oriented

Earliest time for an event is defined as the time at which that event will occur if the preceding activities are started as early as possible. The earliest time for the i-th event is denoted by E(i).

Latest time for an event is defined as the time at which the event can occur without delaying the completion of the project beyond its earliest time. The latest time for the i-th event is denoted by L(i).

Slack for an event is the difference between its latest time and earliest time. The slack for the k-th event is denoted by S(k) and is given by

$$S(k) = L(k) - E(k)$$

Critical Path for the project may be defined as a path through the network such that all the events on this path have zero slack.

Project time is given by the earliest time of the last event in the project network.

Definitions–Activity oriented

Earliest start time for an activity is the earliest time at which it can be started if the preceding activities are started as early as possible. This is denoted by ES(i, j) which is read as Earliest Start for activity (i, j) and is given by

$$ES(i, j) = E(i)$$

Duration of an activity is given by the expected time (t_e) in which an activity will be completed. d(i, j) denotes the duration of the activity (i, j).

Earliest finish time for an activity is the sum of its duration and its earliest start time. This is denoted by EF (i, j) and is given by

$$EF(i, j) = ES(i, j) + d(i, j)$$

Latest finish time for an activity is latest time an activity can be finished without delaying the completion of the project beyond its earliest time. This is denoted by LF (i, j) and is given by

$$LF(i, j) = L(j)$$

Latest start time is the latest time an activity can be started without delaying the completion of the project beyond its earliest time. This is denoted by LS (i, j) and is given by

$$LS(i, j) = LF(i, j) - d(i, j)$$

Total float is the amount of *extra* time available to complete the activity if it is started as early as possible and if it is completed as late as possible without delaying the completion of the project beyond its earliest time.

$$TF(i, j) = E(j) - EF(i, j)$$

Free float is the amount of *extra* time available to complete the activity if all activities are to be started at their respective earliest times.

$$FF(i, j) = E(j) - EF(i, j)$$

Independent float is the float (free time) available to an activity independent of the other activities. It is computed by assuming that the activity is started at the latest start time and yet completed before the earliest time for its end event.

$$IF(i, j) = E(j) - L(i) - d(i, j)$$

Analysis

The example given in Figure 17.2 has brought out all the necessary steps to be taken in analysing a network. If the network is large, then the format used in the examples will not be convenient. Hence, formats 2 and 3 are developed to perform the necessary calculations in an orderly manner.

a	b	c	d	e	f	g	h	i	j
Event No.	Immediate Predecessor			Earliest Time	Immediate Successor			Latest time	Slack
	Event No.	Expected value	Earliest time		Event No.	Expected value	Latest time		
i	j	d (j, i)	E(i)	E(i)	k	d (i, k)	L(k)	L(i)	S(i)
4	1	30	0	30				30	0
	2	24	5						
	3	9	18						
3	1	18	0	18	4	9	30	21	3
	2	7	5						
2	1	5	0	5	3	7	21	6	1
					4	24	30		
1				0	2	5	6	0	0
					3	18	21		
					4	30	30		

FORMAT : 1

(i, j)	d (i, j)	E (i, j)	EF (i, j)	LF (i, j)	LS (i, j)	TF (i, j)	FF (i, j)	IF (i, j)
(1, 2)	5	0	5	6	1	1	0	0
(1, 3)	18	0	18	21	3	3	0	0
(1, 4)	30	0	30	30	0	0	0	0
(2, 3)	7	5	12	21	14	9	6	5
(2, 4)	24	5	29	30	6	1	1	0
(3, 4)	9	18	27	30	21	3	3	0

Procedure for using PERT Form 2

1. Identify sink (last event).
2. Treat this as event i and enter i in column (a).
3. Identify all the events immediately preceding i and list them in column (b).
4. Treat as event j the first event in column (b) against i. Enter the duration d(j, i) in column (c) and the variance = (j, i) in column (e). Repeat this for all j events listed against i.
5. Select event (i–1). If (i--1) = 0 go to step 6; otherwise draw a line below the last entry and go to step 2.
6. Against event 1 enter in columns (g) and (h) a value of 0, i.e., E(1) = 0 and o-² (E1) = 0. Consider event 2.
7. Treat this as event.
8. Treat each event in column (b) as j. Obtain earliest time E(j) from column (g) by visual search and enter it in column (d). Repeat this for all j events listed against event i.
9. For each j, add column (c) and (d). Enter the maximum value in column (g). Select the event j which gives this maximum value. For this j find the sum of o-² (j, i) and o-² (Ej) and enter the sum in column (h).
10. If i is the sink, go to step 11; otherwise select event i+1 and go to step 7.

Procedures to use PERT Form-3 will be similar to those given above. The fact that we are now trying to find out earliest time extent of the latest must be kept in mind.

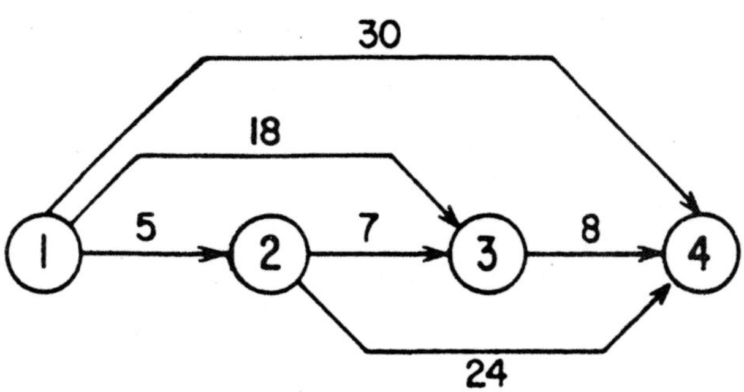

Fig. 17.2

PERT FORM 2

Event i	Immediate Predecessor					Earliest time E(i)	Variance $\sigma^{2}(Ei)$
	Event No. j	Expected value d(j, i)	Earliest time E(j)	Variance $\sigma^{2}(j, i)$	Variance $\sigma^{2}(Ej)$		
a	b	c	d	e	f	g	h

PERT FORM 3

	Immediate Successor								
Event No. i	Event No. k	Expected value d(i, k)	Latest time L (k)	Variance $O^{-}(i, k)$	Variance $O^{-}(LK)$	Latest time	Variance	Earliest time	Slack

Slack

Slack for an event is the time by which that event can be delayed without delaying the completion of the project beyond the earliest time for the project. The extra time available for completing an activity is also called slack.

The planner can concentrate only on those activities having zero slack. These activities, as told earlier, form the critical path. Availability of positive slack for some activities allows the management to shift resources from those activities having positive slacks to those having zero slacks.

Planning

If the earliest time for the project is more than the scheduled time within which the project must be completed, then one or two of the following must be done:

(i) Application of additional resources by overtime or by increasing resources at extra cost;
(ii) re-arranging certain activities (and the necessary resources), which were previously in series, in parallel; and
(iii) deleting, if possible, some of the comparatively less necessary articles.

Probability of Meeting a Schedule

Consider the Figure 17.2. The earliest time within which the project can be completed was found to be 30 days. We shall call this the project time. In probabilistic terms, what this means is that the project can be completed within 30 days with a probability of 0.5. In other words, we consider the earliest time obtained as the expected value of the project duration which is assumed to be distributed normally with this calculated time as the mean and the variance as given in forms 2 and 3.

Considering the same example we find that the project duration is distributed normally with a mean of 30 days. Since we have not calculated the standard deviation in that example, let us assume it to be 5 days. If the planner was told that the project must be completed within 35 days, he can proceed as given below:

mean = 30
Standard deviation = 5
T given = 35

$$\text{Therefore, } Z = \frac{35 - 30}{5} = 1$$

PERT FORM 4

Event No.	Earliest time		Latest time		Slack S(i)	Original Schedule	Probability of meeting schedule P(i)
	Expected value E(i)	Variance $\sigma^2(Ei)$	Expected value L(i)	Variance $\sigma^2(Li)$			

Referring to Table 17.2 giving areas under normal curve we find that probability of meeting a schedule of 35 days is 0.8413.

PERT Form 4 can be conveniently used for evaluating the use of the probability of meeting schedules on various milestones or important events.

Examples in PERT Usage

The following examples are drawn from different sectors, each identifying certain unique problems. While drawing a PERT chart for any project the interdependency of various agencies and resources will automatically come to focus. The recognition of these interdependencies and the planning exercise one goes through in co-ordinating them is one of the major benefits of PERT.

Example 1

National Planning

A country, having recently achieved independence, has drawn up its national plan for economic development. The first objective is in two parts:

(a) Establishment of heavy engineering industry; and
(b) a 20 per cent increase in the area of arable land.

Electricity is essential to heavy engineering, and will be generated by hydroelectric stations. The cement needed for building the power stations and dams is to be manufactured locally, in factories to be financed by World Bank loan. Water from the dams will be taken inconcrete conducts to the barren areas for part 'b' of the plan. Part of the loan will be used to build a fertilizer factory, which will also contribute to part 'b' of plan. Cement will be imported for building the fertilizer and the cement factory.

Let us draw a network for this part of the plan. Some of the points brought out are:

(i) Different levels of network–from highly condensed to extremely detailed;
(ii) level of planning resources needed;

(iii) time constraint for national planning;
(iv) identification of approximate time-schedule and policy for importing cement; and
(v) above all, it provides a framework for having rational discussions (instead of off-the-cuff) towards a feasible plan. The network is shown in Fig. 17.3.

Example 2

Appointment of Land Commission by Parliament

The Ministry of Land and Natural Resources of UK was set up in October, 1964 by the newly elected Labour Government. One of the specific tasks of the Ministry was to give effect to the pledge in the Labour Party's manifesto that it would:

> ". . . . set up a land Commission to buy, for the community, land on which building or rebuilding is to take place. . . .".

An outline network has to be drawn up to bring out the interrelationship of the main activities and to see what could be established initially about the completion date.

After a series of planning meetings the main activities identified for "appointing the land commission" are shown in Table 17.1

The network is shown in Fig. 17.4

The PERT analysis brought out the following points:

(i) The scale of work, on the estimates available, was such that a total staff of over 1,000 was likely and, on grounds of efficiency alone, there was a case for establishing the Commission in a number of offices rather than in one central office;

(ii) The need to make the Land Commission effective at the earliest possible date, it was suggested that office accommodation either existing or in course of erection would be used;

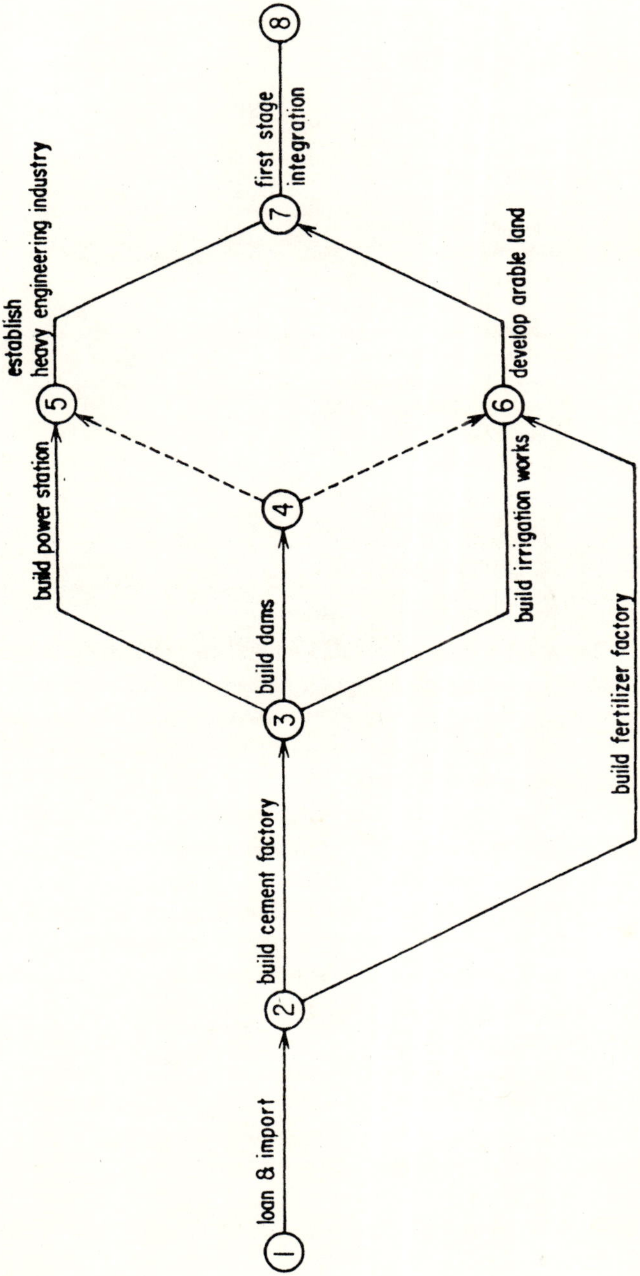
1
loan & import
2
build cement factory
3
build dams
4
build power station
5
establish
heavy engineering industry
build irrigation works
6
develop arable land
build fertilizer factory
7
first stage
integration
8

Fig. 17.3

Table 17.1: Land Commission's Activities

Code	Activity Description	Immediate Predecessor
A	Prepare bill	—
B	Prepare white paper	—
C	Set up project team	—
D	Bill before Parliament	A, B
E	Appoint Commission	D
F	Design system	C
G	Assess staff	C
H	Assess EDP requirements	C
I	Recruit staff	G
J	Assess accommodation required	G
K	Search for accommodation	H
L	Order, receive, install EDP	H
M	Print forms	F
N	Distribute forms	M
O	Trials	F
P	Finalise accommodation	K
Q	Train staff	I, P
R	Test EDP installation	L

(iii) The need for urgency also ruled out the case for installing a Land Commission computer *de novo*, which the scale of operations appeared to require. The use of a Computer service bureau was indicated. It was assumed that computer service bureau capacity would be used;

(iv) It was assumed that the staff would be drawn mainly from the Civil Service but there would also be some direct recruitment. All would require training;

(v) It was desirable that offices should be available and that staff should be in post some time before the Appointed Day so that the staff might become acquainted with each other and their surroundings. It was possible that this step could coincide with the training stage; and

(vi) It was assumed that the day-to-day planning of the project would be carried out by a Project Team reporting to a Steering Committee consisting of senior officers of the Ministry of Land and Natural Resources.

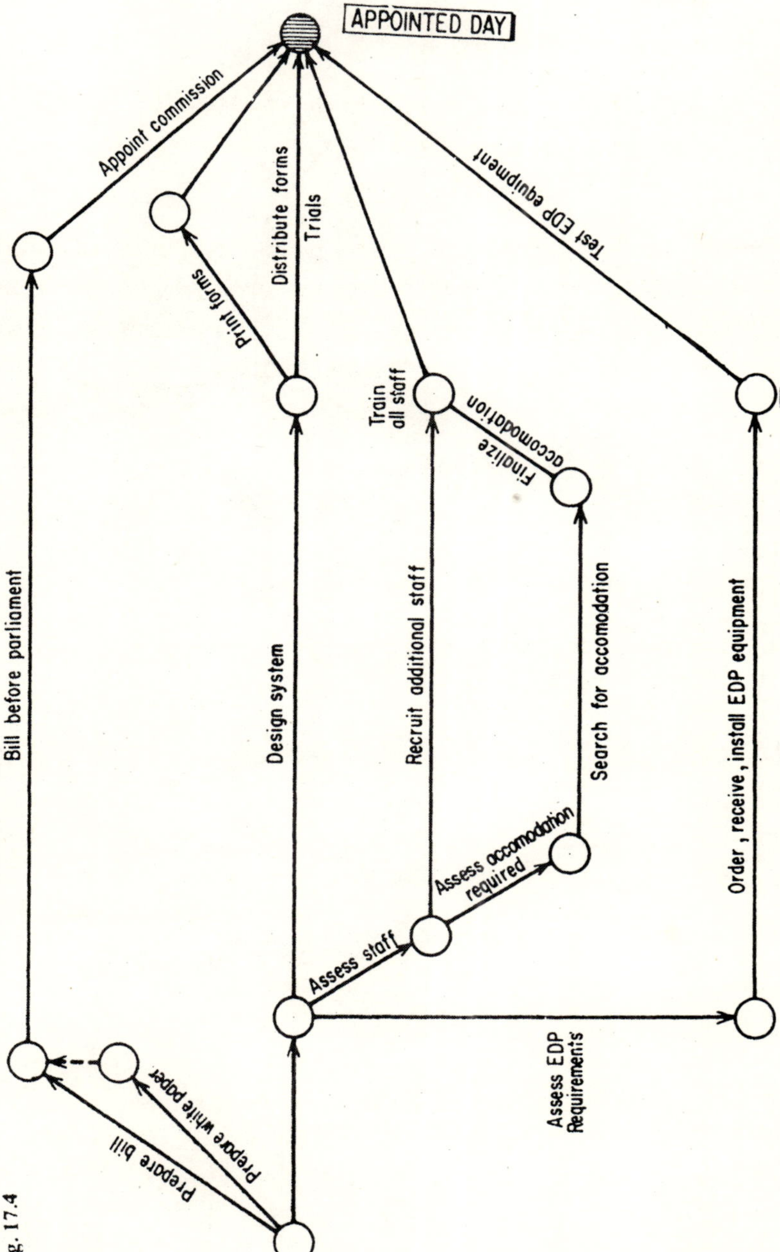
APPOINTED DAY
Appoint commission
Bill before parliament
Prepare bill
Prepare white paper
Print forms
Distribute forms
Trials
Design system
Assess staff
Assess accomodation required
Recruit additional staff
Train all staff
Search for accomodation
Finalize accomodation
Assess EDP Requirements
Order, receive, install EDP equipment
Test EDP equipment

Fig. 17.4

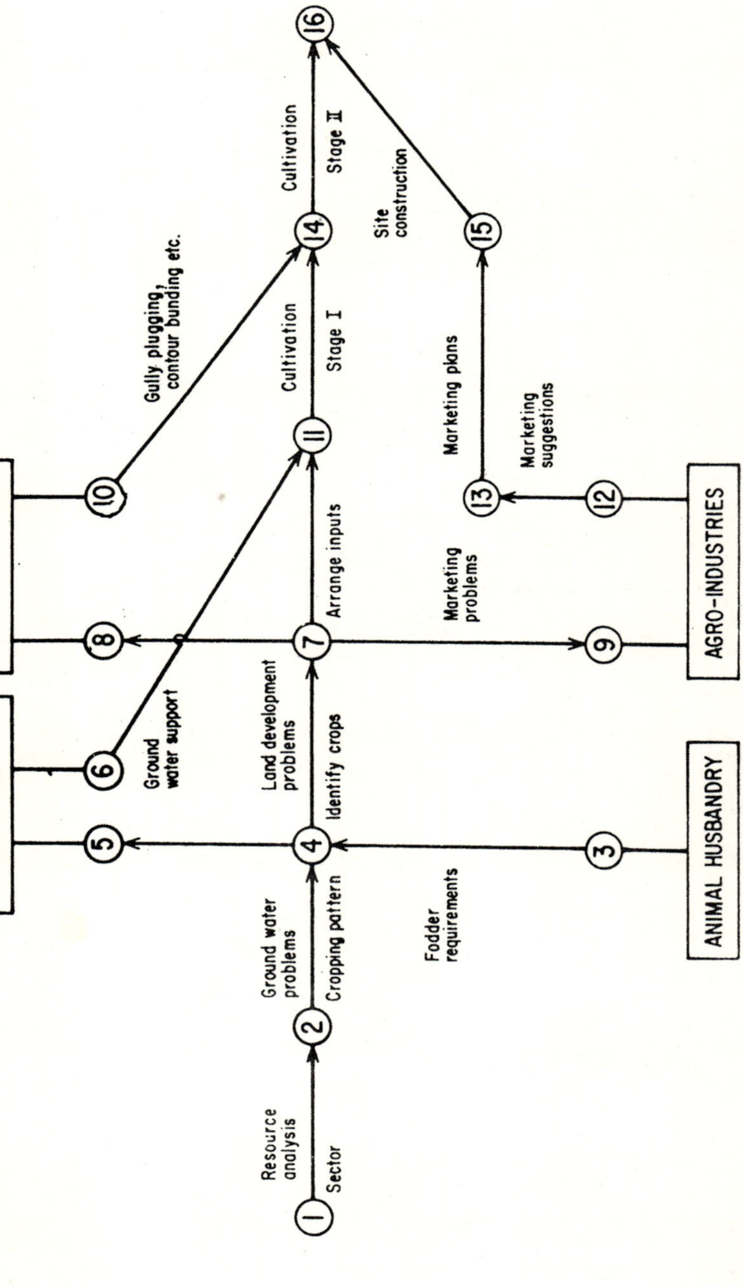
MINOR IRRIGATION
SOIL CONSERVATION
AGRO-INDUSTRIES
ANIMAL HUSBANDRY
Resource analysis
Sector
Ground water problems
Cropping pattern
Fodder requirements
Land development problems
Identify crops
Ground water support
Arrange inputs
Marketing problems
Cultivation
Stage I
Gully plugging, contour bunding etc.
Marketing plans
Marketing suggestions
Site construction
Cultivation
Stage II
1
2
3
4
5
6
7
8
9
10
11
12
13
14
15
16

Fig. 17.5

Example 3

Dry Farming Sector – DPAP and Initial Planning

The DPAP plan for a district involves the participation of many sectors. As an example the overall plan for dry farming is taken up here.

The first activity will be "Resources Analysis and Sectoral Identification". This activity requires the participation of all the sectors. In this example this will be treated as a single activity. However, it will be necessary to develop the detailed PERT chart even for this activity if we want to make effective use of the time and personnel available at the district level.

The second activity will be done by dry farming sector and is titled here as "Cropping Pattern Studies". The third activity is to identify crops. To do this, we also need information from the animal husbandry sector regarding their fodder requirements. Therefore, starting on this we must work with the minor irrigation sector regarding the tapping of the ground-water potential in that area.

Similarly there are many inter-relationship between dry farming and agro-industry corporation and soil conservation sector. The first stage of drawing the network is shown in Fig. 17.5. This must be used as a starting point for detailed planning, including timing.

18

Systematic Monitoring and Evaluation for Management of Development Programmes*

Introduction

AN efficient flow of timely and accurate information is most essential to effectively manage the planning and implementation of development programmes. The need for systematic monitoring and evaluation in order to measure and assess the progress and impact of a development programme is a theme common to most development plans. Yet, in practice, few field operations include systematic programme monitoring and evaluation as integral parts of management.

There are several reasons for this. One is the lack of practical knowledge to accomplish systematic programme monitoring and evaluation. The other is a tendency to look upon systematic programme monitoring and evaluation as an academic research exercise in which costs of obtaining data far outweigh benefits which may be derived in terms of practical information for programme management. Finally, some programme managers feel that monitoring and evaluation only produce bases for negative criticism of a particular development effort.

While there is no doubt that these misgivings have been justified in many instances, the problem is less with the concept of programme monitoring and evaluation than with the methods used. Evaluation and monitoring exist to permit a management framework in which (1) progress toward achieving programme objectives can be measured, (2) whether the most efficient use of resources is being attained and (3) whether the objectives being pursued are the most appropriate in terms of relevance and realism.

---

* Prepared by the Social Development Division, Department of Economic and Social Affairs, United Nations, N.Y.

This study is primarily based on accumulated United Nations experiences. It has been designed to meet the operational requirements of relevant government officials and development practitioners who are responsible for planning new socio-economic development programmes as well as those presently engaged in the implementation of such programmes. The purpose of this study is to define in practical terms the nature of how to obtain a steady flow of information about a programme. It includes an outline of realistic methods for acquiring and utilizing empirical data for planning and management of development programmes. The methods described in this study have been employed and tested under a variety of field conditions and have proven to be low-cost in their execution and effectively provide a high calibre of timely and accurate data on programme operations.

Development Programmes: Their Monitoring and Evaluation

Systematic monitoring and evaluation procedures provide operational and planning staff with practical means for measuring programme progress, assess programme impact and guide programme operations. However, before describing these procedures, it is necessary, first, to clarify a few key concepts. The terms evaluation and monitoring are both so common that it is difficult to use them effectively. They have a specific meaning in this study. To avoid confusion, it is necessary to define these terms with some precision.

Programme, Project and Information Flows

Information systems are discussed in this study with respect to their relationship to integrated socio-economic development programmes. Since the terms programme and project are often used interchangeably, their meaning should be clearly defined at the outset of our discussions. A programme is defined here to mean a set of activities undertaken by a government to resolve a specific group of development problems. Thus, a concerted government effort to build rural housing would be a programme, as would be a campaign to extend adult literacy classes or to develop rural road networks.

In this usage, the programme becomes a means of implementing part of a comprehensive development plan; and a principal characteristic of a development programme is that it is usually executed by a single administrative body. An example of this is the Venezuelan rural housing programme which is executed by the Rural Housing Department of the Ministry of Health and Social Assistance. There are also instances in which a particular development programme may be planned and executed by a number of different agencies. However, any such multi-agency programmes will usually have a central office to ensure co-ordination and control among programme activities.

A development programme may be described as consisting of two principal components and a set of linkages. The elements are the inputs supplied by the programme, such as labour and capital, and the results or programme outputs, produced by these inputs. The linkage between inputs and results consists of those procedures used to convert inputs into results in terms of techniques utilised by field personnel, specific input patterns and sequences of intermediate activities. For example, in an agricultural development programme inputs may consist of land distribution schemes, provision of credit, fertilizer and extension services and organization of co-operatives. These are converted in terms of the amount of land, credit and fertilizer given to each farmer, the agricultural techniques taught by the extension agents and the promotional techniques employed by the extension agents. End result is increased production per hectare, total farm production and net farm income.

Development programmes may also be defined in terms of the specific periods of time that each programme operates; these periods are often termed programme life-cycle. Frequently these are determined by the period covered by the national development plan, and in these cases a programme will be expected to be reviewed prior to the end of the plan period. In other cases the time period for a programme's operations will correspond to the national budgetary cycle, with programme reviews occurring at the end of the budget year. Still other development programmes will have their life-cycle determined by certain internal, administrative targets. For instance, an urban development/redevelopment programme may be broken up into the phases of land clearing and preparation which, when accomplished, is followed by infrastructure development and then by construction of housing and other facilities. However determined, any development will have definable time periods which in turn determine when review and assessment of programme and impact are to be done and when information of programme operations will be required.

The direct United Nations concc with evaluation is in relation with its technical co-operation activities. Since these are usually termed "projects", the term project is used in this study to refer to those internationally supplied inputs to a particular development programme.

In the Rural Works through Co-operation Programme of the Secretariat of Public Health in Mexico, international assistance is provided through a United Nations World Food Programme project of food assistance. Similarly, the land reclamation and settlement programme of the Government of Egypt is assisted by experts from the United Nations development programme assisted project for integrated settlement of the newly reclaimed lands.

Programme evaluation, programme monitoring and project evaluation: There are two categories of desirable information flow which may be identified in a developmental activity. One relates to the relationship between programme inputs and results and is concerned with whether inputs provided are able to produce desired programme outputs at a level which justifies the resource allocations provided programme operations. This process will be termed programme evaluation, and its purpose is to supply national policy-makers and planners with information that will permit them to decide whether to increase support, maintain it at the same level, reduce it, or to terminate a development programme based on its performance as well as its relative contribution to balanced national development.

The second category of information flow focuses upon those methods by which programme inputs are converted to produce the best results. The process by which information is supplied on the combination of inputs required to effect a certain level of results will be termed programme monitoring. Its purpose is to provide programme managers with timely, accurate and complete information on the relative effectiveness with which programme inputs are being utilized so that field operations may be modified in order to realise the most efficient combinations and sequences of inputs to achieve programme objectives.

These relationships among programme elements, and their corresponding information flows, are graphically summarised in Figure 18.1.

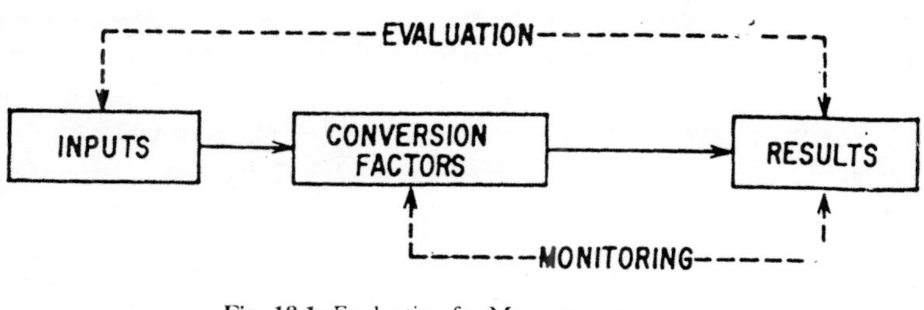

Fig. 18.1: Evaluation for Management

Programme results: Since the essence of the systematic monitoring and evaluation process is relating inputs to results, the definition of what specifically constitutes each is of crucial importance. This is not always easy since a result in one type of a development programme might be an input in another. For each programme, however, inputs must be distinguished from results, or measurement will not be possible.

The most simple way to distinguish inputs from results is to consider a result as what a programme defines as the changes which it expects to achieve among a beneficiary population through its inputs. Results are thus defined as observable changes in a client population. This distinction can be quite subtle. For example, many community development programmes are based on self-help construction of community amenities such as roads. But is the construction of a road a result? Under the definition of changes in a client population, the road itself would not be a result. The results would be, on the one hand, the community organization effects of having built the road in terms of increased solidarity, further community activity and levels of individual participation. On the other hand, a result of the road would be the use made of it by the people. In this sense, the physical road would be the ultimate input in the programme. Similarly, in a programme to supply community services, the construction of a school would not be a result: the use of the school by people would be the result. In contrast, in an educational programme, the result would be qualitative changes in the people's skills and knowledge.

What will be considered a result and what will not is dependent on the nature of the specific development programme. A result is what a programme is specifically trying to accomplish; in that sense, it is the quantitative and qualitative statement of an objective. A result is, in commonsense terms, the answer to the question "if this programme were to achieve what it intends to achieve, what would one expect to see among the beneficiaries?" This also is rather subtle in practice. In one integrated land settlement programme, for example, a major social input was the construction by the government of local schools. When asked what the result of this programme would be, some officials said, "better education for the children of the village. However, others noted that their programme did not provide teachers or school books and, in fact, had no control over the quality of education. They pointed out that their programme merely provided the physical facilities for education, and that the desired result for their specific programme was that the school was attended by the maximum number of village children. The qualitative dimension of education was a result desired specifically by a separate programme of the Ministry of Education. The measurement of the land settlement programme results, in terms of education would be the percentage of school-age children going to school.

Few development programmes tend to have only one or two desired results. Most, in fact, expect a large number of changes to occur as a result of the programme's effort. Of course, not all programme results would be expected to occur at the same time and some would inevitably produce others. For example, in our previous example of the community development programme, promotion of construction of a road should result in greater community activity, which should result in greater co-operation in economic areas, which in turn should result in improved economic conditions for the people in and around the community. What is a result at one time (greater community activity) could in a sense be considered to be an input at a subsequent point in time. To avoid confusing inputs with results it is useful to consider as an input only those resources which come directly from the programme, and recognizing that results may come in sequence, some results having a multiplier effect.

Inputs: Similar care must be shown in defining programme inputs. These may be characterised as those resources and activities which are supplied for programme operations and can usually be expressed quantitatively in terms of personnel (numbers or man-months), materials (wood, bricks, cement, books and paper), equipment, or activities (number of training courses, meetings). To the extent that a programme has established adequate accounting practices, there will be little difficulty in measuring the quantity of inputs supplied.

For systematic monitoring and evaluation, the issue becomes one of how inputs are to be related to results. Each input in a development programme is presumably allocated to produce certain desired results. In fact, this is essential to determine these if the relative efficacy of combinations of inputs is to be accurately determined. Otherwise, utilization of certain inputs may be judged as inefficient simply because the programme as a whole has been deemed a general failure, whereas a specific input may have actually accomplished the result(s) it was intended to achieve but that information on the specific results was not obtained. For example, an analysis in one country showed that, after a number of years of active work in community development, there was no relation between contact with community Development promoters and improvement in family income in these communities. A tentative conclusion was that the personal input had failed. However, when an analysis was made of what the promoters were expected to accomplish in practice and the type of activities in which they were engaged, it was found that there was no reason to have expected an economic result from their work. Promoters were only being used to develop local social organizations, a social result, which, it was found, was achieved. While there could have been some question as to why the community development workers were not also used to provoke economic changes, it was clear that they had, at least, achieved the result which they intended. As a consequence of this analysis, an effective part of the community programme was retained and re-oriented to include economic activities and thus to expand its operational effectiveness.

Just as there are sequences of results which can be expected from a particular development programme, there are also sequences of inputs. Some inputs require inputs of their own in order to achieve results. A case in point is staff training. In an integrated rural development programme, a principal programme input is the work of field extension workers. It is, however, often necessary to provide these field workers with an orientation and specific technical training. The assumption behind this training is that trained extension workers are able to produce better results than untrained ones. In this sense, the training is one input to another programme input. It is possible to measure the direct effect of training in terms of improved skills and levels of knowledge on the part of the field extension workers, but in terms of the development programme itself, the effect of training can only be realistically considered in terms of its impact on the farmers with whom the newly trained extension workers must work. Thus, great care must be taken in examining a programme for purposes of systematic monitoring and evaluation to keep in mind these interrelationships and sequences of programme inputs.

A special class of programme inputs is that which is internationally supplied. Equal care must be taken if the efficiency of international assistance to programmes is to be measured, to assure that these inputs are accounted for separately and are appropriately conceived. Usually international inputs (i.e., projects) are designed to strengthen an existing development programme's inputs rather than produce direct results themselves. This is particularly true of expert advisory and training services. Of course, there are certain classes of international inputs, like the material assistance provided by UNICEF and WEP, which are expected to produce direct programme results.

Non-programmatic inputs: While a development programme is being analysed in order to design procedures for systematic monitoring and evaluation, "non-programmatic" inputs should also be kept in mind. No programme for a given population is likely to exist in a vacuum. In effect, the programme will be one of many forces for change on a population. This situation can easily complicate programme evaluation if outside, i.e., non-programmatic, factors exist which could also be expected to produce the same types of results as programme inputs. For example, in studies of community development it is often found that exposure to ordinary mass media, such as radio and newspapers, for communication is frequently related to participation in voluntary communal activities. The question before the programme evaluators then is whether any increase in community participation was a result of action by community development personnel or merely because of exposure to the mass media. In order to determine which is the real cause of change, information, on both contact with community development workers and level of exposure to the mass media must be related to a particular activity. To analyse it, data must be collected on both the programmatic input (community development workers) and the "non-programmatic" input (exposure to radio).

To avoid the possibility of alternative interpretations laying responsibility for change, key factors which could also produce desired changes should be identified. The number of these should be kept small or the amount of data to be obtained will become unwieldy. The most economical way to identify "non-programmatic" inputs is to consider, for each major objective of a programme, what other inputs, besides those supplied by the programme, could produce the same result.

Conversion factors: While inputs can be accounted for quantitatively, it is also necessary that complete and accurate data are collected on the way in which they are used. For this reason, it is useful to distinguish the conversion factors in a development programme. Conversion factors are the procedures or methods by which programme inputs are transformed into programme results. In this sense, conversion factors are the qualitative dimensions of inputs. In a rural development programme, the main input may be the extension worker. However, an extension worker may perform his tasks in a number of different ways. He may utilise demonstrations, talk to leaders, organise group discussions or organise training courses. There may be different results depending on which method he uses. For programme management, it is essential to know which method is most effective. This is particularly true when training is an important input in the programme.

Under most circumstances, each programme input will have its appropriate conversion factor describing how the input will be used. Where only one method is used to convert a given input into its result, the relationship between input and result indicates the efficacy of the conversion method. However, where two or more methods are in use to convert a given input, the methods themselves must be clearly identified and accurately measured. There is the case of one resettlement programme which aimed at increasing agricultural productivity in which a major input being supplied was land; however, the land was distributed in different ways in different areas. Thus, in order to relate the land input to productivity, it was necessary to measure the conversion factor (i.e., whether plots were distributed in equal-sized lots, whether plot size was determined by soil type). The effect of land as an input was clearly conditioned by the method of distributing the plots. In contrast, an urban housing programme had as a major objective the improvement in sanitary conditions in food preparation through provision of modern stoves. Since only one type of stove was provided, it was only necessary to relate existence of a stove to kitchen cleanliness in order to determine whether the desired result had been achieved from that particular input.

Planning and Implementing the Systematic Programme Monitoring and Evaluation Process

The systematic programme monitoring and evaluation process provides the staff of a development programme with a practical approach to the tasks of monitoring programme progress, guiding operations and assessing impact. The monitoring and evaluation process could be essentially characterised as "quantified commonsense". It should not be looked upon as just another approach to progress reporting, since its principal concerns are with analysis *and* interpretation of data on programme performance and impact. It should also be realised that this process is by no means a substitute for experienced programme management, it is only an aid, an analytical tool to assist in programme decision-making.

As presented in Figure 18.2, the systematic programme monitoring and evaluation process provide an integrated framework for a regular flow of information on the operations of a development programme. It is comprised of the following functional components: problem definition (what is to be done/what is to be measured), data acquisitions (applied research), analysis (review and assessment), and judgement (decision-making).

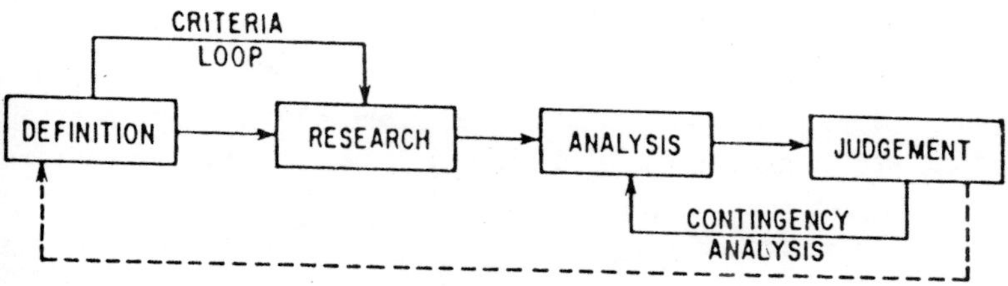

Fig. 18.2: Systematic Programme Monitoring

The constituent components of the systematic monitoring and evaluation process are closely interrelated together, they are able to provide a vast amount of timely, accurate and relevant information for the management of a development programme. On the other hand, if they are employed only as separate elements (research without analysis), only very crude and fragmentary information on programme performance and impact will be obtained.

Of course, continuous monitoring and evaluation of a development programme is the ideal. In actual practice this ideal will be modified in light of politico-administrative conditions which, in turn, determine the amount of resources to be allocated to monitoring and evaluation of a development programme.

Monitoring and Evaluation as a Staff Responsibility

Since the systematic monitoring and evaluation process has been assigned to assist the tasks of planning and managing a development programme rather than to its academic study, principal responsibility for its conduct should rest with the programme staff rather than with special, outside consultants. It may be argued that the programme staff may not always be completely impartial in their assessments, nor might they have the necessary technical competence to execute effectively all aspects of the systematic evaluation process. In such cases, it may be useful to use outside experts to undertake special, technical activities and to train programme staff. However, their continual presence could prove to be detrimental to overall programme operations.

In the first place, outside personnel does not have the same knowledge of local conditions and of the populace as does the programme staff. This consideration becomes especially important where the development activity has been designed to promote socio-cultural progress as well as economic growth. If the programme staff has been performing its tasks conscientiously and effectively, it will be trusted and respected by the programme's beneficiaries. In contrast, repeated visits by outside personnel may create an impression among the local people that these individuals have come to conduct studies (or experiments) on them for purely personal purposes. Once programme credibility has been challenged, maintenance of programme momentum becomes difficult.

A second difficulty arising from the use of outside personnel to carry out systematic evaluation is that many of the individuals connected with a development programme (programme staff, counterparts, volunteers, etc.) may tend to look upon such periodic review and assessment as little more than a check upon their own functions and/or as a conscious attempt to detect programme difficulties or shortcomings. Staff morale is equally critical to effective operations as is over-all programme credibility.

With respect to the design and execution of a programme monitoring and evaluation system, there are certain instances in which outside assistance may be of great advantage in elaborating the monitoring and evaluation concept. These would include formulation of the monitoring and evaluative strategy and assistance with the initial analysis of performance data and with executing re-studies.

In all such instances, the role of the outside expert should be that of adviser. He has come to work *with* the programme staff–and not to supplant their mandated responsibilities, to inspect programme operations or to audit programme accounts. The adviser who acts as a comptroller is of little use either to a field programme or to the headquarters of a sectoral ministry or of an international organization. The most effective expert input is often that which is least obtrusive.

The process: The following discussion will focus upon certain basic conceptual and operational considerations relating to each component of the monitoring and evaluation process.

Definition: (Fig. 18.3).

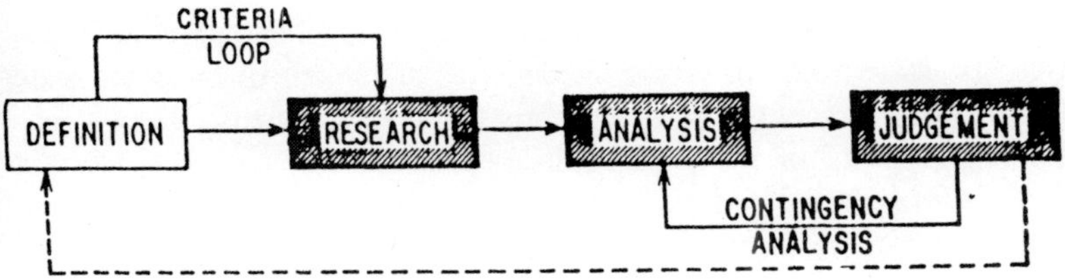

Fig. 18.3

The principal concerns of the definition phase are formulation of an operational statement on programme purpose(s) and determination of the most effective means for accomplishing programme ends.

- delimit the problem and describe its political environments;
- define principal issues of concern and functions to be performed;
- clarify the objectives;
- identify alternative courses of action to meet programme objectives; and
- define economic and non-economic cost criteria.

The first step in the systematic monitoring and evaluation process is to arrive at a clear statement of what the development programme is attempting to accomplish. If the major problems can be accurately and succinctly defined, it is possible to measure progress in resolving them.

In formulating the statement on programme purposes, the programme staff needs to make a distinction between long-term and short-term purposes. Long-term purposes generally reflect current national goals and aspirations and provide the policy framework for the elaboration of a development activity. In contrast, short-term purposes reflect how a particular development activity is supposed to contribute to furthering these longer-term considerations.

A brief example may help in clarifying the distinction made above. One common national goal is reduction in the incidence of infant mortality. In the context of a socio-economic development programme (a child and maternal health-care programme), this proposition could be translated into the following short-term objective function: to achieve a reduction in the incidence of infant mortality from its present rate of four times the global average to half the global average within five years.

What is at issue is not the requirement that all programme objectives be stated *quantitatively*. Rather, the statement of purposes does need to be expressed clearly in terms for which a qualitative or quantitative measure of progress could be defined. Only in this way are programme objectives susceptible to periodic review and assessment. Systematic monitoring and evaluation are difficult enough without compounding these tasks with considerations of overall national aspirations in addition to the programme's explicit operational concerns.

Although the operational statement of a programme's objectives will probably be different in each developmental activity, there are a number of considerations which are basic to all such statements:

(1) what is to be done (what is the programme's anticipated output);
(2) who benefits;
(3) how are benefits to be measured (performance data categories and evaluative criteria);
(4) who pays (what benefits will be forgone and by whom);
(5) how are economic and non-economic costs measured;
(6) when are benefits and costs supposed to occur (what is their time frame);
(7) what are politico-administrative constraints (the "rules of the game").

Once the objectives have been operationally formulated, it becomes the task of the programme staff to identify clearly and objectively the alternative means by which programme purposes may be accomplished and to estimate the resource implications for each such alternative.

Although a programme work-plan usually contains a general scheme for programme execution, it rarely contains sufficient operational data on which the programme staff can develop the most efficient approach for achieving programme ends. Consequently, for each specified objective, a realistic indication must be given as to the means by which it is to be achieved: method of execution, resource inputs, personnel requirements, timetable of operations and possible difficulties. Resource considerations, and not simply costs, are particularly critical, since what they really represent are the extent to which certain inputs are no longer available for other programme purposes. To plan in the absence of resource considerations is to lose sight of reality.

Analysis of programme means is the identification and definition of the functions which the programme will perform. This is an equally critical stage in the planning and organization of a development programme. However, a common shortcoming of many of these functions is that their planning has not been completed until after programme operations have begun and that this planning has been based on subjective and superficial data. As a result, programmes tend to get behind schedule and incur cost over-runs (Fig. 18.4).

Research

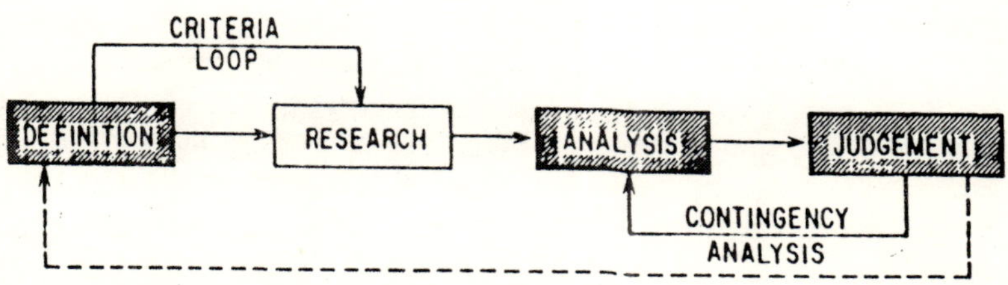

Fig. 18.4: The Research Phase

During the research phase, data on programme operations are collected to assist in the periodic review and assessment of programme progress and impact.

- identify types of data which are needed;
- determine measures of how well a programme is performing.
- formulate a strategy on how to acquire data;
- undertake baseline studies;
- analyse data in a preliminary way; and
- schedule re-survey data collection.

An analysis of the purposes to be served by a development programme also involves identification of the types of data needed about performance and specific indicators of performance. Just as the programme staff need to estimate the resource implications of each alternative for achieving programme purposes, they must also develop workable measures to gauge programme progress and impact. The basis for such measures should be the operational statement of programme purposes (the programme's objective function). Realistic indicators of programme performance and other relevant types of data cannot be determined solely on an intuitive basis.

System Constraints

There are two principal constraints which will affect the effectiveness of a monitoring and evaluation system for management of a development programme. First, the results of the studies must be known rapidly if they are to effect policy and management decisions, i.e., the evaluation of a given year's performance must be known before the next year's activities are programmed. Second, the system must not cost too much. Since the purpose of the system is to assist management, it should not divert programme resources to the extent that operations are impaired. Under normal circumstances the two factors are closely related in that the more rapidly information is required, the more resources must be allocated to obtain it, or, in other words, the faster, the costlier.

However, three considerations can modify this general rule. First, the lesser the volume of information obtained and analysed, the lesser the time and resources required. Thus, if information to be collected is reduced to the absolute minimum necessary, i.e., absolute minimum necessary, the information can be collected within normal resource and time limits. Second, the more information can be reduced in volume beforehand, the less will be the time necessary to analyse it. Thus, if the most efficient procedures possible are used to obtain each type of information, and steps are taken to tabulate data while in the field, costs can be reduced. Third, if the data collection phase can be used for other programme purposes in addition to evaluation, the relative cost of evaluation is decreased. Thus, for example, if data collection is integrated with staff training, or evaluation studies are also used for action research purposes, their cost can be more easily justified.

Determination of the Information to be obtained

Great care must be exercised in determining the content of a monitoring and evaluation system since this will affect both the system's cost and its usefulness to the programme staff.

An integrated socio-economic development programme deals with a potentially infinite number of variables which could be measured in order to facilitate assessment of programme progress and impact. Collection of these data itself could easily become the most expensive element of a monitoring and evaluation system unless great caution is exercised to ensure that data are not acquired simply for their own sake but to provide a quantitative basis for programme decision-making. From a managerial standpoint, data are collected:

(1) to obtain factual knowledge about particular problem areas;
(2) to facilitate an accurate diagnosis of a problem and to provide a basis for alternative solutions; and
(3) to evaluate subsequent changes that result.

In order to keep monitoring and evaluation activities to a manageable scale, managers should seek only that information, which is otherwise not readily available, which permits relating of fundamental inputs to basic results.

The first step, therefore, consists in determining, from the statement of programme objectives, those specific observable changes which are expected to occur as a result of programme operations. As has been noted previously this is frequently difficult, especially with social development objectives since they are at times expressed in very general terms.

On the basis of this analysis of programme objectives and determination of changes programme inputs are expected to achieve, it is then possible to develop a list of variables representing programme results which may be observed and measured. It is similarly possible to identify variables representing programme inputs in the form in which these inputs arrive at the site of programme operations. These lists of variables should be subjected to a critical examination based upon the following two questions: (1) Are we really trying to accomplish *this*? (2) Are we really supplying this *input*. The purpose of this examination is to reduce further the number of variables for observation and measurement to the minimum number necessary.

The next step is to discuss each variable, one by one, both among the programme staff and with other relevant governmental officials, in order to determine where information about each variable can best be obtained. There are two purposes to be served by this exercise: (1) to identify relevant information sources which exist and are available so that this information need not be collected again and, in turn; and (2) to reduce the amount of information which must be collected through systematic observations and surveys.

This master list of variables, which indicates potential sources of information about each item, whether programme result or input, constitutes the blueprint for a programme monitoring and evaluation system.

Criteria Loop: Considerations for Internal Programme Management

Indicators and criteria on programme cost and performance need to be established to assist in the management of a development programme. Since developmental emphasis and purposes vary from programme to programme, generalized standards and norms are not applicable. Such indicators and criteria can only be developed on the basis of a programme's stated objectives.

The chief purpose of this set of indicators and criteria is to provide programme management with an indication of the performance and cost of major activities as based upon data obtained from periodic review and assessment. In this manner, these indicators and criteria for internal programme management serve to link planning considerations with those of implementation.

It should be recognized that these indicators and criteria are not permanent and absolute. Since it is conceivable that programme purposes may be modified in the course of the programme life-cycle—on the basis of new information and/or socio-politico-economic changes—these indicators and criteria will need to reflect the changes in priorities. The means by which this is accomplished is through interaction between the stated objectives of a development programme and the findings from periodic review and assessment.

The indicators and criteria selected for analyses of programme cost and performance should ideally have the following properties:

(1) Each criterion should be relevant and important to the specific problem area for which it is to be used;
(2) Together, the criteria used for a specific problem area should consider all major effects relative to programme objectives. Evaluative criteria must relate to all major programme activities

or else very misleading findings will result. For example, programmes to improve housing should consider not only the acres of sub-standard housing removed but also the socio-cultural and economic effects upon the persons displaced. Furthermore, expressing the criteria in terms of one or a limited number of units will facilitate neat, analytically optimizable solutions. However, forcing the analysis into oversimplified forms may obscure certain significant programme results. It is unlikely that multiple criteria are to be avoided;

(3) Each criterion and indicator should be capable of meaningful quantification.[1]

Where to Relate Inputs to Results

The question of where to obtain measurements which will permit relating inputs and conversion factors to results is largely answered by the operational definition of each programme element. Results are changes in a population caused by the programme's inputs. These must be measured in terms of individuals or of aggregates of individuals. The most appropriate point of observation, then, is where inputs reach the target population of a development programme. While this point will vary according to the specific type of development programme involved, it will usually beat the lowest politico-administrative unit where most programme inputs are delivered to the people.

Except for those programmes which deal with people exclusively on an individual basis, the point at which people receive inputs is usually some form of settlement or politico-administrative unit such as a village, neighbourhood or district. For example, an education programme does not reach people individually; in integrated rural development, the point of intersection, for example, is usually a village which has a single school. All educational inputs for that programme would be distributed through the school. Similarly, many agrarian reform programmes distribute land and other productive inputs through special settlements; sometimes these are smaller than a village, yet often they may be larger than the boundaries of a particular programme. The key point is that for any specific development *the settlement*, however defined, is the point at which all programme inputs reach their intended beneficiaries.

A rule of thumb, for determining where inputs can be directly related to results, is to ask the following question: where do the most inputs reach the most people? Any development programme has such a point. In one country, most of the inputs in a resettlement programme were channeled through farms, which although consist of several villages do have a central administrative structure. The farm was, therefore, identified as the lowest politico-administrative unit where results and inputs could best be related. In another country, an integrated rural development programme was being executed within the context of a comprehensive socio-political reform, which was based on the sub-municipality (corregimiento) as the primary unit for popular participation in national development efforts. The *corregimiento* became the appropriate point at which to relate inputs to results. In a third country, with a traditional village structure, most government programmes centred on the individual village; and in yet another country, which was executing an urban social development programme, services were dispensed through neighbourhoods whose boundaries had been defined by the residents themselves. Thus, whatever the nature of a particular development programme, it is critical that this lowest politico-administrative unit for programme operations be carefully defined so that desired changes may be appropriately measured and related to programme inputs.

How to Relate Inputs to Results

A result has been defined as an observable change in the target population of a development programme; this change is achieved through utilisation of various programme inputs. If only results were to be measured for the purposes of monitoring and evaluation, then the sample survey would be the most appropriate technique to achieve this. However, measures on input delivery and utilization are also necessary. These measurements become somewhat complicated due to the fact that programme inputs are provided through a variety of organizational structures such as associations, co-operatives and block, neighbourhood or settlement groups.

The lowest politico-administrative unit at which different inputs reach the individuals who are to benefit from programme operations has been identified as the most appropriate point where relationships between inputs and results may be observed and measured. An effective approach to accomplish this is the case study. However, the individual case study cannot describe the pattern of results for a programme. Thus, the appropriate method would be a sample of case studies representative of all the communities, or their politico-administrative units, participating in a programme and, therefore, representative of the individuals benefiting from the programme. For this reason, the system of data collection points should be based upon a network of case studies, selected so as to represent the entire programme area, both in terms of inputs and results.

The actual relating the inputs to results is not always a simple task. The first consideration is to ensure that results have been measured. There are three basic approaches to accomplish this–each has certain advantages and disadvantages. The most appropriate means of determining results is on the basis of changes occurring over time in the target population of a development programme. The presumption is that if there is a desired change in a particular behaviour where a programme input is present and no change (or substantially less change) where the input is not present, this would serve as evidence that the input is at least one cause of the change. For example, if farmers' incomes increase over a period of time in communities where agricultural extension workers have been present but do not increase where there has been no contact with agricultural extension workers, it can be presumed that the extension work has been effective. This approach is advantageous in that it permits causal relations to be imputed. It also has certain disadvantages in that such causal relationships may not always be clear, or that several inputs may be related to a given result. This approach also requires a "control" group, where the input has been absent, as well as at least two observations in time.

A second means is to relate programme results to established targets. Rather than measuring change over time, results are compared to a desirable standard or target. If the targets have been reached in those areas where inputs are present, but not reached where inputs are absent, a case can be made that a relationship with inputs exists. An advantage of this approach is that a judgement can be made with relatively little information, since all that is involved is a comparison with a predetermined norm. One disadvantage of this approach is that in the absence of knowledge about conditions before the programme, it cannot be precisely stated that achieving a target represents change. Those places where targets apparently have been reached may have already been at that level. Furthermore, the targets themselves may have been unrealistic (too high to attain, or too low to require much change to achieve). For these reasons, this approach to relating inputs to results is best used in conjunction with other methods.

A third means for relating inputs to results is through comparison of those places with highest results with those with lowest levels of results. The presumption is that those inputs, or conversion factors, which are present in the places with highest results but are absent in those with lowest results are the most effective. The advantage of this approach, based on internal comparisons of a programme, is that judgement can be made from a single set of data taken at only one period of time. The main disadvantage is that without baseline data it is impossible to determine whether highest and lowest results actually represent changes caused by the programme. In fact, such places might have always had the highest and lowest results respectively. This fact makes the assumption that programme inputs caused the observed differences to be very tentative. Consequently, this mode of relating inputs to outputs must be used with great care and preferably as a supplement to other means for measuring results.

Structuring the Sample of Case Studies

The most effective method for obtaining information which relates changes (programme results) to inputs for the purposes of monitoring and evaluation would be through a network of case studies involving at least two measurements at different points in time–one to establish baseline data and the other to indicate observed changes, inputs utilized, and conversion factors.

Data are best collected through a *sample* of case studies. A sample is used simply because in most development programmes the number of communities, or that organizational unit through which programme inputs are supplied, is far too large to allow investigation of each individual "community". To ensure the cases selected are truly representative of overall conditions, the sample must be random (in a perfectly random sample, every member of the population to be surveyed has an *equal chance* of being selected). Representativeness of a sample also depends on the absolute size of the sample: the larger the sample, the more it is guaranteed to be representative.

The question then becomes "how large a sample"? Two considerations determine the size of the sample of case studies: (1) The amount of resources available for data collection and analysis, and (2) the method of sampling. In reality, the amount of resources available is the more important determinant. This implies, as a first step, determining how many people are available for how much time to collect and analyse data. For example, suppose a development programme includes 500 villages, and each case study is expected to require one week by a team of five to collect the data, plus another week to tabulate and pre-analyse these data. If a total of 100 persons are available for two weeks each to participate in the conduct of case studies, it is clear that no more than 25 cases can be studied.

The next question is whether 25 villages are sufficient to represent, with acceptable precision, 500 villages. At this point, the issue of sampling method arises. While a principle of sampling is "the larger the sample size, the more precise the sample", a related principle is that "the more which is known in advance about the units in a sample, the smaller the number of cases needed to provide adequate representativeness". This means that if all of the "communities" in a development programme (the sampling universe) can be classified according to criteria which it is known in advance account for much of the variation among "communities", the cases can be selected proportionately according to categories with much of the possible variation already substantially reduced. This sampling technique, the single stage stratified random sample with proportional selection among strata, requires fewer case studies to be undertaken to ensure representativeness than a simple random selection.

Sample Selection

Once the number of case studies to be selected is known, the procedure for drawing this single stage stratified random sample consists of classifying the sampling units (the lowest organizational unit at which programme inputs are delivered) into strata. By doing this, much of the potential variation within the sample is already accounted for by the respective strata. The critical consideration then is to ensure that the strata are able to account for the variations which exist. The stratification factors employed should be based upon data which exist for all "communities", should be able to account for major differences among sampling units and should not duplicate one another. Of all these considerations, data availability is most important since it is quite common that those data which are available for all sampling units are limited.

Once the strata have been determined, the number of case studies can be drawn proportionately from each stratum. These cases within the respective stratum should be selected randomly.

If there exists a set of data known in advance for all "communities" in a programme and not used as a stratification factor, it is wise to compare the sample to the whole population to determine the degrees to which sample values estimate the population values. If the sample values differ by an appreciable amount, the stratification factors should be changed, and a new sample drawn and tested.

Data Collection

Data for the case studies are collected at a number of levels: from individual families, at the community level (local leader and government officials) and at the area level. To standardize information collection among cases, questionnaires are used. These vary from relatively structured questionnaires at the individual level to general guidelines for interviewing local leaders and government workers. The content of these questionnaires is based on the master list of information which was previously determined by the analysis of programme purposes. The questionnaires should include all information which is needed, but no more.

Two principles should be maintained in drafting the questionnaires: (1) The questions should express only a single and uncomplicated idea, not include unfamiliar words as frames of reference and require only a simple reply, and (2) the use of each question should be known in advance. Simplicity in interpretation implies that the questions should refer primarily to actual or past behaviour; known use of each question implies that only those questions, which, it is assured will be analysed should be included, especially at the individual level.

Baseline Studies

The baseline data provide a quantitative picture of the programme environment prior to the initiation of programme operations. These data, collected from the initial series of sample case studies, serve two purposes: (1) To establish a base for comparison in order to assess changes over time, and (2) to permit a diagnosis of the existing situation for planning purposes. The structure of sample case studies is such that each case study is analysed as a single entity and results are subsequently pooled to obtain a representative picture of the area for programme operations.

The vital importance of baseline data to effective programme management cannot be over-emphasized. Their collection helps in the establishment of procedures for continuous and comprehensive programme records. Such data also greatly facilitate the definition of major problem areas to be resolved as well as principal programme purposes to be achieved.

For the baseline data to be of greatest value, they need to be collected before programme operations commence–and, if possible, before the programme's work plan has been finalised. An equally important consideration is that the precise location of programme activities and selection of control or comparison areas need to be decided upon prior to the collection of baseline data. If not, these data may fail to represent some of the most significant aspects of programme operations and results achieved.

Collection of Baseline Data

The data collection methodology utilized for each sampling unit (the community or other organizational unit) consists of a series of different techniques. For collection of data at the level of the individual or the family or household a sample survey is made within each sampling unit (case).

The size of this sample will depend upon time and resources available and can be either a fixed number for all of the sampling units or a fixed percentage. There are certain advantages and disadvantages which may be associated with either of these approaches. In the case where a fixed percentage is applied to each sampling unit, the size of the resulting sample will vary as a function of the population of the respective sampling unit. In some cases, this number of individuals to be surveyed may be so small that the sampling unit is not accurately represented, or the number may be larger than time and resources available for the conduct of the survey. The advantage of fixed percentage approach to determine sample size is that the results of the individual surveys of all sampling units may be added together to provide a representative picture of entire population affected by programme operations. On the other hand, in the case where a fixed number of individual surveys to be conducted in each sampling unit is established, these individual data cannot be added together unless a weighting factor is applied which accounts for the variation in size among sampling units. A principal advantage of the fixed number approach is that a sample size is established which is consistent with time and resources available for conducting the sample surveys.

Whatever approach is taken, it is best that a stratified random sample is utilized in the determination of those individuals to be surveyed within a particular sampling unit; this will ensure that maximum possible representativeness is obtained for a given sample size.

To collect individual-level information, a survey questionnaire, supplemented by informal interviewing, is employed. For collection of information at the community or neighbourhood-level, effective methods are in depth interviews with local leaders and systematic observations of group activities, such as meetings, market functions and productive endeavours.

Once the baseline data have been collected, the same team which conducted the sample surveys should tabulate these data as well as prepare a tentative analysis of their findings for a particular sampling unit in order to reduce the amount of time required for analysis by the programme staff. This requires prior preparation of a tabulation and pre-analysis form which specifies both the tabulations to be made and the analysis required from the survey team. This form, supplemented by the various questionnaires is the primary data source for analysis at the level of the programme's central staff.

Executing the Re-studies

The core of the systematic programme monitoring and evaluation process is the re-study of the case studies included in the baseline surveys. Only through this approach can an accurate determination of the relationships between programme inputs and results be obtained. In essence, the re-study procedure consists of returning to the sampling unit (community or other organizational unit) previously studied and collecting approximately the same type of information as in the base-line study, comparing the two, and, on the basis of what inputs have been supplied in the meantime, determining the effect of programme inputs.

Because the analysis of the re-studies is more complex and detailed than that required for the baseline studies, and because it is desirable to assure a constant flow of timely and accurate information to programme managers, it is preferable to stagger the re-studies over time. For example, in a programme whose current stage will run for three years, and for which 30 baseline studies were made, it would be appropriate to re-study 10 cases each year to assess programme progress and impact. The cases to be re-studied each year should be randomly selected to assure relative representativeness of all "communities" affected by programme operations. For example, if in 30 of the cases 15 have heavy capital investments, then five of the re-studies each year should be made of cases with similar investment patterns.

Analysis (Figure 18.5)

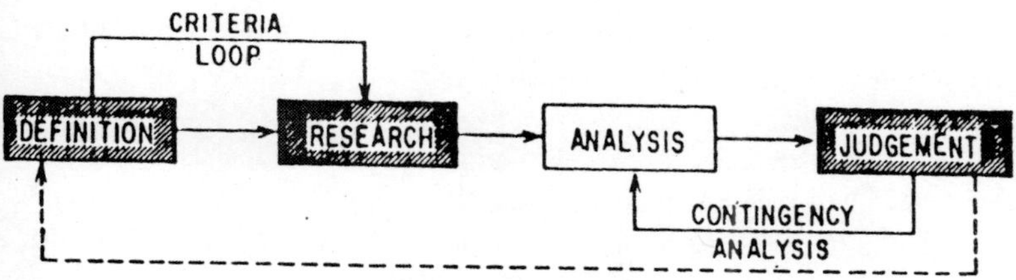

Fig. 18.5: The Analysis Phase

In the analysis phase, attention is directed to identifying observed regularities (similarities and differences) in data on performance and to drawing inferences about causes and effects.

- determines how well the data assess programmes progress and results;
- examines whether anticipated results are observed;
- determines relationships between results and programme elements; and
- establishes an estimate of the relative cost of programme elements in terms of their results.

Data collection and analysis need to be accomplished as quickly and efficiently as possible since there is little value for management purposes in outdated or incomplete data on performance. In addition, prompt analysis and utilization of data on performance reduce the amount of staff time which must be diverted to the monitoring and evaluation task.

There are two extremes to be avoided in approaching the task. On the one hand, data analysis can be so general that the conclusions are weak (the data are under-analysed); on the other, data can be analysed so fully that results become trivial in that unimportant findings are given equal standing with important ones (the data are over-analysed). The solution is to strike a balance between these extremes, based on the quality of the data and the information needs of the programme. If this is done, data analysis can be straightforward and useful. It should be kept in mind that certain types of data, especially those which measure qualitative aspects of development, are not precise whereas other, such as economic data, are more precise. One should not over-analyse less precise data nor under-analyse that which is precise. A good rule is that if a result is important, it should be easily observable in the data, without requiring sophisticated use of statistics and other types of analysis procedures. Commonsense should be the main tool of analysis.

The process of analysis of socio-economic data consists of reduction of raw data to empirically-supported conclusions. In order to ensure that this process takes place with dispatch, care must be taken to assure that analysis procedures are kept simple.

Tabulation of Results:

The first stage of analysis is tabulation of raw data. Without proper procedures this can be a very time-consuming process whether the tabulation is to be done manually or by electronic computer. This is principally a problem with respect to individual interviews since these are the most numerous sources of data. For example, in a system with twenty case studies, and twenty-five interviews per case study, there would be 500 individual questionnaires. If each questionnaire had 75 variables, there would be 37,500 individual pieces of data to be dealt with.

A method which has been found appropriate in a number of countries for tabulating this information is to utilize the most abundant source of manpower available for evaluation (the interviewers). This is done in two steps. First, complex individual computations (individual indices, calculation of economic data) are done by the interviewer on the questionnaire itself. Then, since the primary unit in the system is the case study, the individual responses in each community are tabulated *on a single community-level tabulation form before the interview team leaves the area*. This has two advantages: (1) The interviewers will be able to identify incomplete or possibly erroneous data and return to rectify them; and (2) at the central level, analysts will only have to deal with 20 data sets instead of 500. The individual questionnaires are also forwarded for possible limited future use on any matter which requires more detailed analysis based on the individual-level data.

Because of this procedure, analysis can proceed based on three sets of data: *a community tabulation form* summarizing individual interviews; a form (or forms) containing *information on institutions obtained at the community level*, and a form containing relevant *information obtained from other government offices* as necessary.

Analysis of Baseline Studies

The first stage in the evaluation system concerns the baseline studies. The analysts must keep in mind that these represent observations at a single point in time and, therefore, cannot be used directly for analysis of cause and effect. The process consists of two types of analysis: descriptive analysis and explanatory analysis. The first analyses the data, one variable at a time, the second involves inter-relating variables. *The unit of analysis is usually the community.* While it would be possible to analyse the relationships among variables at the individual level, this would be rather time-consuming and is only justified in cases where results of comparisons among communities indicate a phenomenon for which it is crucial to provide a more complete explanation.

Descriptive Analysis

Descriptive analysis is presenting data on a variable by variable basis. The primary conclusions which may be drawn from this analysis are the overall levels of results obtained where the baseline data have been acquired after a programme has been underway or the type of existing behaviours which are to be changed by the programme. In addition, it is possible to note the variation which exists in the target population in terms of "best" or highest-level community and "worst" or lowest-level community. This analysis can best be done by rank-ordering cases (communities) on each variable and calculating measures of central tendency (mean, median, quartiles, minima and maxima). For example, income measures might be presented as in Table. 18.1

Table 18.1: Income by Different Measures in Communities Income Measure

(Example from self-weighted sample)

Communities*	Net Cash Farm	Net Farm	Net Cash Family	Net Family
Mean	125	205	210	250
First Quartile	270	355	345	405
Median	110	175	160	200
Third Quartile	75	150	105	160
Maximum	635	735	835	935
Minimum	0	10	25	35

The mean is calculated by totalling the income of all interviews in the communities (the total for each community is already pre-tabulated) and dividing the sum by the number of communities. The median is the point above which are found 50 per cent of the communities, i.e., the median would be the difference between the incomes of the 10th and 11th ranked communities divided by two and added to the value of the 11th ranked community. The first Quartile is the point above which 25 per cent of the communities fall, and the Third Quartile the point above which 75 per cent of the communities fall, i.e., the difference between the 15th and 16th ranked communities divided by two and added to the value of the 16th ranked community.

For data expressed in percentage the procedures are similar. For example, Table 18.2 presents the measures of central tendency and dispersion of communities in terms of participation in community development societies on a number of measures.

Table 18.2: Per Cent of Participation in Community Development Societies

	Percentage of families who are members	Percentage regularly attending meetings	Percentage expressing opinions of meetings
Mean	65	35	15
First Quartile	85	75	40
Median	50	40	10
Third Quartile	35	20	0
Maximum	100	95	65
Minimum	0	0	0

These data may be compared, for first conclusions, with targets. For example, if the target for net farm income is $ 350 per family, Table 18.1 would indicate that the target has not been reached, on the average, but that in 25 per cent of the communities, the target has been reached and surpassed. This permits evaluation in terms of targets, although it should be kept in mind that targets may be excessively conservative or optimistic.

For further descriptive purposes and preparatory to explanatory analysis, the various variables may be combined to classify communities along a number of dimensions. Suppose, for example that a comprehensive ranking of communities is desired, based on degree to which various behaviour changes desired by the programme have been relatively achieved in the communities, e.g., increased income improved social conditions and increased citizen involvement in community activities. A possible procedure would be to determine the average rank of all communities on result measures and utilise this to rank-order communities on overall level of development.

To avoid giving excessive weight to any one aspect of the integrated approach to development, the first step would be to determine rank-ordering of communities in economic, social and popular participation aspects. If, for example, social output consists of various behaviours in housing, social integration, health and education, the various measures of each should first be combined into a sub-aspect ranking. This consists of taking rank ordering of communities on each measure, as in Table 18.3 which deals with health output, then calculating the average rank, and, finally, using the average rank to create a new rank order. These can then be combined with other combined rank-orderings to create a rank-order on social aspects (Table 18.4). This can be combined in turn with rank-orders on economic and popular participation aspects to create an overall rank-order on integrated development (Table 18.5).

This would permit identifying and describing the overall "best" results obtained through such statements as "in the community with the highest overall level of results, income is $ 600, 85 per cent of head of families participate in meetings of the co-operative, the percentage of school attendance among schoolage children is 90 per cent etc." Similar statements could be made about the middle and lowest community, and tentative conclusions could be drawn about the nature of the area being affected by the programme.

Explanatory analysis: Once data are presented descriptively, the analyst's task is to seek to identify relationships among variables, especially between inputs and results. If the descriptive analysis process has converted all variables into the ordinal level of measurement through rank-ordering communities on both qualitative variables and interval-type quantitative variables, such as income, the variables which in their pure form could not be correlated may be jointly analysed.

Table 18.3: Computation of Community Rank Order on Health Output

	Rank of community in:				
Community	Frequency use of health clinic	Average number of workdays lost due to illness	Percentage of children ill during year	Average rank	New rank
A	8	7	5	6.7	6.5
B	2	1	1	1.3	1
C	5	6	4	5.0	5
D	1	3	2	2.0	2
E	10	9	9	9.3	9
F	4	4	6	4.7	4
G	3	2	3	2.7	3
H	7	5	8	6.7	6.5
I	9	10	10	9.7	10
J	6	8	7	7.0	8

Table 18.4: Computation of Community Rank Order on Social Aspects

Community	Health rank	Education rank	Social integra-ion rank	Housing rank	Average rank	New rank
A	6.5	5	7	6	6.1	6
B	1	2	1	3	1.8	1
C	5	4	5	4	4.5	5
D	2	1	3	2	2.0	2
E	9	9	10	9	9.3	10
F	4	3	4	5	4.0	4
G	3	6	2	1	3.0	3
H	6.5	7.5	6	7	6.8	7
I	10	7.5	8	10	8.9	9
J	8	10	9	8	8.8	8

Table 18.5: Computation of Community Rank Order on Integrated Development

Community	Social rank	Economic rank	Popular participation rank	Average rank	New rank
A	6	4	5	5	5
B	1	3	3	2.3	2
C	5	7	6	6.0	6
D	2	1	1	1.3	1
E	10	10	9	9.7	10
F	4	2	2	2.7	3
G	3	5	4	4.0	4
H	7	8	7	7.3	7
I	9	6	8	7.7	8
J	8	9	10	9.0	9

The process consists of further reducing the number of variables through discarding those input variables which show no relationship with results. An appropriate statistic for correlating these ordinal variables is Spearman's Ranking Correlation Coefficient, a measure of ordinal association which can be tested for significance.[2] For example, it may be desirable to relate level of investment on farms (an input measure) to overall development. The Spearman's *rho* calculation would be shown in Table 18.6. On this basis it can be determined whether or not there is a relationship between investment and level of integrated development.

$$\rho = 1 - \frac{-6\Sigma(r_1 - r_2)^2}{n(n^2-1)} = 1 - \frac{54}{990} = +0.95$$

$P < .001$ in normal distribution

This type of procedure can be followed for the major types of relationships which must be determined for planning purposes. The relationships include:

Table 18.6: Relationship Between Level of Investment and Overall Level of Development in Communities

(Spearman's *rho*)

Community	Rank in level of investment	Rank in overall level of development	Difference	Squared difference
A	5	5	0	0
B	1	2	–1	1
C	7	6	1	1
D	2	1	1	1
E	10	10	0	0
F	3	3	0	0
G	4	4	0	0
H	5	7	–2	4
I	9	8	1	1
J	8	9	–1	1
			Total	9

– Relationships among outputs (economic to social popular participation to economic, popular participation to social);
– Relationships between input variables and result variables;
– Relationships between conversion factors to the extent they are known at this stage, and result variables.

The process continues until those major groups of related variables are identified, on the basis of which policy conclusions should be drawn. If, for example, in those communities with high economic output, a major related factor is high level of popular participation in the co-operative, whereas communities with low economic output also have low participation in their co-operatives, it would follow that the programme should give priority to encouraging popular participation in co-operatives.

Analysis of the re-studies: The re-studies, which form the core of the evaluation system, require a different type of analysis from the baseline studies. This is because the baseline studies involve observation at a single point in time and thus *permit* only comparisons among communities and with targets. In contrast, the re-studies when combined with the baselines represent observations at two points in time. Hence, the principal type of comparison is community by community over time. The individual-level data to a large extent must, therefore, be analysed at that level, or at least as sub-groups within the community. There are, in analysing the re-studies, three phases: intra-community descriptive analysis, intra-community explanatory analysis, and finally, *inter-community* analysis to help determine policy.

Intra-community descriptive analysis: The first step consists of identifying and describing changes that have occurred between the time of the baseline study and the re-study. This is done by comparing, on a variable by variable basis, the two studies. For example, this might result in the case of net farm income in a Table 18.7. This indicates that net farm income has improved for all families in the community (and that the target of $ 300 has been surpassed by over half the families).

Similarly, percentage-based variables can be expressed in change tables, as shown in Table 18.8. This would indicate that participation had decreased over time and suggest that a careful analysis of the community development society would be in order.

Once changes (or lack of them) have been identified for major clusters of variables, the purpose of the explanatory analysis is to indicate why these changes have occurred or have not occurred.

Intra-community explanatory analysis: The process of explaining changes over time is one of rigid application of scientific norms but more of detective work. The analyst is required to seek and test possible explanations and then seek new possible explanations until he has reduced the number of possible factors to a minimum. As such, there are no hard and fast rules which can be given. Rather, one can suggest general principles. The first is that whenever a change in result is observed, the analyst should seek to determine whether there has been a corresponding change in inputs. If there has been no quantitative change in the relevant inputs, he should see whether the method of conversion has changed, i.e., the quality of inputs has changed.

Table 18.7: Changes in Net Farm Income in Community 'A'

	1974	1976	Change
Mean	275	375	+100
First Quartile	350	480	+130
Median	250	365	+115
Third Quartile	100	250	+150
Maximum	550	625	+ 75
Minimum	60	175	+115

Table 18.8: Changes in Levels of Participation in Community 'A'

	1974	1976	Change
Percentage members of community development society	50	30	–20
Percentage regularly attending meetings	40	10	–30
Percentage expressing opinions in meetings	10	0	–10

The process can best be illustrated by an example. Suppose farm income has changed as in Table 18.9. This suggests that only part of the population has shown an improvement in income, primarily those in the upper half of the distribution of population.

Table 18.9: Changes in Net Farm Income in Community 'G'

	1974	1976	Change
Mean	150	220	+ 70
First Quartile	200	300	+100
Median	140	200	+ 60
Third Quartile	75	75	+ 0
Maximum	635	700	+ 65
Minimum	10	10	+ 0

Comparing individuals, it is found that the individual changes were quite variable: some of those in the first quartile in 1974 are in the third quartile in 1976 and *vice versa*. This indicates that the changes are not natural, i.e., good farmers simply becoming better, poor farmers remaining the same. Suppose that between 1974 and 1976 the major input change was that two co-operatives had been formed for different sectors of the community and with equal numbers of farmers in each, then it would be logical to see whether this had any effect. Suppose we find when comparing the two co-operatives in terms of net farm income the type of result shown in Table 18.10. This suggests that a major factor in determining income is the specific co-operative to which an individual belongs. The next step would be to see what difference might exist between the two co-operatives. This might include comparing cropping patterns, use of inputs, technical assistance, organizational structure, participation rates, etc. If, between the two co-operatives, there is no difference on a given variable, that variable is eliminated. Suppose, for example, that in both co-operatives the farmers raise the same crops, on the same type of soil with the same inputs, but that technical assistance from extension agents is more frequent in one and the rate of participation and quality of leadership is higher in one. It would then be possible to assert that the principal factors in income are technical assistance and popular participation. This type of procedure would be applied to different output variables in an attempt to determine the patterns of relationships among inputs, conversion factors and results.

Table 18.10: Net Farm Income in Two Co-operatives in Community 'G'

	Co-operative I	Co-operative II
Mean	340	100
Median	320	110
Average change (1974—1976)	+190	–50

Inter-community Comparisons

Once the possible factors explaining changes have been reduced to a minimum for each re-studied community, it is possible to compare communities in order to suggest policy and management changes. This is necessary to assure that input factors observed in a given community represent a general tendency and are not merely local idiosyncrasies. Thus, for example, if in all re-studied communities extension agent's effectiveness in raising productivity was related to degree of training it could be concluded that training should be increased. Suppose, however, it is found that cropping patterns are only important in explaining productivity in one re-studied community but not in others. The conclusion would be that while cropping pattern should be noted as something to continue observing, it would not be necessary to change cropping patterns in the whole programme in order to raise productivity.

From these comparisons among communities it is possible to present a series of empirically derived recommendations of three types:

- Recommendations about inputs and procedures which, because they produce desired changes in all communities, should be favoured in the programme;
- Recommendations about inputs and procedures which because they produce desired changes in some communities and not in others should be continued but at a lower priority and on a selected basis, depending on the type of community; and
- Recommendations about inputs and procedures which, because they do not produce desired changes in most or all communities, should be discontinued.

With this information in hand the programme's policy-makers and managers can continually alter and improve the programme's operations on the basis of greater information about the working of the programme and a reduced degree of uncertainty.

Judgement: (Fig. 18.6)

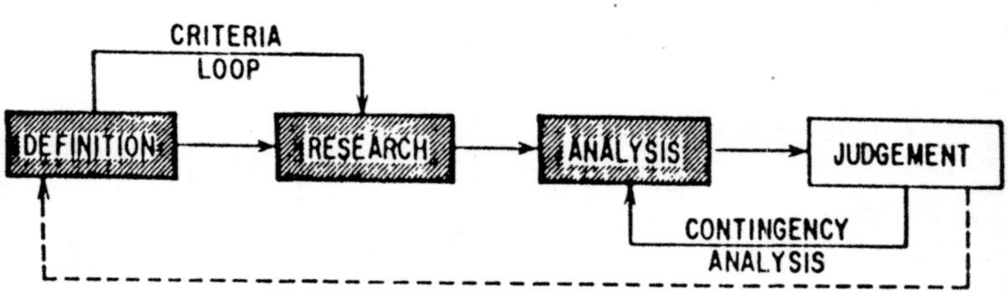

Fig. 18.6: The Judgement Phase

On the basis of analyses of data on performance, choices among alternatives are made by programme management to guide subsequent programme operations.

- Review and question analysis of performance in light of programme objectives;
- Comparison of programme assumptions with findings;
- Compare progress, consequences, risk and uncertainty;
- Make necessary management changes to achieve programme objectives; and

  Judgement becomes a new data input.

From an operational standpoint, the judgement phase provides the pay-off of the staff work performed in the preceding phases of the systematic evaluation process. In the judgement phase, the programme management must review and interpret the conclusions and recommendations coming out of the analysis of data. They must, at the same time, critically question the sufficiency of these findings before taking decisions about subsequent programme operations.

The tasks of analysis and judgement are so closely related that they often appear to be the same. It is necessary to keep them separately, mentally if not temporally. Proper analysis provides conclusions based on available data; judgement is the process of determining whether these conclusions are feasible and what, if anything, should be done about them in the programme's operations. Data analysis, at its best, will reduce uncertainty about the likelihood that any given decision will have its desired results. No analysis will eliminate uncertainty. In this sense, the systematic evaluation process is no substitute for wisdom and experience in programme decision-making; it is a tool for enhancing experience and directing the application of wisdom.

Because the systematic monitoring and evaluation process can only be an aid to programme decision-making, programme managers should never be content simply with the analyses and conclusions as they have been submitted by the programme staff. These must be critically reviewed and challenged and their implications interpreted in terms of overall programme purposes prior to its becoming the basis for decisions as to subsequent programme activities.

As a cardinal rule, programme managers should never receive a single analysis of a body or data on performance for decisional choice. Reliance upon only a single interpretation of the data may force decisions to be made without due consideration being given to risk and uncertainty. Furthermore, any staff analysis must be critically examined within the context of the overall programme. Failure to subject staff work to a contingency analysis, i.e., giving consideration to risk, to uncertainty and to implications of the findings to subsequent programme operations, can only lead to decisions that are often narrow and superficial.

The essential responsibilities of programme management are not simply routine supervision of efforts but rather a longer vision involving review of what has occurred and why, interpretation and judgement as to what should be done in the future. Nevertheless, there is a common tendency for a programme staff which is technically proficient to be an ineffective management and decision-making body. There are two common reasons for such a situation: (1) Greater reliance may be placed upon intuitive rather than empirically-based decision processes because of a belief that certain innovative aspects of an applied programme are not susceptible to measurement, or (2) failure to challenge and penetrate technical analyses and evaluations.[3]

The first consideration can be resolved simply through a conscious effort by the programme staff, and allied co-ordinating bodies, in fully utilising the managerial potential of systematic monitoring and evaluation processes in which both qualitative and quantitative factors can be accommodated. The issue is not numbers versus judgement, but clarity and specificity in expressing objectives in measurable terms.

The second might well involve a change in the manner in which the staff undertakes its programme responsibilities. Failure to conduct analyses, of how good data and their underlying assumptions are (contingency analysis), is often due to a tendency to take decisions on the basis of a consensus of opinion rather than on the basis of organised professional deliberations. Promotion of these deliberations frequently leads to conclusions that are different from established and/or majority opinions.

Programme management which allows incomplete or superficial data inputs to go unchallenged cannot hope to take sound and relevant decisions; persistence of such tendencies mostly leads to programme delays and cost over-runs. A rule of thumb is that events which are unanticipated tend to create increasing problems usually resulting in the need for substantial expenditures of additional programme resources to resolve them.

Avoiding unanticipated events based on uncritical acceptance of information depends on the programme staff's gaining a better understanding of managerial decision-making:

(1) Effective programme management need take very few decisions; however, those choices which are made are critical to subsequent programme operations;
(2) An essential factor in managerial decision-making is understanding rather than speed. The essential characteristic of decision-making for a development programme should be choice among complex alternatives in the varying degrees of uncertainty about the probable outcomes of the decision;

(3) Technical personnel are trained to see only one aspect of the larger problem to which they are assigned to develop solutions. The technician may develop certain associations that hold within a limited range of circumstances; programme managers must recognise that in the larger programme context these findings are, in reality, opinions. A programme manager must also take his decisions against a larger socio-politico context which is often represented by periodic data on programme performance. Consequently, the task for programme management then becomes one of encouraging a wide range of professional opinion and then to test these opinions against the reality of programme purpose and resources and socio-political environment.[4]

An acceptance of this more process-oriented approach to programme management, rather than becoming concerned with specific problems, can contribute significantly to the overall efficiency in execution of a development programme as well as to the effectiveness of that programme's activities. Moreover, incorporation of review and interpretation elements to the task of judgement can only lead to an improved quality of programme decision-making.

Summary and Conclusions

Why Systematic Evaluation

Progress reporting, operational research and evaluation are the indispensable tools of development planners and administrators. In the context of executing an integrate socio-economic development programme, such periodic review and appraisal activities become particularly critical. The planning and administering any development activity is, necessarily, a continuing and complex enterprise, and in the absence of a well organised system for information flow it becomes exceedingly difficult to manage and may involve waste of scarce resources to no good effect.

There are a number of approaches to periodic review and assessment of a development programme; certain of these alternatives are *ad hoc* reviews, mid-term and end-of-programme appraisal, and intuition. Although each has found application, to varying degrees, in the field environment, neither one has been able to demonstrate a real capacity for providing complete, timely and accurate management information on key operational elements of a development programme nor on its impact.

As an alternative, the systematic programme monitoring and evaluation process offers and approach which has been devised to provide programme staff with timely and accurate data that go beyond simple measures of programme expenditures and operations.

Yet, in this context, it is well to remember that the systematic programme monitoring and evaluation process is not being advocated as the definitive technique for periodic review and appraisal of programme performance: only an approach and not a universal model is being offered to assist in resolving certain of the central problems associated with management of development programmes.

REFERENCES

1. Harry P. Hatry, "Criteria for Evaluation in Planning State and Local Programmes", in Harley H. Hinrichs and Graeme M. Taylor (eds.), *Programme Budgeting and Benefit-Cost Analysis*: cases, texts and readings (Pacific Palisades, California. Goodyear Publishing, 1969), pp. 99-100.
2. Kendall's tau may also be used, but its manual calculation is extremely time-consuming.
3. James Bain, Jr., *Systematic Decision-making* (Estimate of System Worth) (Columbus, Ohio: The Ohio State University Research Foundation, 1968), p. 15.
4. James Bain, *op. cit.*, p. 17.

Index